Excel 2023

Unlock the Power of EXCEL 2023: The All-in-One Guide to Mastering
Excel, from Basics to Advanced Techniques, with Step-by-Step Tutorials and
Real-Life Accounting Examples.

CONTENTS

List business cases where excel is used...................................1

CHAPTER 1.   WHEN SHOULD YOU USE EXCEL?........2

CHAPTER 2.   7 THINGS YOU SHOULD KNOW ABOUT MICROSOFT EXCEL...3

    Customize Your Mouse 3
    Input Data on Screen 3
    Master Numbers in Excel 3
    Create a Drop down List 3
    Create Formulas on the Fly 3
    Learn To Use the Command Button 3
    Analyze Your Spreadsheet..3

CHAPTER 3.   EXCEL'S ADVANCED FEATURES AND FUNCTIONS   4

    The Fill Handle 4
    Copy from reference cells 4
    Clipboard viewer 4
    Formulas and calculations 4
    MsgBox 4
    Wrap text 4
    VLOOKUP 4
    Filter 4
    Trim...4
    Pivot table 5
    Text to Columns 5
    Paste Special 5
    Paste as Picture 5
    Ribbon icon Functions 5

CHAPTER 4.   5 WAYS TO MASTER EXCEL 6

CHAPTER 5.   EXCEL TIPS AND TRICKS....................7

    Excel Tips 7

CHAPTER 6.   BASIC DEFINITION AND TERMINOLOGY 9

    Using the Ribbon 9
    Creating a spreadsheet from scratch 10
    Formatting Cells and Text 10
    Formatting the worksheet 11

CHAPTER 7.   DATA PRESENTING TECHNIQUES 13

    Data Visualization 13
    Data Validation 13
    Validation rules 13
    Data Presenting Techniques:.. 14
    Varying Levels of Difficulty 15
    Asynchronous Processes 15

CHAPTER 8.   BASIC FUNCTIONALITIES....................16

    Adding new rows and columns 16
    Creating charts 17
    Calculators 18
    Conditional formatting 20
    Text-to-columns 20
    Color Schemes 21
    AutoFilter 22
    Cursor 22
    Dragging 23
    Multi-threading 23
    Cell numerical operation 24
    Sorting 24
    Add-in-Excel 25
    Cell comments 25
    Drawing freehand shapes 26
    Customizing Ribbons 28
    Importing and exporting data 29
    Converting text to cells 29
    Adding Watermark and Background Pictures 30

CHAPTER 9.   FORMATTING.......................................31

    Characters, colors, size 31
    Alignment, merge, wrap 32
    All cell data types and common issues 34
    Conditional formatting and Table format............................. 35
    Add and remove columns/cells.. 36

CHAPTER 10.   MERGING CELLS IN EXCEL USING THE MERGE COMMAND 38

    How the merge command works 38
    Merging cells using the contents menu 38

CHAPTER 11.   INSERTING 40

    Pivot Table 40
    Illustration 43
    Charts 45
    Links and Comments 50

CHAPTER 12.   UNDERSTANDING THE PIVOT TABLE   54

    What is a Pivot table? 54
    Why use pivot tables? 54
    How do we use pivot tables? 54

CHAPTER 13.   MASTERING THE DIFFERENT PARTS OF A PIVOT TABLE 55

    Field List 55
    Pivot Table Area 56
    The Filter area 57
    The Rows area 58
    The Columns area 59
    The Values area 60
    Using the commands to accomplish a pivot table 60
    Sum Value 65
    Count Value 66
    Average Value... 68
    Max value 69
    Min Value 69
    Product Value 70
    Count Numbers Value 70
    StdDev Value 71
    StdDevp 71
    Var Value 72
    Varp Value 72
    Excel tips for Pivot tables 73

CHAPTER 14.   ENHANCING YOUR PIVOT TABLE PRESENTATIONS 74

    How to use a Subtotals option on pivot table 74
    How to use Grand total option on pivot table 76
    How to use Report Lay out: 76
    Pivot chart and Pivot Chart Options 80
    Insert Slicer.. 81
    Selection Pane 83

CHAPTER 15.   GETTING TO KNOW FORMULAS 85

    Arithmetic Formulas.. 85
    Financial Formulas.. 85
    Look-Up Formulas.. 85
    Defining Functions in Excel 85
    User-defined Functions 85
    Built-In Functions 85
    Understanding Arguments 86
    Reasons for Using Formulas in Excel 86
    Important Things to Know about Functions........................... 87

CHAPTER 16.   FORMULAS...88

    SUM 89
    AVERAGE 90
    MATCH... 91

SUBTOTAL 92
IF FUNCTION 92
TRIM FUNCTION 94
MAX AND MIN 95
DATE AND TIME FUNCTION 96
VPLOOKUP 100
INDEX 102
XLOOKUP 104
HLOOKUP 107
CHAPTER 17.   VARIOUS FORMULAS 108
Present Value Function 110
Future Function 111
Standard Deviation 112
Financial formulas for interest and mortgage calculations 112
CHAPTER 18.   TRACING FUNCTIONALITY 114
Input Functions 114
Output Functions 114
Basic Functions 114
Input vs. output: 114
Output vs. input: 114
Tracing Formulas 114
SUMPRODUCT 115
Other Logical Functions 117
CHAPTER 19.   DATA 118

Importing data text file 118
Sorting and Filtering 119
Auto Filter 120
Advanced Filter 120
Data Validation 120
Remove Duplicates 129
CHAPTER 20.   CODING 131
CHAPTER 21.   MACROS IN MICROSOFT EXCEL AND
REMINDERS   132
Advantages of Macro in Excel 133
Disadvantages of Macro in Excel 133
CHAPTER 22.   EXCEL SHORTCUTS AND TIPS 134
Keyboard Shortcuts 134
Formatting Tips 134
Tools Shortcuts 135
CHAPTER 23.   NEWEST FEATURES 2023 137
CHAPTER 24.   BONUSES – VIDEO LECTURES AND
TEMPLATES   139
CHAPTER 25.   BONUS - ACCOUNTING SPREADSHEET
IN LESS THAN 15 MINUTES! 140
CHAPTER 26.   FAQS 152
CONCLUSION 156

INTRODUCTION

Excel is a powerful spreadsheet application from Microsoft, with a long history dating back over 30 years. It has evolved from a simple calculator tool to a comprehensive software for financial analysis, business intelligence, and data visualization. In this book, we will introduce you to the latest version of Excel and its most exciting new features.

Even if you are already familiar with previous versions of Microsoft Excel, this guide will serve as a great starting point for getting up-to-date with the latest features. The goal is to provide you with the information you need to work more efficiently and effectively. You can then delve deeper into the new features at your own pace.

Excel users are in for an exciting time, as Microsoft continues its tradition of offering free upgrades with each new release of the software. The best way to upgrade is by installing Office 365 on your computer. Linking your Microsoft account with Office 365 gives you seamless access to updates and all the latest features, such as docs.com, OneDrive for Business, and Skype for Business. Microsoft continues to add new features, but it's up to you and your team to determine how best to use them. The good news is that no special skills or training are required, just an existing knowledge of Excel that you can build upon with these new resources.

In addition to new features, Excel has also seen improvements in usability and security, allowing you to work faster and more accurately. These improvements make it an even more valuable tool for individuals and teams alike.

LIST BUSINESS CASES WHERE EXCEL IS USED

Excel is a widely used spreadsheet application from Microsoft that has evolved from a simple calculator to a comprehensive tool for financial analysis, business intelligence, and data visualization. The newest version of Excel offers exciting new features and improvements in usability and security.

Uses of Excel in Business:

1. Financial analysis: Excel can simplify complex processes in areas such as financial analysis, sales forecasting, and budgeting.
2. Everyday tasks: It can be used to facilitate tasks in various professions such as inventory control, human resources management, and product development planning.
3. Data management: Excel can streamline tedious operations such as data entry and manual calculations and be used to manage and track data in areas such as business intelligence and health care.
4. Data presentation: Excel can easily present data in report form in government, education, and healthcare and be used to create advanced graphics in business intelligence, engineering, and scientific research.
5. Visualizations: It can create 2D and 3D visualizations of data for stakeholders in areas such as geology, meteorology, and astronomy.
6. Cost analysis: Excel can analyze and control costs in inventory management, capital budgeting, and purchasing.
7. Product feedback: It can provide feedback on products in product design, marketing, and quality assurance.
8. Dashboards: Excel can create dashboards in areas such as operating information, engineering, and human resources management.

In today's office environment, computers and electronic devices are widely used, and it is essential to have specific security measures in place. This includes malware protection through antivirus software or a firewall, and Microsoft Excel is no exception.

Excel is a versatile tool with numerous uses in business. The sheer number of uses can be overwhelming, but with the right knowledge, anyone can become an Excel user. This guide provides an overview of the most common uses of Excel in business, and once you get past the initial learning curve, you'll discover how easy it is to create Excel spreadsheets and charts on your own.

Chapter 1. WHEN SHOULD YOU USE EXCEL?

Excel is a versatile and powerful tool that can be used in a variety of ways, but it's important to understand when it is the best tool for the job. The three examples listed, financial reports, sales reports, and inventory management, all involve tracking data over time, which is where Excel excels.

However, it's important to remember that Excel may not be the best tool for every situation, and if you're not familiar with the software, it can be frustrating to use. That's why it's essential to have a good understanding of Excel and its various features and functions, in order to work effectively and efficiently.

By starting with the simpler, more accessible techniques and gradually learning more advanced concepts, you'll be able to handle more complex tasks with ease. The goal should always be to find the tool that works best for your needs and to master it, so that you can work effectively and efficiently.

Once you have a solid understanding of how Excel works, you'll be able to automate certain tasks to save time. For example, you can set up a formula that automatically calculates the difference between two numbers, or you can use conditional formatting to highlight cells with certain values. These tools make it easy to manage and analyze data, so it's essential to take advantage of them.

Additionally, Excel has a range of built-in functions and tools for working with financial data. This includes functions for calculating interest rates, loan payments, depreciation, and more. This makes Excel an excellent tool for managing financial reports, budgeting, and other financial tasks.

Overall, Excel can be an incredibly valuable tool for businesses and individuals who need to manage and analyze data. By taking the time to learn how it works and how to use its features efficiently, you can save time and streamline your workflow.

Chapter 2.   7 Things You Should Know About Microsoft Excel

Many people think Excel is just for mathematicians and accounting professionals. Still, the truth is that this versatile spreadsheet application has grown to be a must-have tool for graphic designers, educators, and even writers. Whether you're an expert with Excel or a novice, not having a good skill level in this program can prevent you from advancing your career. And sometimes, even if you have some experience in Excel, the very nature of the program can be challenging to master. So here are 7 things every excel user should know about mastering this versatile software. If you're ready to take your skills with Excel beyond the beginner level, read on.

Customize Your Mouse

Configuring your mouse for Excel navigation is the quickest and simplest method to get more out of Excel. Select the View tab, followed by the Customize Quick Access Toolbar button on the ribbon. Choose Commands Not in the Ribbon from the Choose Commands From drop-down menu.

Find "Grid" in the list and select it by clicking on it once, then click Add.

Input Data on Screen

It is easy to have your spreadsheet on-screen, but it can also be distracting. To prevent interruptions, store your data in a separate document, such as a spreadsheet. Then, while you are working in Excel, you can just open the paper instead of the spreadsheet to make changes.

Master Numbers in Excel

Excel novices may find learning how to use numbers to be a demanding undertaking. However, do not berate yourself. Excel's new user interface makes entering and editing numbers easier than ever.

First, activate the navigation pane by clicking on the View tab > Show View Options dropdown > Navigation Pane checkbox. Then, in the left column, choose "Number" to open a number grid in Excel that allows you to enter numbers and formulas as though using a calculator.

Create a Drop down List

Sorting and analyzing data is one of Excel's most valuable capabilities. Manually sorting and analyzing data, however, can be laborious. If you have typed over a drop-down list, select the entire list and then go to the Data tab > Validation. Click "allow" next to each of the listed things, excluding your drop-down menu item, which should say "list."

Create Formulas on the Fly

Formulae are a major reason why many people shy away from Excel, but formulas may be simple — even for spreadsheet novices. Instead of repeatedly retyping formulas, type the formula once and then press Alt+Shift+Enter. This will provide the required formula in each row.

Learn To Use the Command Button

Utilizing formula columns is the simplest method for learning Excel. By default, when you enter information into a column, the application will attempt to calculate a result and display it. You can convert these columns into "user input" columns that allow you to opt in or out of the automatic calculation with only two clicks.

Analyze Your Spreadsheet

One of the most significant limitations of spreadsheets is that you can only analyze and evaluate your work when you're in Excel, but what if you could explore your spreadsheet without opening it? That's precisely what the VLookup function is for.

Like the SUM function, VLookup automatically charts your data when you use it and produces an output table that collates all results. In addition, you can "group" statistics by different criteria – even if your data doesn't follow a normal distribution. For example, you can put all the sales figures in column B but gather all the sales figures by product in column C – even though they're not both related to product prices.

One of the most repeated misconceptions people have about Excel is that it can only analyze numerical data. It's an excellent tool for analyzing almost any data or process – whether you're calculating sales figures or tracking your weekly weight loss.

The Microsoft Excel 2019 user interface is intuitive and robust – giving you unprecedented control over the data in your spreadsheet, regardless of your skill level.

Chapter 3. EXCEL'S ADVANCED FEATURES AND FUNCTIONS

Excel is an advantageous and versatile spreadsheet application used for many purposes. However, like any application, Excel has certain features that are not always obvious but can make the user experience more efficient. Below we'll look at some of these lesser-known features and see what benefits they provide:

THE FILL HANDLE

This feature will allow you to easily copy the value from one cell to another nearby partition. For your convenience, the fill handle is located on either side of the fill handle button on the bottom portion of the formula bar. This makes it very convenient to copy from one cell to a nearby cell without using the mouse quickly.

COPY FROM REFERENCE CELLS

If you are using references in your formula, you can copy a value from a reference cell and paste it into another cell by holding down the SHIFT key and clicking on the desired reference cell.

CLIPBOARD VIEWER

You can quickly see what is currently on the clipboard by holding down shift and clicking on the fill handle. The fill handle will change from a clipboard shape to a clipboard with a checkmark. This represents what is currently on the clipboard in your current workbook. If you want to paste something from your workbook, click on the checkmark, and away you go.

FORMULAS AND CALCULATIONS

In Excel, formulas are the backbone of everything. Formula is simply a string of text containing a set of numbers. This is one way Excel makes formulas easy to use and understand. You can use the F2 key to run a formula in the formula bar. However, if you want to see what your formula will look like when inserted into a cell, press on the cell that contains the formula and then select Formulas > Formulas and calculations.

MSGBOX

This feature allows you to quickly see what is on your clipboard by showing a message box containing whatever is currently on your clipboard. This is useful when you need to copy something, such as a web address, and do not want to make any other changes to your original copy. To use the MsgBox feature, all you must do is press F2 on your keyboard, type or paste the message or text you want to see in a message box and click on OK.

WRAP TEXT

This feature allows you to easily format text by wrapping it around another cell's text value. This is done by clicking on the cell you want the text to appear in, clicking on Home > Alignment, and clicking Wrap Text. You then highlight the cell you want to wrap text around, and lastly, type your text into the second cell.

VLOOKUP

The Vlookup function allows you to search for a specific value in one or many columns based on the values in other columns. This is useful when searching for a particular value based on the values in different columns. When searching for a bargain, you must give the VLOOKUP function at least two arguments. The first argument must be the column where you want to find the value, and the second argument is the column(s) that want to be searched. In return, VLOOKUP will return a number representing how many rows in that column(s) contain the exact value you specified in your first argument.

FILTER

The Filter feature allows you to search for a specific value based on more columns in an Excel spreadsheet. This is useful when searching in a particular matter in one or more columns in your spreadsheet. To use the filter feature, select the range you want to filter, and then go to Data > Filter. You will be enquired to select the one or more columns to be filtered. In return, Excel will search for your specified value in that column.

TRIM

The TRIM function allows you to remove any spaces from the beginning or end of a string of text. This is useful when you have data with spaces at the beginning or end of each cell and remove them. To use this function, highlight the cell you want to trim spaces from and click on Formulas > Trim. In your dialog box, type the exact name of the trim function you want to run.

PIVOT TABLE

Pivot tables allow you to quickly summarize large amounts of data without the need to do a lot of analysis. It is useful when you have lots of data that you need to summarize. To use the Pivot table, select the cell where you want your pivot table to appear and click on either Insert > Tables > PivotTable or go to Insert > Table, then click on PivotTable. Give it a name and, if needed, specify the range that it should use as its source data. After this is completed, you will be provided with a blank pivot table with fields listed along the top and data in columns below. You can then enter your data into this pivot table and see how it will summarize the data by looking at the fields along the top. To add more lots or see what the summarized data looks like, click on any of the fields along the top. These fields will then be added at the bottom, and your original data will be summarized in each column you selected for this pivot table.

TEXT TO COLUMNS

This method is an Excel version of what some call a "Conditional Formatting" method which requires Microsoft Access. This method allows you to apply formatting/colors/etc. To a column of cells based on a value in an adjacent cell. To use this method, highlight a cell containing the value you want to apply the condition to, then click on the Home > Conditional Formatting button. In this dialog box, all you must do is choose the format that should be applied and apply it where you want. For example, if you wanted to use a specific color for all the cells in the column that was highlighted, click on "Fill Color" in the upper right corner. In return, Excel will apply your color/format to all cells in the highlighted column based on your value.

PASTE SPECIAL

The Paste Special feature is useful when you need to paste a cell's formatting or value but not its cell location. This is useful for copying values, but not the formulas that use those values. To use this feature, select the cells you want to copy. Next, highlight the cells where you want to paste those copied values and click on Home > Paste > Paste Special.

PASTE AS PICTURE

The Paste as Picture feature is useful when you want to paste values as pictures. This is handy when you want to paste an image of a formula but not its cell location. To use this feature, select the cells you want to copy. Next, highlight the cells where you want to paste those copied values and click on Home > Paste > Paste Special. Select "Paste as Picture" and click OK in the dialog box that appears.

RIBBON ICON FUNCTIONS

Although there is nothing wrong with the classic menu system that was found in previous versions of Excel, the Ribbon brings some features to the table that were previously unavailable. When you click on a Ribbon icon, it will expand to display additional commands and buttons. One of the best things about the Ribbon is that it provides fast access to various commands and tools.

These are just certain of the features in Excel that you should know how to use. There are many more features that you should learn that will make your time in Excel much more effortless. Continue reading this book to learn more.

Chapter 4.   5 WAYS TO MASTER EXCEL

Excel mastery can be a difficult and scary endeavor, given the ever-growing array of features and functions to master. Nevertheless, with the appropriate attitude, you can advance your Excel skills and make the most of this flexible software. Here are some suggestions to get you started:

1. Before getting into Excel, determine what you wish to accomplish and which abilities you must acquire first. This will provide you with direction and help you maintain concentration.

2. Learn shortcuts and workarounds: Once you have mastered the fundamentals, focus on the aspects that frustrate or confound you. Examine Excel models for shortcuts and workarounds that can save you time and effort.

3. Be patient and persistent: Excel mastery requires time and practice, so don't give up if you don't notice results immediately. Schedule daily time, even if it's only 15 or 30 minutes, to continue developing your talents.

4. When you feel stuck, don't be afraid to contact your management, coworkers, or even search the Internet for information and solutions to your problems. You are not alone in your pursuit of knowledge!

5. Remember that there is always more to learn in Excel, so be receptive to new features and functions and continue to push yourself to develop your skills.

You will be well on your way to learning Excel and unleashing its full potential if you keep these ideas in mind. Do not be scared to take the jump and begin your journey to Excel mastery now.

Chapter 5. Excel tips and Tricks

Excel is a very effective and versatile program that has revolutionized the method in which people interact with data. However, its extensive array of features and functionalities can be intimidating for beginners. Fear of the unknown should not hold you back. This guide is intended to equip you with all the skills and knowledge necessary to master Excel and unlock its full potential. With a little effort and resolve, you can quickly become an Excel expert.

EXCEL TIPS

- Develop expertise with Pivot Tables, Filters, and the VLOOKUP tool. These sophisticated tools enable efficient and effective analysis and summarization of vast quantities of data.
- Master Excel chart and graph making. Excel supports a variety of complex chart formats, including 3D pie charts, line graphs with polar axes and square root scaling, Gantt charts, and stacked bar charts, which are familiar to most Excel users.
- Set absolute references in your calculations to generate intelligent ranges. This facilitates data entry in numerous columns simultaneously, saving you time and effort.
- Become familiar with Excel worksheets by dividing your spreadsheet into many rows or columns and selecting which cells to display on each worksheet.
- Learn how to simultaneously use two spreadsheets.
- Use Excel's built-in AutoSum tool to calculate sums fast and precisely, particularly when it comes to accounting duties such as calculating profit margins and net worth.
- Utilize Excel's Mail Merge feature to automate the distribution of personalized documents such as letters and labels.

Excel is one of the most popular programs in the office. However, even professional users often forget about some of its advanced features.

Here are some of the most advanced tricks that will take your Excel knowledge to the next level.

1. Track how much time it takes you to do specific tasks in one day with conditional formatting. If it takes less than 10 minutes, highlight the cells green. If it takes more than 10 minutes but less than 30 minutes, highlight them yellow, and if it gives you more than 30 minutes but less than 60 minutes, highlight them orange. This will give you a clear visual representation of how much time-specific tasks take you to do, and you can use your newfound knowledge to streamline your processes.
2. Use the pivot table and sort data. It's easy to see the average amount of time that something takes you to do. You can also filter the data by category or value to determine which task takes up the most of your time.
3. Sometimes, it is hard to find the value you are looking for if there are a lot of other values on the same row. Using the formula =VLOOKUP(), you can look up the value of a particular column at any given position in your data table.
4. If you have a massive table of data and you need to find the average for the entire table, instead of manually doing it, use this formula: =AVERAGEIF(some cell, C5:C8,")=. This will allow you to enter your average formula in one cell as an average and then use conditional formatting, and it will highlight the cells that meet that condition. This way, you can change the numbers in your function without retyping them into every cell.
5. If you want a number with specific formatting within an Excel formula, you can use the "=" operator. For example, if you're going to display $100 but in a currency format in the spreadsheet, instead of using =",=Currency," you can set up the number format in the HOME option and select CURRENCY. This will display $100 within your document in the currency format that is specified.
6. When you have a large table of data and you want to filter specific columns using a drop-down list, it can be challenging to keep track of what column will apply each time. Using this formula is as easy as typing in a number between 1-7. This formula will filter through all the numbers in your table and check if they were used before. Then it will output the number that has been used before, making it very easy to find which value is being used from the list.
7. This formula is a variation of the "IFS" formula, which allows you to create conditional logic in Excel and compares two values based on a specified condition. The IF function is commonly used to compare two values logically. However, it will only work for single values or when you compare by less than, equal to, or greater than. To fix this, use a variation of the IFS formula. This will result in a more efficient procedure not encumbered by single values and logical comparisons.
8. A common problem many users have is selecting data from within a table. Often it is easy to choose the wrong cell because you don't know what cell you are choosing from. To fix this problem, you can use the FIND method. For example, if you have a table that is sorted by dates and you want to select the date for a particular cell, use the formula =FIND(B4, "date"). This formula will select your date from within the table and put it into a cell.

9. It is often complicated to see what cells are highlighted in Excel. There are a few ways you can use to do this. The first way is using conditional formatting. Highlight the cells you want to see highlighted, and then select the "Conditional Formatting" option from the home tab that will let you to highlight specific cells based on certain formulas in your sheet. This will allow you to quickly scan your data and see which duplicated numbers.

10. Sometimes, it is necessary to perform extensive calculations in Excel, and it would take too long if you were to do them manually. You can use the "SUMIF()" formula in Excel to do this. This formula is used to sum up, cells based on specific criteria. This will allow you to enter multiple formulas with the same function, and Excel will combine them into one formula and perform the task for you instantly.

11. Another advanced trick is to use the INDEX and MATCH functions together. The INDEX function returns the value of a cell in a specified range, while the MATCH function returns the position of a value in a specified range. By combining these two functions, you can create a powerful lookup formula that can find values in large data sets based on specific conditions.

12. You can also use the "Text to Columns" feature to split cells with multiple values into separate columns. This is especially useful when working with data imported from external sources that may not be in the desired format.

13. Another advanced feature is to use the "Data Validation" option to ensure that data entered in a specific cell or range conforms to certain conditions. For example, you can use data validation to enforce a certain data type, such as a date or a number, or to limit the range of allowed values.

14. Another useful trick is to use the "IFERROR" function to handle errors in your formulas. The IFERROR function checks the result of a formula and returns a specified value if an error occurs. This is especially useful when working with complex formulas that may generate errors, such as #DIV/0!.

15. Finally, you can use the "Goal Seek" feature to find the value that makes a formula return a specific result. This is useful when working with financial models or other scenarios where you need to find the value that results in a specific outcome.

Now, you got the tips and tricks that will take your Excel knowledge to the next level and will help you improve your workplace efficiency. You can maximize your productivity with minimal effort. Learn how to use these tips and tricks!

Chapter 6. BASIC DEFINITION AND TERMINOLOGY

Basic definition and terminology are crucial aspects of this book, aimed at helping you master Microsoft Excel functions to conduct standard data analysis and business calculations. As a business professional using Microsoft Excel, a strong understanding of basic definition and terminology is crucial to your success in performing tasks efficiently and effectively.

This chapter focuses on the central topics that will aid in your mastery of the Microsoft Excel software:

- Utilizing the Ribbon Interface
- Building a Spreadsheet from the Ground Up
- Formatting Cells and Text in Excel
- Enhancing the Overall Look and Feel of the Worksheet

If you have Office 365, you already have access to the latest version of Microsoft Excel (2016) with the Ribbon interface. This modern interface replaces the traditional menu system found in older versions, providing quick access to common commands and tools via icons. This chapter will guide you on how to effectively utilize the Ribbon interface to create a spreadsheet, format cells and text, and understand key terminology and definitions in Microsoft Excel.

USING THE RIBBON

The basic idea behind the Ribbon interface is that all the tools, menus, and buttons are organized in a vertical column directly on top of the spreadsheet. This column has a row of self-explanatory icons in most cases, and they can be run through a command by clicking on them, such as the Insert Ribbon icon. Icons for the most common controls, such as Cut, Copy, Paste, and Print. It also shows a particular tool relevant to the task you're doing. For example, if you're formatting text in Excel on a spreadsheet, it will show a drop-down menu that contains options for formatting the text in that column.

The Ribbon is organized into groups of related tasks and tools. The groups are:

Home: Contains the options for formatting cells and text, inserting new columns and rows, using AutoFormat options, and inserting comments.

Insert: Contains the options for inserting objects into the spreadsheet-like tables, charts, or SmartArt. Object insertion is covered later in this tutorial.

Page Layout: Contains only two groups of commands that deal with how the entire spreadsheet prints on paper. It doesn't deal with how individual cells print out on a printer.

Formulas: Contains the groups to add new cells to the spreadsheet, set up functions and formulas, and create data tables. These are covered later in this tutorial.

Data: Contains the groups for dealing with types of data in the spreadsheet, such as sorting, filtering, or using PivotTables. These are covered later in this tutorial.

Analyze: Contains two groups that deal with how Excel deals with data analysis calculations and charts. You can find out more about charts later in this tutorial.

Review: Contains the groups for working with comments and reviews. There are two other groups to print out the worksheet to a printer or save and share data.

View: Contains the groups for viewing a spreadsheet and customizing the screen elements.

Developer: Contains the groups using Visual Basic to customize Excel, create your tools, or use macros.

Tools: Contains the groups for exporting data to PDF, export data to picture, data to XML, and other tools.

The Ribbon also has tabs along its top, which will change depending on what task you're doing. For example, when you're using a cell to enter text, the Home tab will have options for formatting the text. But if you have a chart selected on the screen, it will display tabs with commands specifically relevant to that chart. The Ribbon can also be customized to show only the relevant commands or tools you want to use most often. You can customize the Ribbon by choosing the Home tab and then clicking on any of its icons. This will set up a drop-down menu that contains other options for commands and tools available on that tab. Once you've got the extend of using the Ribbon and its layout, it's relatively intuitive and easy to use. It would be best to remember that there is more than one way to perform specific tasks in Excel. These groups are essential to learning about since they contain unique commands and tools that you need to master to be proficient in Excel. The goal of this part of the tutorial is to go over and understand the various groups on the Ribbon and how it works.

CREATING A SPREADSHEET FROM SCRATCH

This is a tremendous place to start if you're learning how to use the Ribbon in Excel. Open the program and create a fresh spreadsheet by selecting 'New → Blank Workbook' from the File menu. If you use Office 365, this will most likely be called Blank Workbook.

Once created, you'll see the first few rows of cells at the top of the screen. The first row will be the 'Title' row and is usually used to give instructions or outline the purpose of your spreadsheet. Below this is a group called 'Rows' that has basic information about what information is in each column. The actual data itself follow this.

To add data to a row, you first need to select it. You can do this by clicking on the empty cell in that row or highlighting the entire row of cells if they're contiguous (meaning there are no empty cells in between). If a cell is highlighted in red, Excel has automatically entered data into that cell for you. This is called a 'formula,' and it's covered later in this tutorial.

To add data to a cell, you'll need to select the cell first. Click on any cell in the row, or right-click and then choose 'Select' or anywhere else on your sheet that contains a cell. Then you can start typing in the data in the cells. If there are no empty cells between two of these cells, Excel automatically adjusts them to fit your data. You can also have your keyboard shortcuts to quickly jump between rows and columns without having to scroll up and down or use any menus or toolbars. The entire purpose of creating a spreadsheet is to store data to be viewed, manipulated, and analyzed.

Once you have your data sorted correctly, analyzing the data becomes easy. Excel has tools that allow you to quickly see how your data is arranged, how it compares across groups and groups within a category, or how changes in the values of a column affect other columns or the total.

FORMATTING CELLS AND TEXT

The options available will depend upon what type of cell it is, for example, a number or text entry. You can also set custom sizes and styles here in most cases. The easiest way to format cells and text is by using the button found in the Home tab. This is the 'Cells Dropdown.' It contains formatting options relevant to the entire sheet, so they can be used to format any cells in a spreadsheet.

Just click on any cell, or highlight some of them, and this menu should pop up.

Below stands a list of most of the standard formatting options:

- Bold
- Strikeout
- Italicize
- Underline

Apply to Selection and Apply to Entire Selection.

To adjust the font type in cells, you'll need to click on the 'Font' dropdown and then choose the one you want.

Notice that this dropdown menu is different from the other one. This is because it isn't specific to a single cell or a group of cells; instead, it contains formatting options relevant to all fonts and text in your spreadsheet. You should also see how this affects the text once you apply it.

The 'Style' dropdown only contains two options: Normal and Classic. To change the size or style of text, you can also use this option. The different styles will be explained later in this tutorial.

There are numerous other options for styling cells, but most of them aren't used often, so we'll go over them later in the tutorial.

FORMATTING THE WORKSHEET

The "**Number**" dropdown only contains one option: 'Normal.' This is used for formatting cells and numbers on the spreadsheet. It will change the color of the number, add a decimal point, and add lines to make it easier to read large numbers. The other options are used for formatting text (for example, bold or italicized).

The "**Currency**" dropdown contains the same options as the 'Number' dropdown, except it adds an extra option for using a specific currency symbol in numbers. This is usually used for accounting or business applications.

The "**Percentage**" dropdown works similarly to the other formatting options, except that it will format cells as percentages instead of currency or numbers. This is useful since it displays values in comparison to 100% instead of a certain number or currency amount.

The "**Font**" option can be used to change the size, type, or style of any text on the spreadsheet.

The "**Alignment**" dropdown contains all the other options for formatting and aligning text. Left, Center, Right, Top and Bottom.

When used on their own, they will only align single cells that you select. If you choose multiple cells, they will all be aligned in the same direction (for example, all right-aligned or center-aligned).

Using the **'Drawing Tools'** group

The Drawing Tools group contains tools used to draw, resize, or delete data on a sheet. The menu bar above of a sheet is only used to display the commands and tools you can use in each group. The drawing tools are no exception; the menu that pops up when you click on the Drawing Tools button will contain all the options.

A few other valuable things you can do with drawing tools draw a specific shape over an existing shape or select an area on a sheet and then copy it to another location on the page (for example, if you want to create a table of contents at the beginning of your spreadsheets).

The "**Borders and Shading**" option adds a border around a cell that you select. This can be useful for highlighting the value of a cell or simply giving cells more emphasis on your spreadsheet. The options are the same as the 'Borders' option in the Format Cells dropdown menu; you can choose to have a 'Line', 'Dashed Line', 'Dash-Dot Line', or nothing around your cells.

The last part is used for changing the color and style of borders on individual cells. To reform the color of a cell, you first need to select the cell and then click on the 'Fill Color' option. This will show a panel where you can choose different shades of color. The 'No Fill' option is used to delete the color from a cell and make it white (or whatever color your text is).

The "**Conditional Formatting**" option adds certain effects to cells based on their values. It is not used often, but it can be useful for highlighting certain values with color or changing the cells style, size or borders.

This menu has three main options:

- New Rule
- Edit Rule
- Delete Rule.'

The "**New Rule**" option will allow you to add new rules, which allows you to format multiple cells at once with the same setting (for example, all text in the cell should be bold). You can select from the different options under this group, including setting how many spaces to leave after a period or comma and the font used for it.

The "**Edit Rule**" option is used for adding new conditional formatting rules. This will give you access to even more settings and options.

The "**Delete Rule**" option is like 'Edit Rule,' but it will remove all the conditional formatting rules from your current sheet, which can be helpful if you don't want specific cells to have certain effects.

There are also two other options for setting or deleting a rule in this menu. The "**Remove All Rules**" option will delete all the rules and conditionals you currently set on your sheet. The other option, "**Manage Rules**" will launch a new window where you can set even more rules for a specific number of cells. It's not used often, but it is helpful for setting specific effects for large sets of data.

The **'Merge and Center'** option is used for merging cells to the left and right of a selected cell. This command can be helpful when you have data that spans several columns or rows and want to make it fit in a particular area.

The **'Unmerge'** option will reverse 'Merge and Center', which will separate merged cells back into individual ones. Merged cells only remain the same after they are merged. If you change the content of a previously merged cell, then it will no longer be merged when you unmerge it.

The **'Wrap Text'** option is used for wrapping the text in a cell to the next line. This is useful if a cell contains something too long to fit in it (for example, a company name that is longer than the cell itself).

The **'Fill'** option is used for filling in empty cells to the left, right, above or below a selected cell. This is useful if you have data that partially fills a cell and want the remaining content to appear in empty cells beside it.

The **'Interior'** option is used to change the background or interior of a selected cell. It will also allow you to change things like the shading and style.

The **'Toggle Cell Names'** option is used to toggle the display of each cell's name on or off. The names are what you would typically see in a spreadsheet, which can make it easier to use and identify cells (for example, if you don't know where a column is being displayed or what data it has). To toggle the names on or off simply click on this button (it will toggle the feature on and off). To display the cell's name again, click on this button once more (the characters will be shown in a thin black box next to each cell).

The **'Toggle Formula Auditing'** option is used for adding an auditing style to your spreadsheet. This adds a box around the cells you have manually entered your data in (for example, if you have filled in all the data or used a formula to update your data). It can be helpful if you want to highlight certain things or simply add a visual effect.

The **'Toggle Formula Bar'** option will display a blue bar at the bottom of your spreadsheet. This is like the Auditing style; in that it shows which cells have been manually entered into and which cells have been filled with a formula. It can be helpful for people who use formulas often as it gives them an easier way to find where their data is coming from (instead of searching every cell individually).

The **'Insert'** option is used for inserting comments, images and shapes into your spreadsheets. This option will bring up a new panel to insert these objects. You can always add comments at the end of your worksheets, but they are often not seen by other people or they may be too long to be relevant. The images and shapes are useful for adding tiny graphics or icons in your workbook to make it more aesthetically pleasing.

There are two dissimilar styles that you can use for inserting an image or shape in a cell: 'Insert Shapes' and 'Insert Pictures'. The 'Insert Shapes' option will allow you to insert shapes that can be used for things like borders and glares. These can look good, depending on what you are trying to do with it. The 'Insert Pictures' option will insert images into a cell. This allows you to use images that can be quite complex and make your spreadsheet look interesting (for example, an image of a map of the world).

The **'Create a Comment'** option is used for adding a comment to your spreadsheet. Comments are usually used to describe the content of a cell and what each number or formula means. They can also ask someone else a question about the data. This is useful when you want people to see what your data means without looking at all of it first.

The right-most button on this panel, 'Change Comment,' is used for editing an existing comment in your spreadsheet.

The **'Add Attachment'** option adds external files to your spreadsheet. This is useful if you want to comprise an image or a large amount of text somewhere else. To set this, you will need to add the file that you are uploading into the same folder as your spreadsheet, then go to the 'Insert' option, and from where it has been attached, you can use it.

The **'Add a Chart'** option is meant for adding charts to your spreadsheet. Charts can be used to display any data in the world (other than numbers). They are usually used to show icons, pictures, maps, or data that needs a visual representation.

The options discussed so far are primarily used for formatting and adding extra features to spreadsheets. This will help you make your workbook the way you want it. The rest of the buttons on this panel are mainly used for analyzing data and finding specific information. These options are not very important to make your workbook look good, but they can be helpful if you want to analyze it.

Chapter 7. DATA PRESENTING TECHNIQUES

Presentation plays an integral part in any field - including statistics and data analysis. In general, data visualization is a framework for analyzing data, presenting the results, and learning more about the underlying factors.

There are many dissimilar ways to view the data in your spreadsheet. You can let the data tell for itself, or you can choose to analyze it and extract knowledge from it. This is a material of personal preference, and you should use whatever displays your results in the best way.

DATA VISUALIZATION

The idea of data visualization is to present large quantities of numerical information in meaningful ways to the human eye. The use of data visualization techniques can help you communicate your findings statistically, reduce stress caused by large amounts of information, and improve productivity.

The Benefits: Data Visualization Techniques

Improve accuracy: Make sure your data is reliable by presenting it visually. It is easier to see where errors are in your work - find them earlier and save time.

Save time: Reduce the amount of time spent analyzing data by presenting it visually. - Reduce stress: Data visualization techniques can help alleviate stress caused by large amounts of information and improve productivity.

Communicate results: Presenting a paper visually, rather than just with text, is more exciting and engaging for readers.

Enhance learning: Visualization tools help learn about data.

Stay organized: If a visualization helps keep you organized, then it can help you stay organized.

Reduce stress caused by large amounts of information: You will feel less stressed if you can make sense of the huge volume of information and identify patterns in your data. - Make complex concepts easier to understand: Sometimes, we struggle to understand significant ideas because they are difficult to explain verbally, even with simple diagrams. Visualization can help make complex ideas more understandable.

DATA VALIDATION

Many types of errors can occur during data entry. These include: - Data entry errors: Dropping a digit, transposing two numbers, etc. While entering the data, it's easy to make mistakes that may not be obvious to you until much later.

Quantitative errors: The most common quantitative mistake is when someone puts the wrong number in a cell. Simple multiplication or division of cells can easily result in an incorrect value.

Value errors: A value error occurs when someone inputs a data type that Excel doesn't recognize. This can happen when someone misuses a function, or it could be an entirely new function.

Content errors: These are errors that occur with the content of the data itself. It could be characters in a string exceeding the capacity of the cell (less than 255 characters) or an invalid name, text, or logical value.

Type Mismatch: This is an error that occurs when someone attempts to enter the wrong type of data in a specific cell. For example, you can't put a number into a cell designated for text.

Logical errors occur when someone inputs a value for one thing, but Excel interprets it to mean something else.

Data type errors: This is like the type mismatch error, except Excel recognizes the data as being in the wrong format.

VALIDATION RULES

Validation rules are set up to make sure the accuracy of your data. In the case of Excel, you can use validation rules to set up certain functions and formulas so that they will only be carried out if the input is correct. You can have validation rules for ranges, columns, and individual cells. If a validation rule exists for a cell, it won't accept an entry unless it complies with that rule.

Data integrity: Data integrity is when your data doesn't have any errors or problems. You should have validation rules for data integrity to ensure sloppy or careless data entry does not ruin your work.

Accuracy: In Excel, a validation rule is called an error rule. It ensures that your cell entries are accurate and not just any old random string.

Find and fix errors: You attempt to find and fix errors that occur when you enter the data into your spreadsheet. Most of them will appear as minor errors that can be corrected later by editing the worksheet or changing the cell with the error. However, you will also want to prevent the mistakes from occurring in the first place.

Prevent errors: Validation rules are a good tool in your spreadsheet to prevent data entry errors. However, you also should spend lots of time ensuring that all the data entered your spreadsheet is accurate and proper. Some familiar sources of errors include typos, logical fallacies, and invalid function calls.

Here are some tips to teach you effectively present your data:

Color coding: Most people appreciate color coding, as it makes it easy to see patterns in the data. Typically, you use color to represent sales, expenses, and gross profit.

Shapes: There are many shapes in the Excel library that you can use to organize your data visually. For example, if you want to display a pie chart for each quarter of your data, you can map out the pie charts in a column and then outline them with a single shape.

Gridlines: You can hide gridlines or show them as dotted lines (this makes it easier to see the boundaries between columns). The grid lines can be used to create a 2D graph or used in a 3D graph.

BAR(graph): This is a bar graph because it has one dominant value and multiple values that fall on top of the principal value. You can make your bar graphs easier to read by centering the bars within their columns and showing the above or below the bars.

Atlas: An atlas represents data from multiple source documents as one big picture. An atlas allows you to see the relationships between various data sources.

Timelines: A timeline allows you to organize your data based on dates. This makes it smoother for viewers to see patterns in the data.

Clustering: Clustered charts group similar data items together in a single bar or column, making it easier to see patterns and trends within that grouping.

3D: 3D is a way to present data in a manner that is easy to read and understand.

Data Visualization can help the visually impaired navigate through data in a meaningful way. Data visualization projects aim to give people who cannot access visual information and use assistive technology a chance to understand the data presented.

DATA PRESENTING TECHNIQUES:

Data Analysis- Spreadsheets are great, but what if we're trying to present our data in a more digestible and aesthetically appealing way? If that sounds like something you're in, you might want to brush up on your Excel skills. So, are you ready to be an Excel master?

Four Techniques for Presenting Data

1. Visual Profit Chart

This is pretty much like a visual histogram, only instead of giving percentages, the scale is a logarithmic one. The idea is to show the "distribution" of your data. So instead of just showing the percent difference between two points, you can visualize everything in a percentage-less way by using this technique.

2. Insightful Pivot Tables

Excel allows you to create pivot tables that show insights into your work. It's a good idea to use simple colors (red, yellow, and green) to denote positive/negative values. You can also use it to create a visual table of data sorted by specific criteria. Not only does this method make the data easier to process, but it also gives a more visual presentation.

3. Showing Change with Formulas

This is where using the IF function helps. In a spreadsheet, it is possible to create a formula to change the color of cells depending upon what factors you choose. For example, you can change color depending on whether the sales are increasing or decreasing.

4. Categorizing with Chart Groups

Charts are great, but they can get confusing quite quickly. Therefore, it's a good idea to group specific charts so that everything looks more organized and tidier. Not only that, but it's also easy to digest.

If you adore what you do, why not share the love? That's right – since you're efficient at Excel, why not take the time to teach others how to be just like you? Doing so will not only show that they should respect your skills, but it will also give them something valuable in return. Make sure you're performing what you love and teaching others to follow their dreams as well.

VARYING LEVELS OF DIFFICULTY

Some Excel tasks are simple, even if you've never touched an Excel spreadsheet in your life. Then, those tasks require a bit more knowledge and practice to complete. Many times, it's best to start on the more accessible side of the spectrum before you move on to more complex topics.

For example, if you want to learn how to create a Pivot Table, it's best not to skip the first step. You don't want to drip the ball in this area and then have no idea what you're supposed to do in the second step. If you can complete step one, it wouldn't be that hard for you to move on with step two.

In the end, you'll be able to do whatever it is that you need to do with Excel.

ASYNCHRONOUS PROCESSES

If you're just like me, you find yourself working on multiple projects at one time, with one thing constantly distracting you from working on something else. If you place one enormous task in front of you at a time, it can be challenging to maintain your focus. The most acceptable way to handle this is to break your larger project into multiple parts. This way, you're able to work on several different things simultaneously, which will help keep you focused on the task at hand. In that way, you won't be distracted by something else while completing a project.

The only headache with this method is that it might take longer to complete a project because you're splitting your focus, but it's better this way than the alternative. You can always work on one task at a time after all your "pieces" have been completed.

One of the huge gest reasons people don't work as effectively as they can is because they try to complete everything all at once. Also, they continuously restructure their projects as they go. By splitting up your work into different parts, you force yourself to complete each one of these separate tasks. This helps you stay on task and prevent distractions from other projects that may be going on simultaneously.

Here are a few different techniques that can help improve your efficiency in Excel:

1. Work with Multiple Projects at Once

When you're on a large project, it's possible that several parts of it can be completed simultaneously. There might be some tasks that only take a few minutes, so you may as well handle them while you're working on something else. Then other tasks can only be accomplished once those smaller tasks have been finished.

2. Work with the Same Data in Multiple Spreadsheets

If you're on a large project, the chances are good that there will be several different Excel spreadsheets associated with it. These various spreadsheets might be spread out over several days or even weeks. The best way to handle this work is to always work with the same data in each spreadsheet. This way, if you need to reference it for something else, later, you know where it's located.

A very typical example is if you're creating a sales report. You'll probably want to start by creating a spreadsheet that has all your products listed on it. As you complete each invoice, you'll need to keep this spreadsheet updated with the latest information. Then, you might have another sheet that has all your products listed in it again, but this time it includes their current inventory level. You'll also want to create a report that calculates the difference between these two numbers. Likewise, if you always work with the same data in every spreadsheet throughout your project, everything should fall into place once you're done.

3. Work with a Time-Based Schedule

This is one of the leading ways to ensure you're staying on task. If you're working on different parts of your project simultaneously, you'll be able to break them up into sections based on their due dates. You can then schedule your work based on how long it will take to complete each part. This will help you avoid procrastinating and keep yourself on track. Some people can also use their schedule as a reward for completing certain portions of their work.

Chapter 8. BASIC FUNCTIONALITIES

Most features and functions are the most widely used spreadsheet application for personal and business purposes. The application has maintained its popularity due to its ease of use, dependability, and adaptability. Excel is used throughout the world to manage data and make informed business decisions. It is currently the most used spreadsheet program. In this area, we have gathered a list of the majority of Excel's features and functionalities for your perusal. Excel further enables you to make charts. This permits you to modify your data's representation so that it can be easily visualized. Excel provides both 2D and 3D charts for this function, allowing you to generate visual representations of your data in 2D and 3D forms. This tool allows you to generate pie charts, histograms, and even gauge bars in only minutes.

ADDING NEW ROWS AND COLUMNS

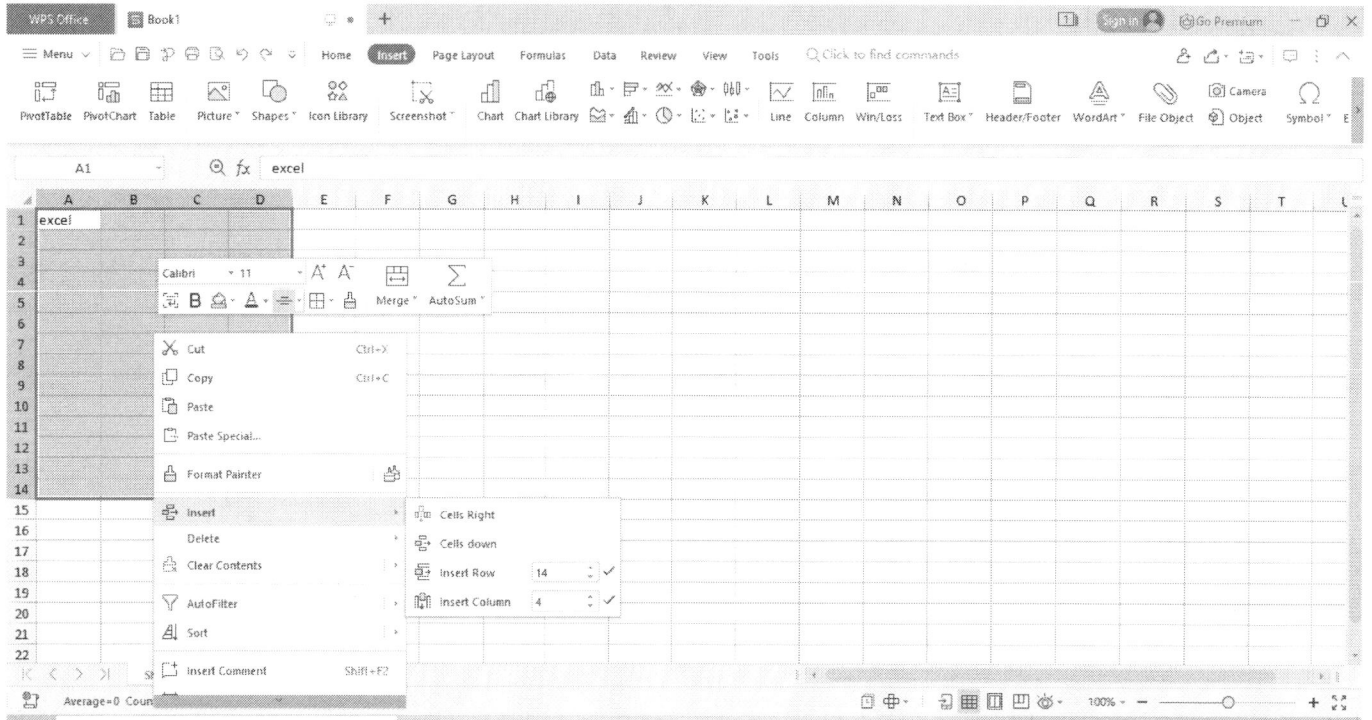

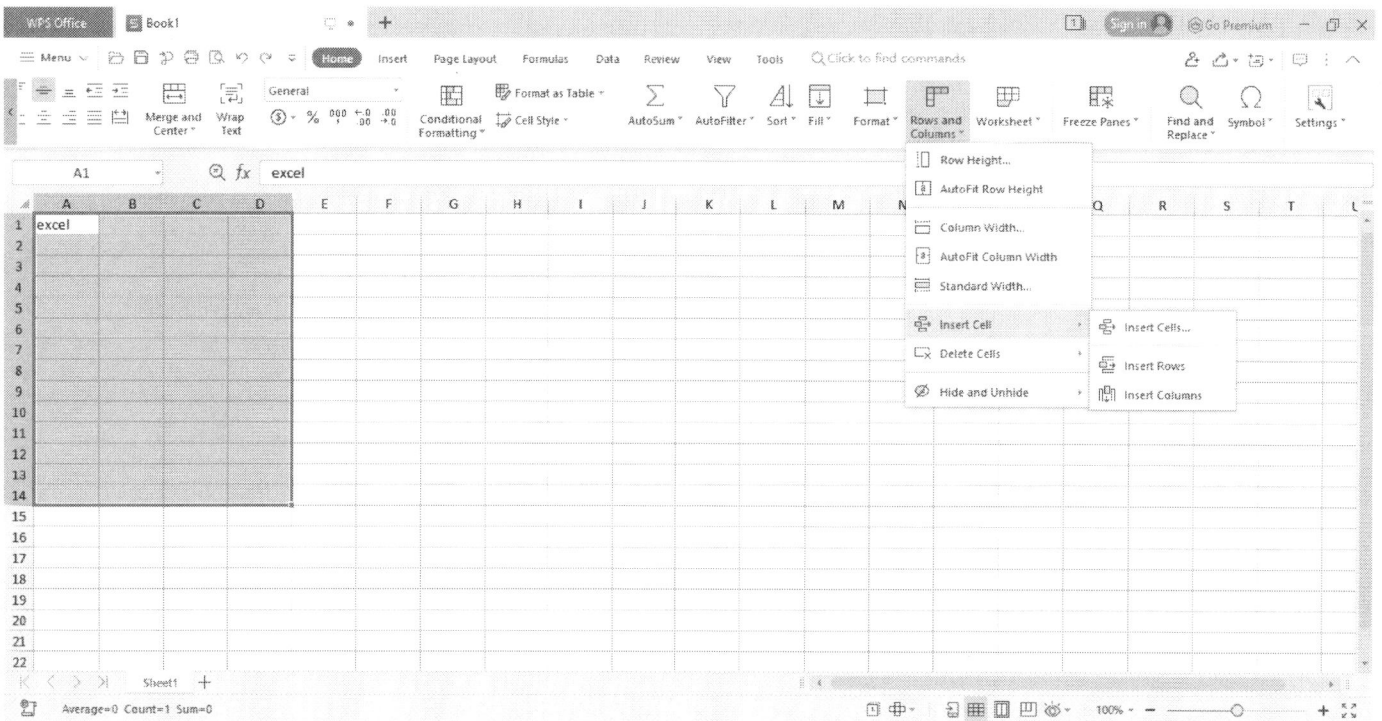

Excel facilitates the addition of new rows and columns to a workbook. This allows you to generate more comprehensive assessments of your data. Additionally, this allows you to be creative and display more data points simultaneously in a chart. Excel also permits you to hide or reposition existing rows and columns, if required for your study. Excel also provides the ability to enter and change material, including text and numbers. This can be accomplished by manually entering them into your worksheets or by importing data from raw text files.

CREATING CHARTS

Excel also gives you the opportunity to construct numerous types of charts to make your job more aesthetically appealing (line, graph, bar, image). It provides a variety of choices for customizing the style of your charts to make your data appear more plain and assured. This feature allows you to modify the color scheme, column widths, and borders. It also allows you to improve the visual appeal of your charts by adding photos and changing or removing chart elements such as names and axes.

CALCULATORS

SUMIF | fx =SUM(C4:C9)

CALCULATOR WITH FORMULAS

SUPPLIES	2020		SUPPLIES	2021		SUPPLIES	2020	Months		SUPPLIES	2021	Months
APPLES	13,000		APPLES	11,000		APPLES	13,000	156,000		APPLES	11,000	917
LIMES	9,000		LIMES	5,000		LIMES	9,000	108,000		LIMES	5,000	417
PINEAPPLES	3,000		PINEAPPLES	1,500		PINEAPPLES	3,000	36,000		PINEAPPLES	1,500	125
BERRIES	21,000		BERRIES	19,000		BERRIES	21,000	252,000		BERRIES	19,000	1,583
ORANGES	12,000		ORANGES	11,000		ORANGES	12,000	144,000		ORANGES	11,000	917
GRAPES	6,000		GRAPES	35,000		GRAPES	6,000	72,000		GRAPES	35,000	2,917
	=SUM(C4:C9)			-80,479								

ADDITION

SUMIF | fx =G3-G4-G5-G6-G7-G8-G9

CALCULATOR WITH FORMULAS

SUPPLIES	2020		SUPPLIES	2021		SUPPLIES	2020	Months		SUPPLIES	2021	Months
APPLES	13,000		APPLES	11,000		APPLES	13,000	156,000		APPLES	11,000	917
LIMES	9,000		LIMES	5,000		LIMES	9,000	108,000		LIMES	5,000	417
PINEAPPLES	3,000		PINEAPPLES	1,500		PINEAPPLES	3,000	36,000		PINEAPPLES	1,500	125
BERRIES	21,000		BERRIES	19,000		BERRIES	21,000	252,000		BERRIES	19,000	1,583
ORANGES	12,000		ORANGES	11,000		ORANGES	12,000	144,000		ORANGES	11,000	917
GRAPES	6,000		GRAPES	35,000		GRAPES	6,000	72,000		GRAPES	35,000	2,917
	64,000			=G3-G4-G5-G6-G7-G8-G9								

SUBTRACTION

Screenshot 1 — Formula bar: =K4*12

CALCULATOR WITH FORMULAS

SUPPLIES	2020		SUPPLIES	2021		SUPPLIES	2020	Months		SUPPLIES	2021	Months
APPLES	13,000		APPLES	11,000		APPLES	13,000	=K4 *12		APPLES	11,000	917
LIMES	9,000		LIMES	5,000		LIMES	9,000	108,000		LIMES	5,000	417
PINEAPPLES	3,000		PINEAPPLES	1,500		PINEAPPLES	3,000	36,000		PINEAPPLES	1,500	125
BERRIES	21,000		BERRIES	19,000		BERRIES	21,000	252,000		BERRIES	19,000	1,583
ORANGES	12,000		ORANGES	11,000		ORANGES	12,000	144,000		ORANGES	11,000	917
GRAPES	6,000		GRAPES	35,000		GRAPES	6,000	72,000		GRAPES	35,000	2,917
	64,000			-80,479								

MULTIPLICATION

Screenshot 2 — Formula bar: =P4/12

CALCULATOR WITH FORMULAS

SUPPLIES	2020		SUPPLIES	2021		SUPPLIES	2020	Months		SUPPLIES	2021	Months
APPLES	13,000		APPLES	11,000		APPLES	13,000	156,000		APPLES	11,000	=P4 /12
LIMES	9,000		LIMES	5,000		LIMES	9,000	108,000		LIMES	5,000	417
PINEAPPLES	3,000		PINEAPPLES	1,500		PINEAPPLES	3,000	36,000		PINEAPPLES	1,500	125
BERRIES	21,000		BERRIES	19,000		BERRIES	21,000	252,000		BERRIES	19,000	1,583
ORANGES	12,000		ORANGES	11,000		ORANGES	12,000	144,000		ORANGES	11,000	917
GRAPES	6,000		GRAPES	35,000		GRAPES	6,000	72,000		GRAPES	35,000	2,917
	64,000			-80,479								

DIVISION

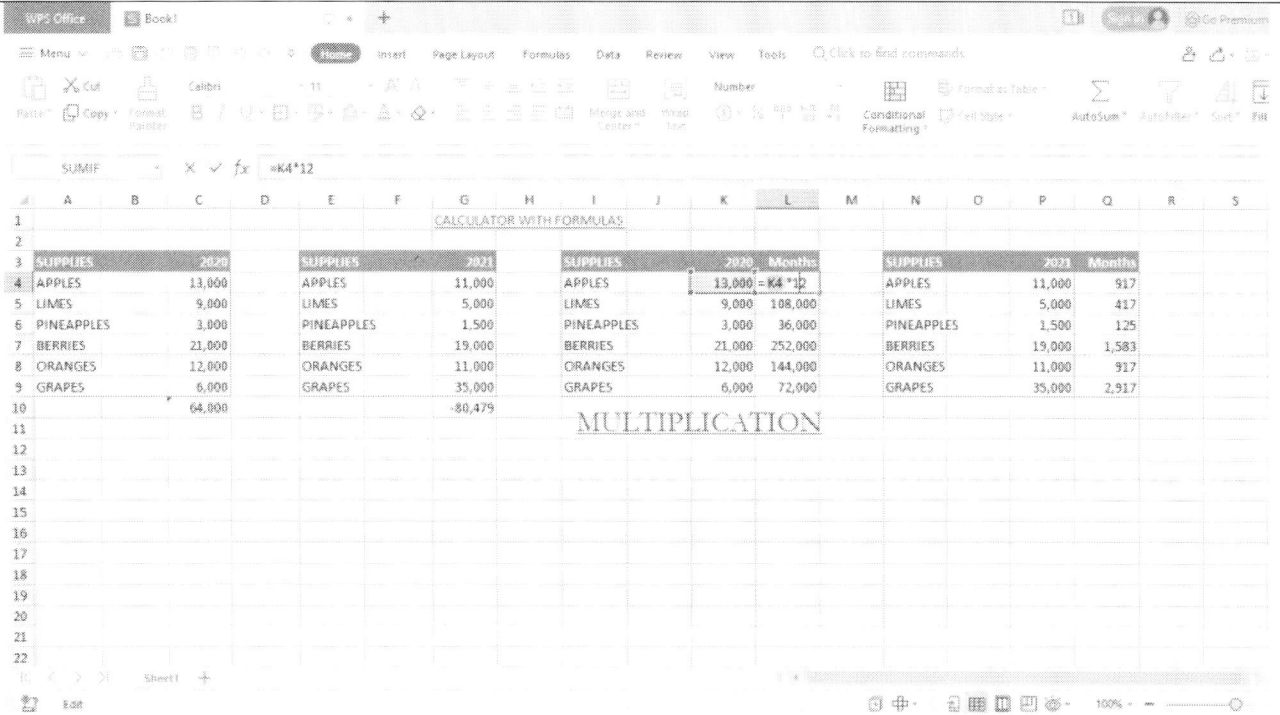

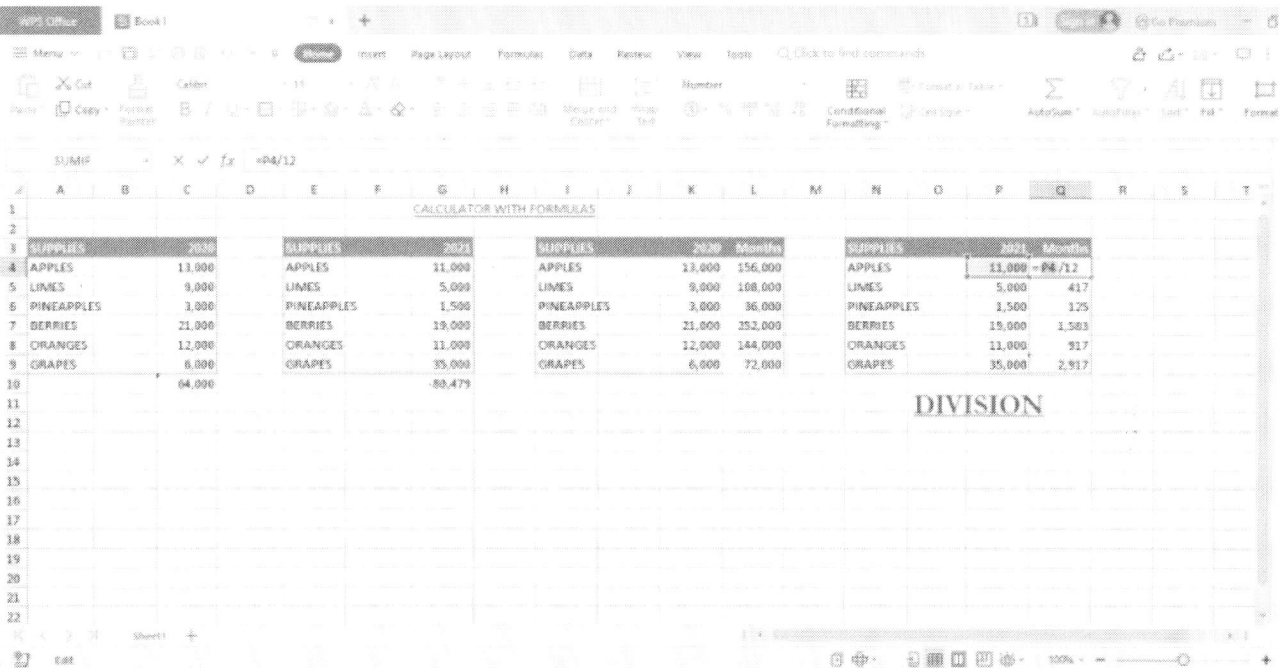

This is the most popular spreadsheet function. It makes addition, subtraction, multiplication, and division simple. Thus, you can efficiently manipulate numbers without needing to launch a separate program.

CONDITIONAL FORMATTING

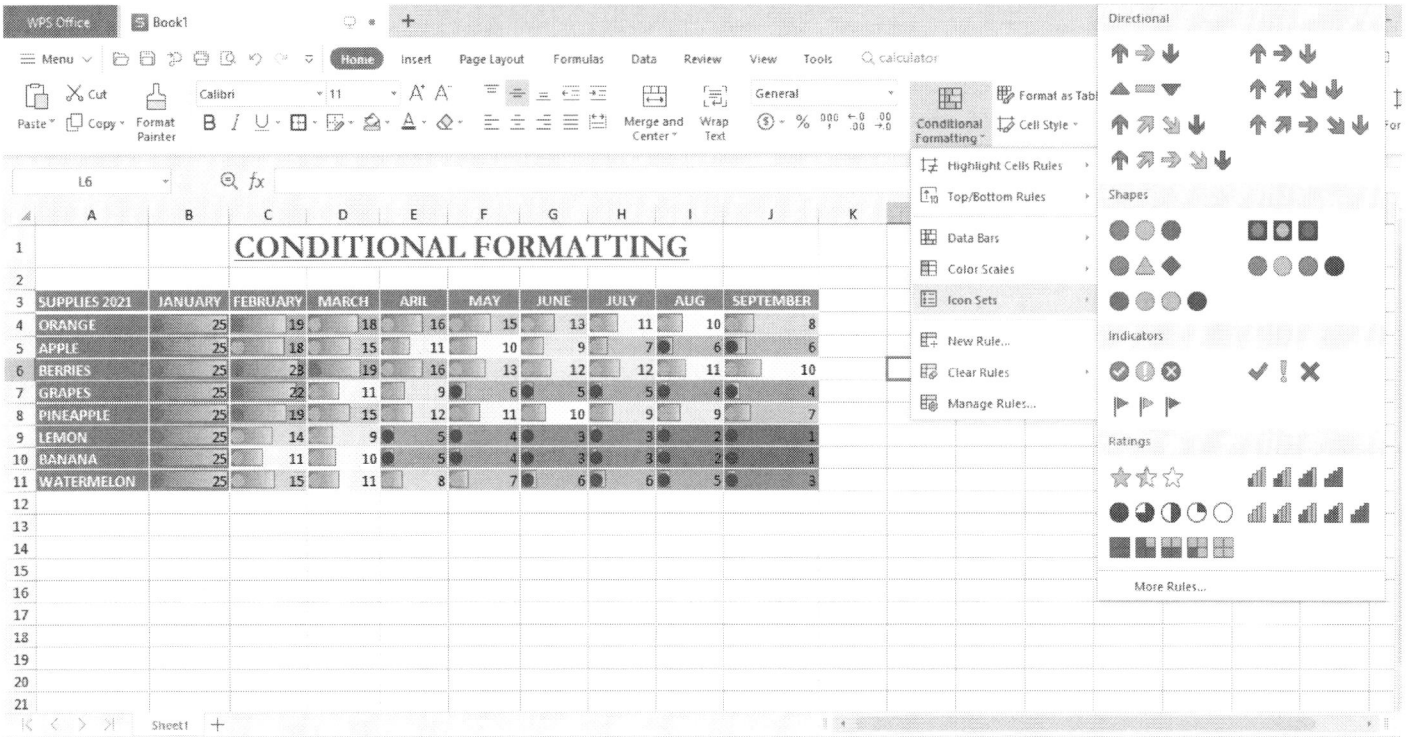

This feature enables the creation of charts and graphs that highlight various features of data based on current and historical situations. This is helpful for showing data trends and patterns as well as deviations from critical requirements. In addition to conditional formatting, Excel has several other features, including percentile charts, pivot tables, and charts with multiple series.

TEXT-TO-COLUMNS

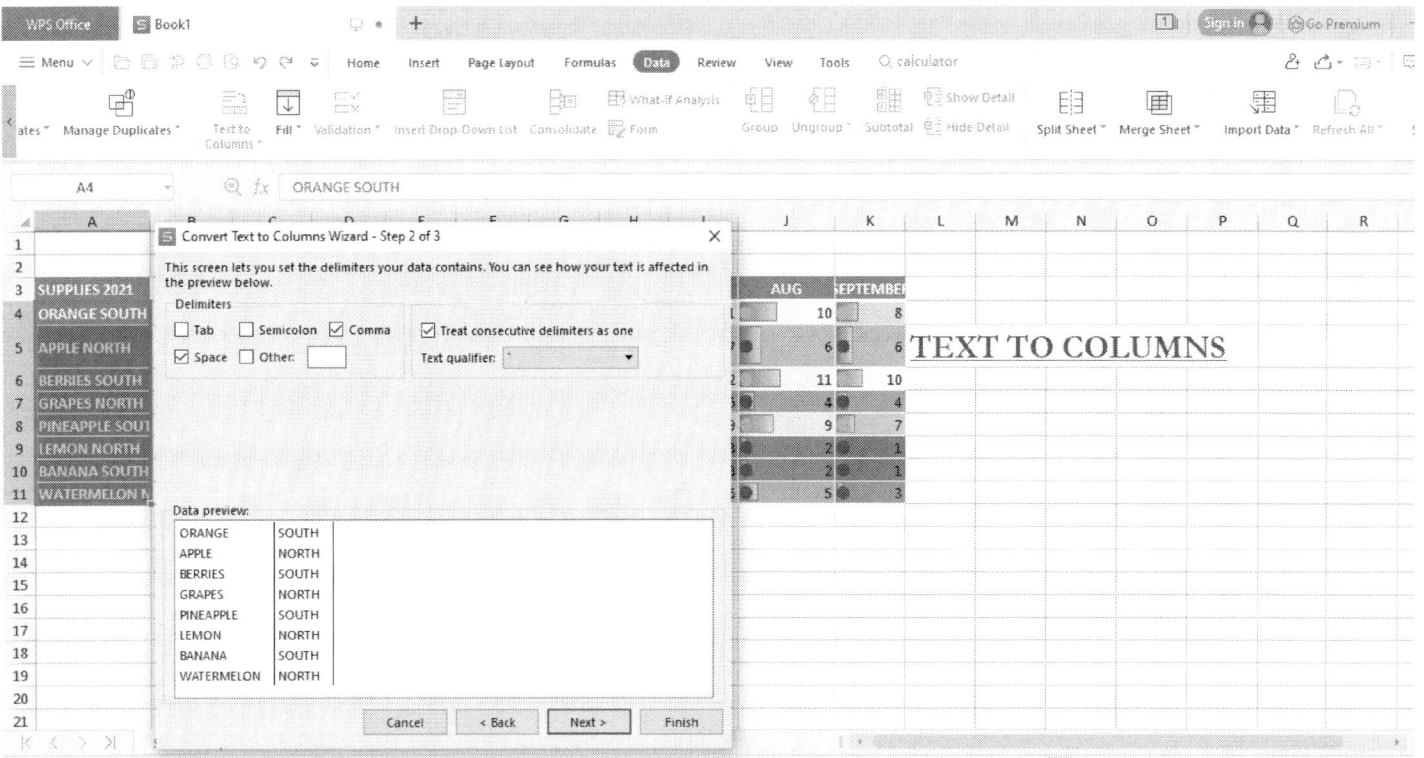

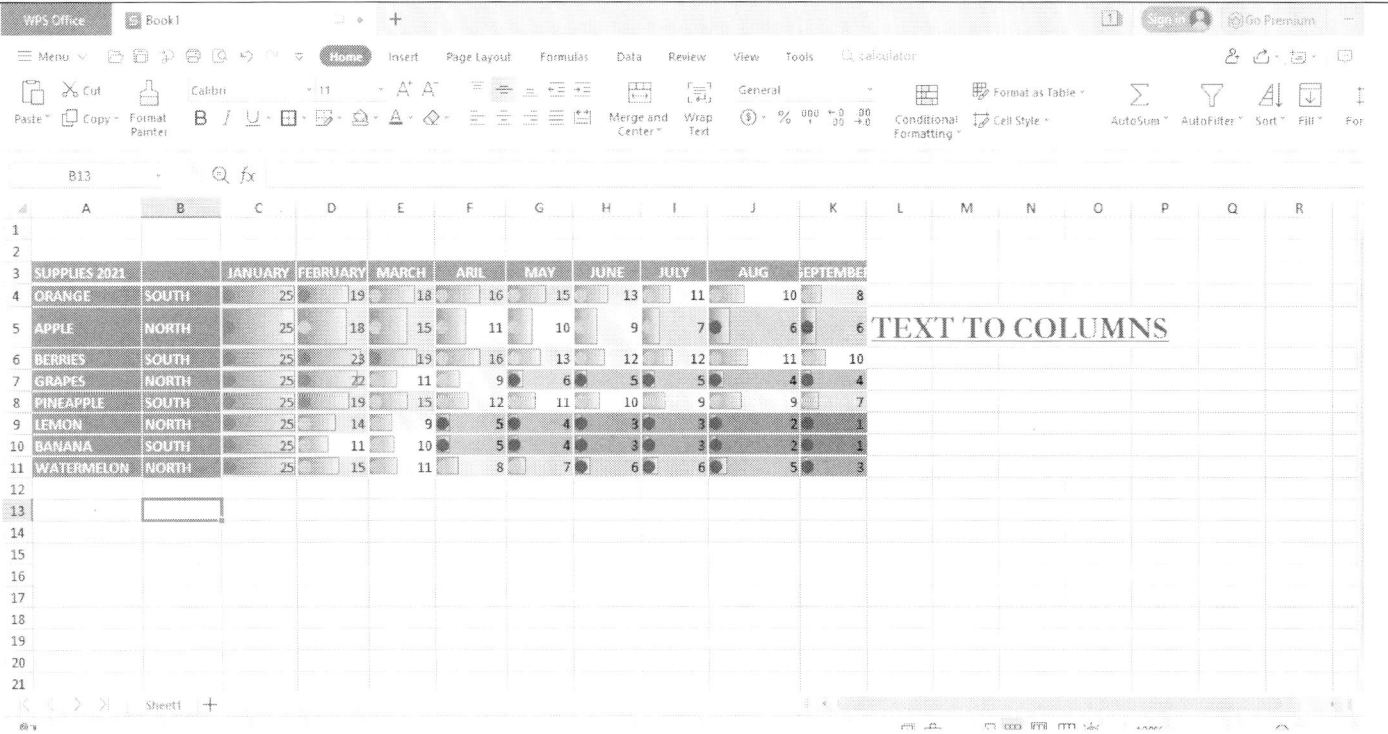

This function enables you to separate a text into columns and mix it with other data, such as dates and numbers. This will allow you to conveniently organize numbers and dates in rows rather than columns.

COLOR SCHEMES

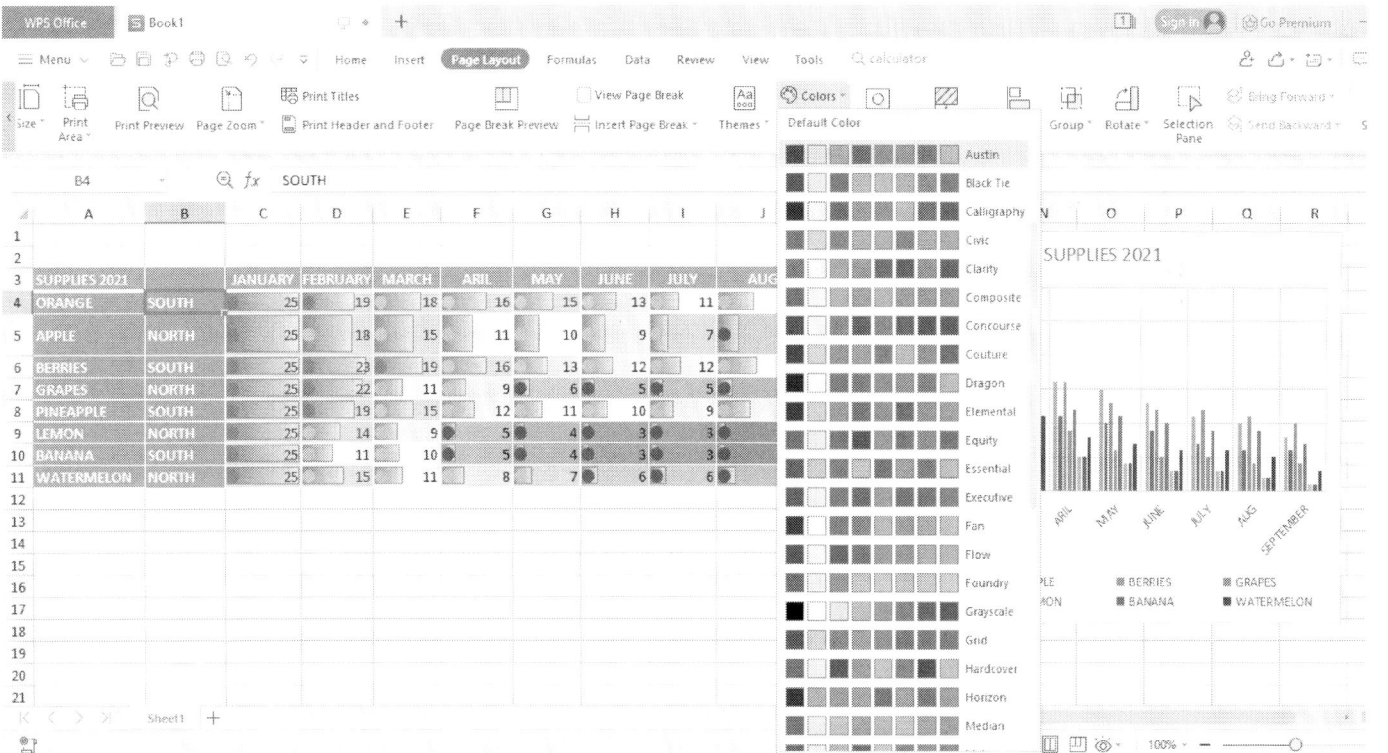

You may automatically colorize cells based on their values with this tool. This facilitates the visualization of a distribution or trend in your workbook.

AUTOFILTER

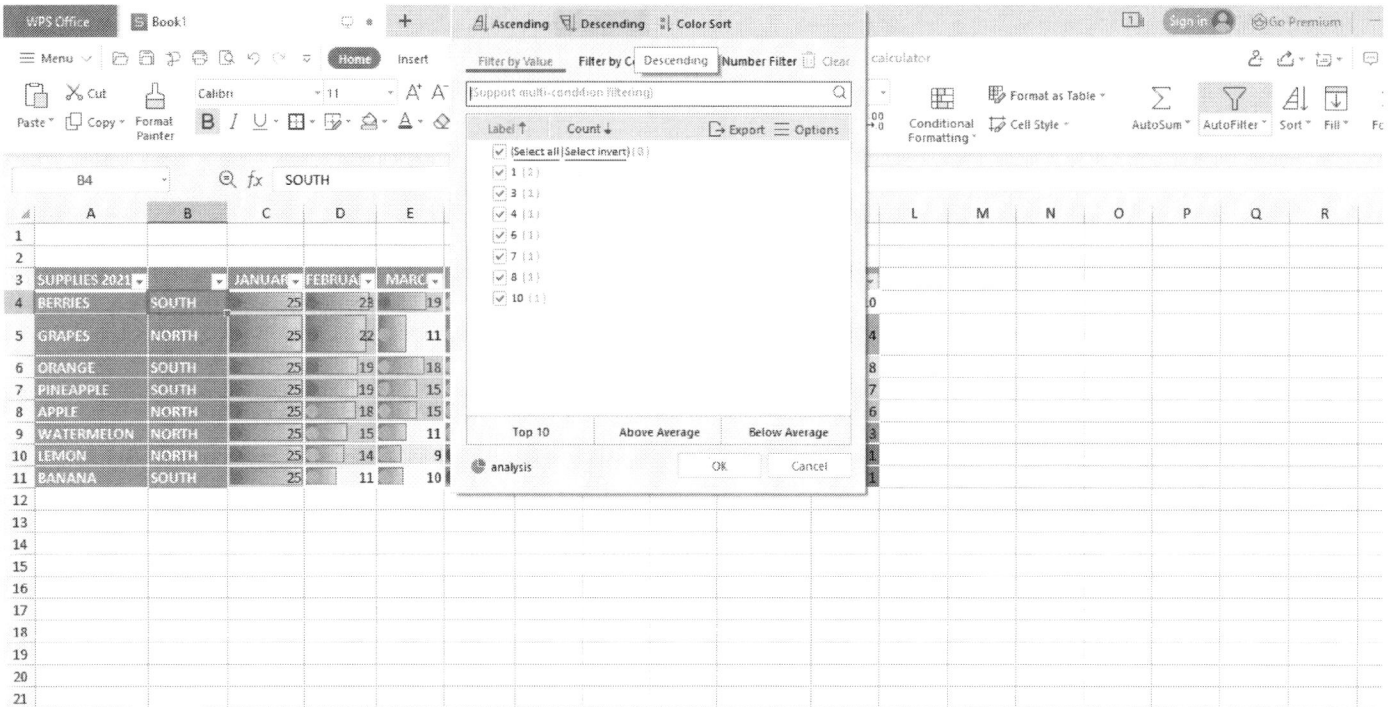

This function highlights rows of data that fulfill a given set of criteria. This application enables you to automatically filter material by substituting certain portions of your data with data from other sources. AutoFilter is an amazing tool for rapidly filtering data, allowing you to focus on what matters most at any given time. This method allows you to rapidly sort enormous volumes of data to reveal only the most essential information. It enables you to filter data by column or row, and in several orientations.

CURSOR

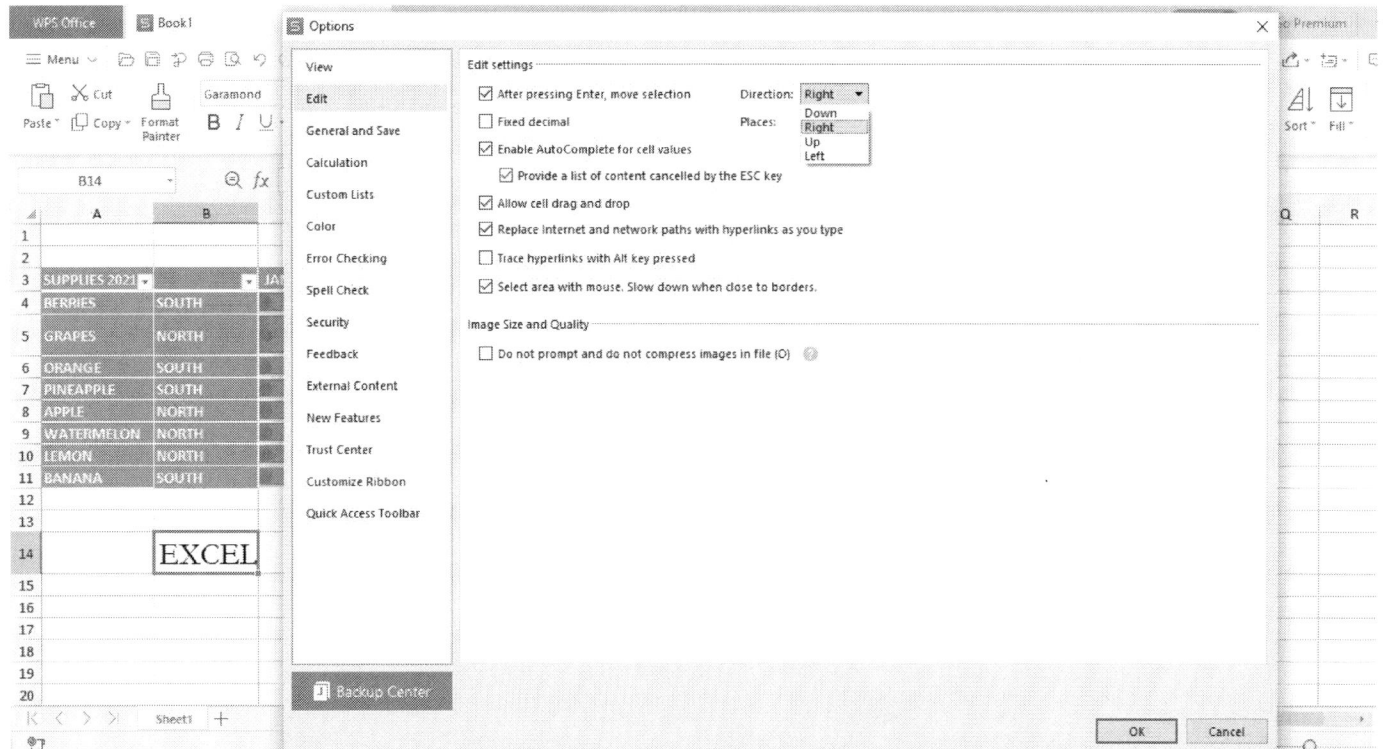

The cursor represents the location where new text will be input. This tool allows you to move the pointer to a different cell to view a different section of your data. This allows you to swiftly navigate between different sections of your workbook without the need for numerous tools.

DRAGGING

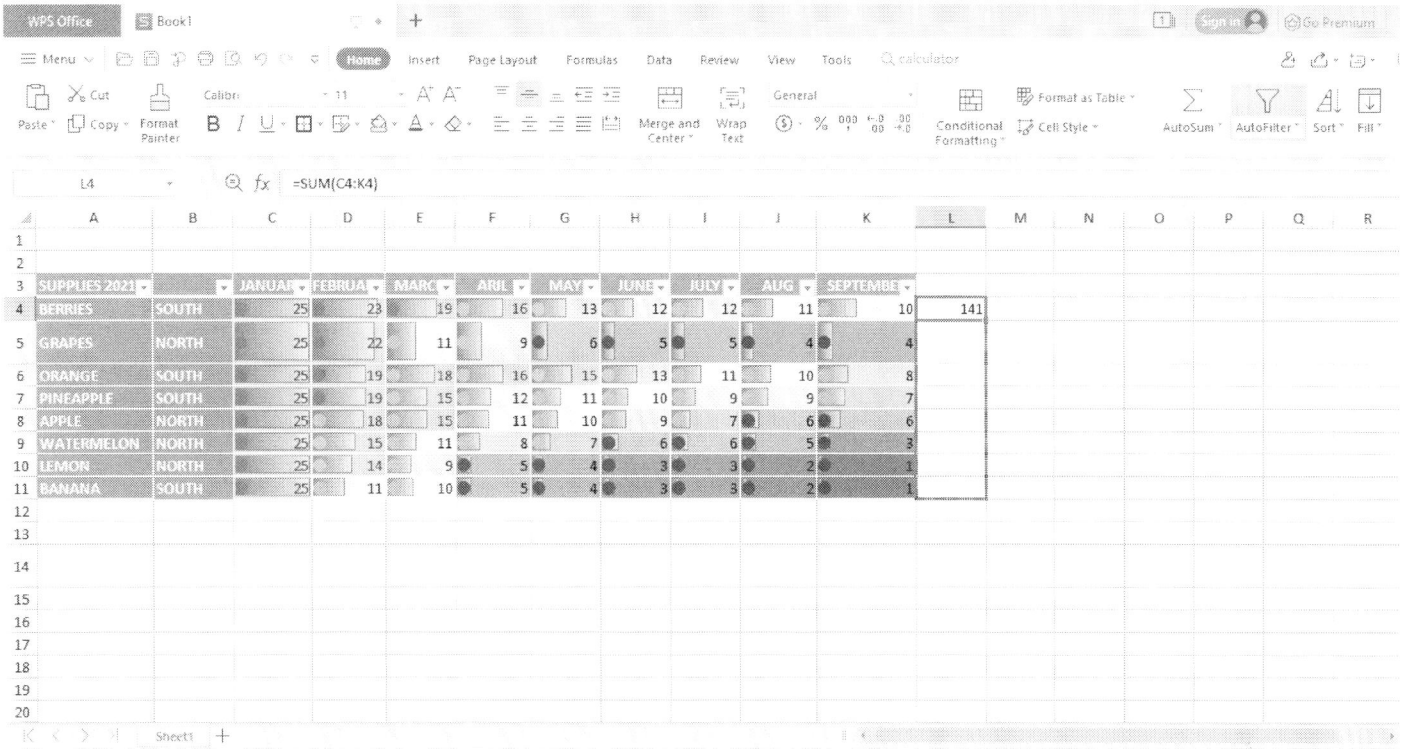

The entire column will follow the column's label when it is dragged in a spreadsheet. This tool allows you to rapidly reorganize worksheet sections. It allows you to transfer information between cells, folders, and even other files.

MULTI-THREADING

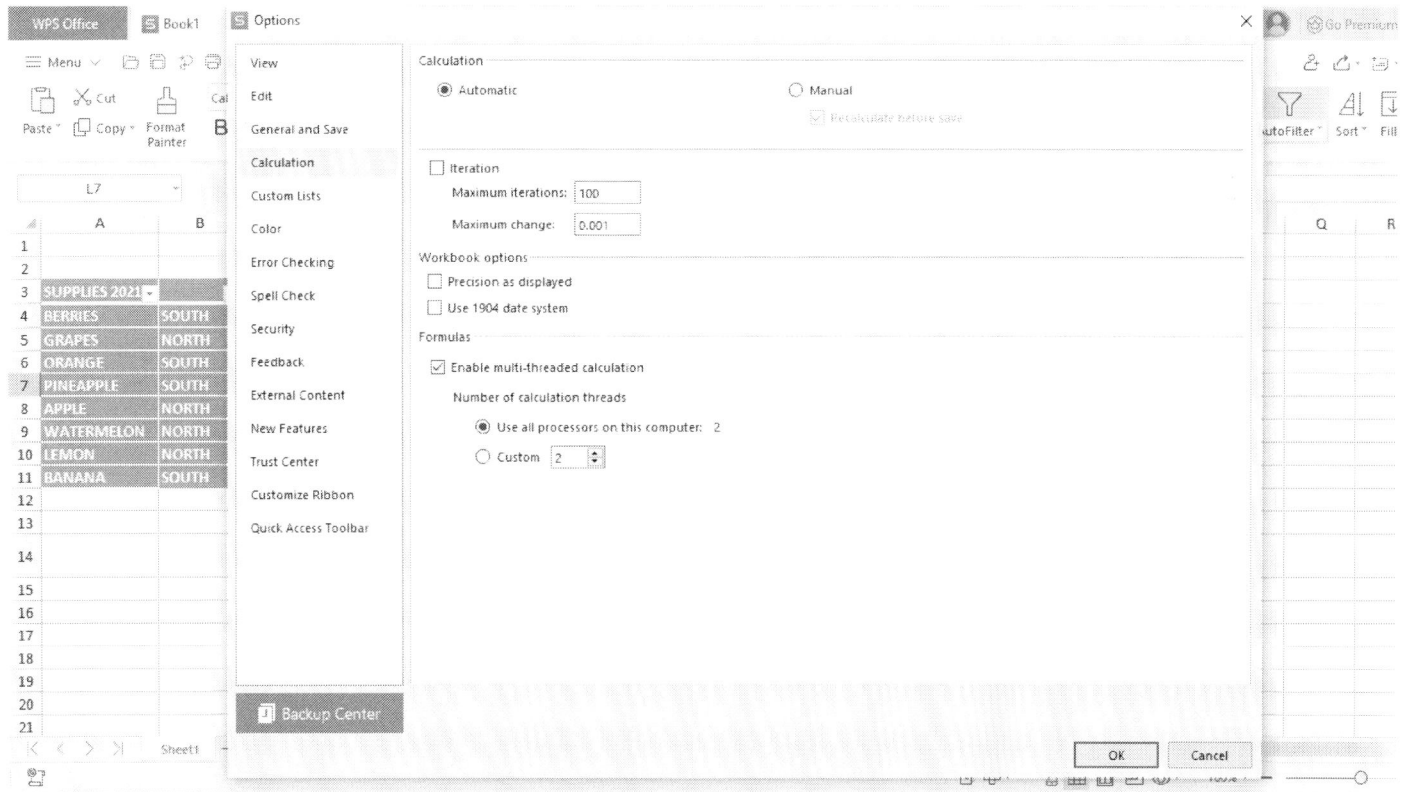

This function allows Excel to optimally utilize the computer's resources by doing several calculations in parallel. It has a significant impact on the computation speed of your spreadsheet. This allows you to execute numerous things simultaneously on your computer. It can offer additional functionality such as spellchecking while entering text in a cell while maintaining an open and accessible software interface.

CELL NUMERICAL OPERATION

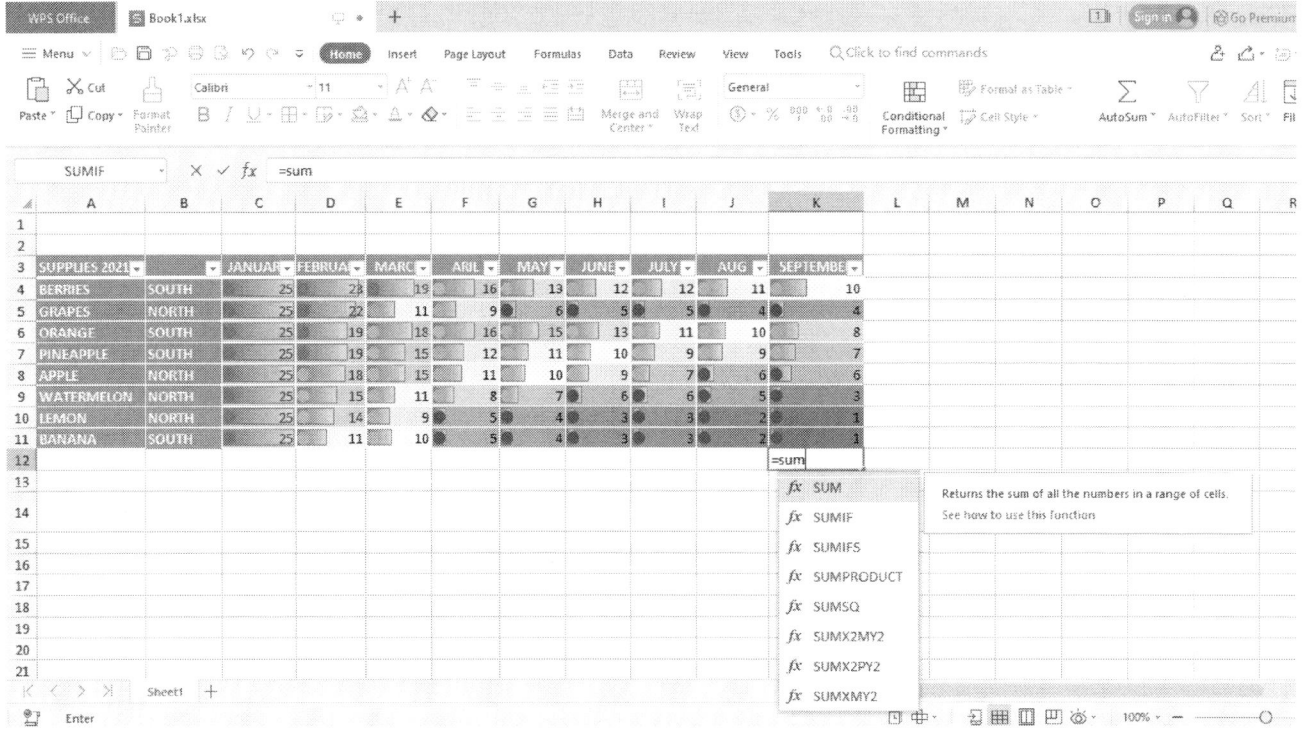

This tool enables you to apply mathematical functions to cell values. You can use this tool, for instance, to add, subtract, or multiply integers in a cell.

SORTING

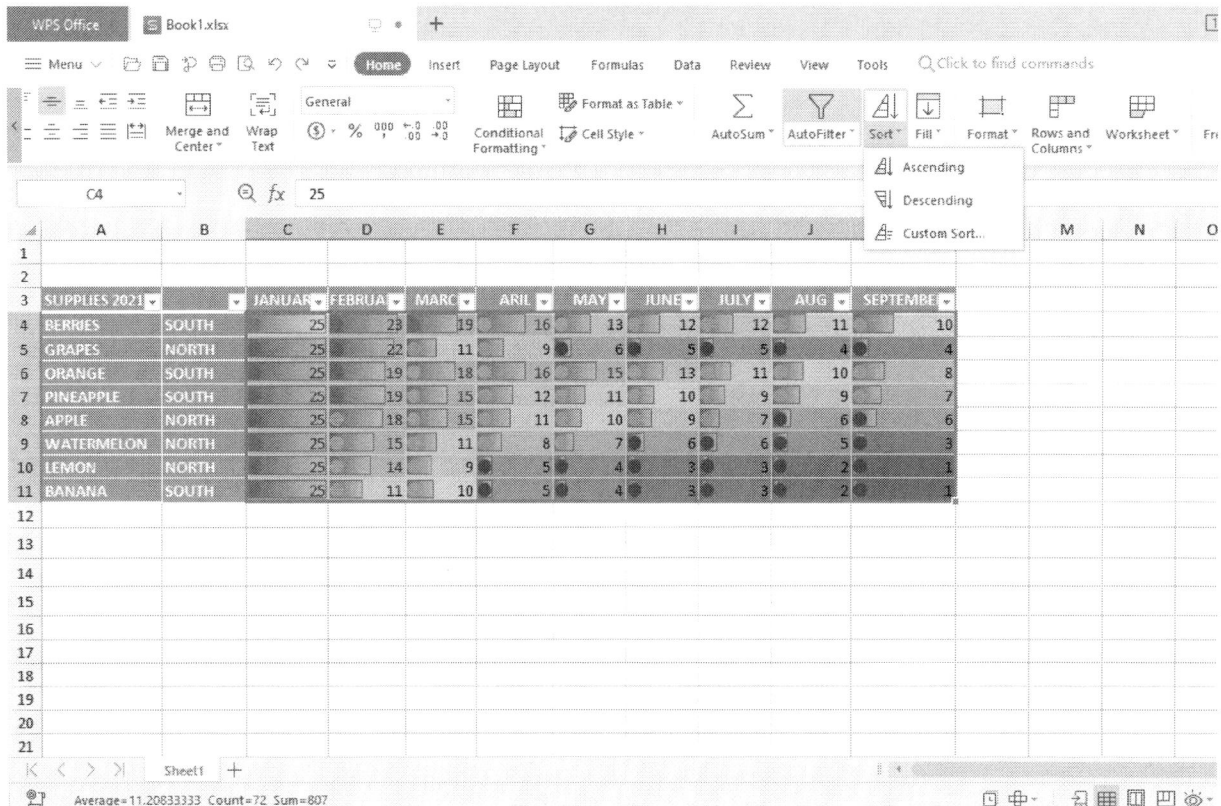

This feature allows you to rapidly organize content in a variety of ways. It allows you to sort data, for instance, in ascending or descending order.

ADD-IN-EXCEL

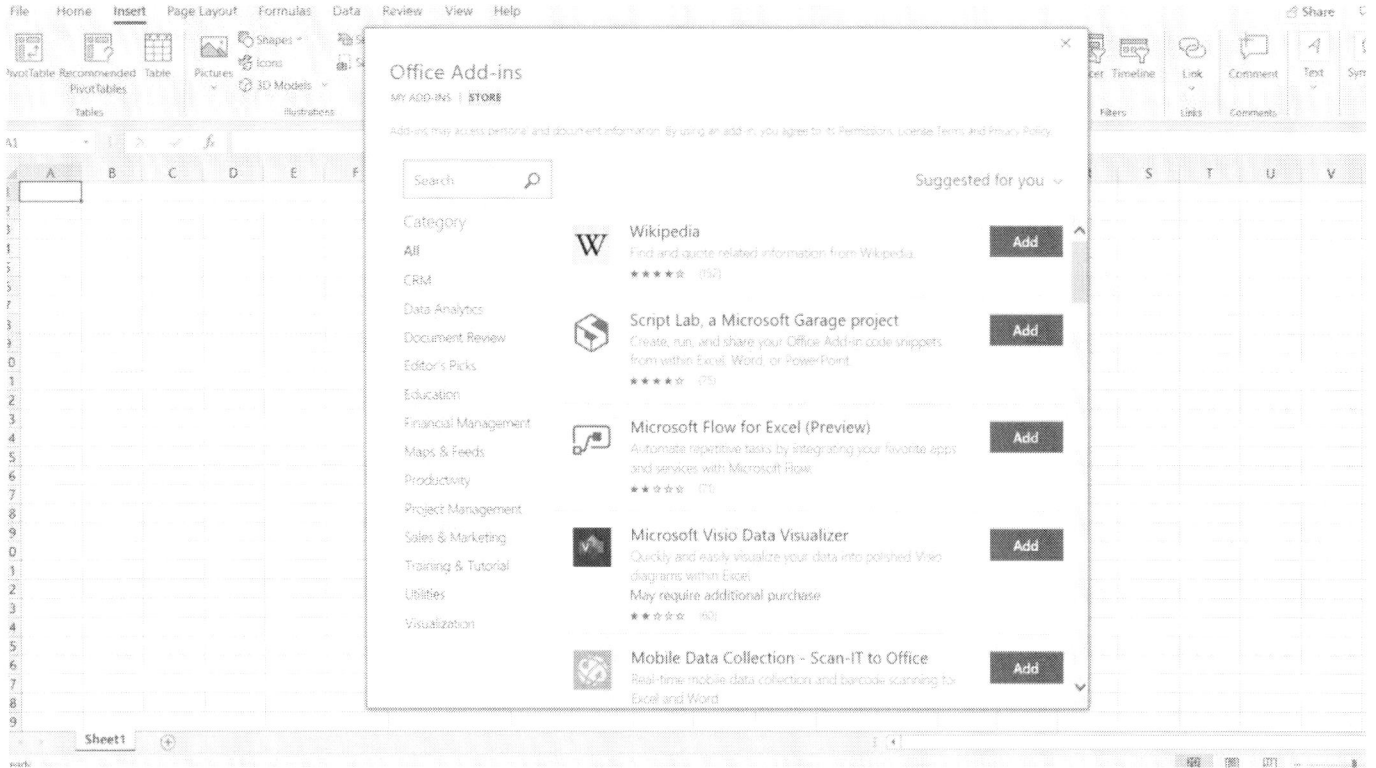

Permits the installation of add-ins, which extend the functionality of the base program. This implies that you may add tools for visualizing data from numerous sources, retrieving information from the internet, and generating content on the fly.

CELL COMMENTS

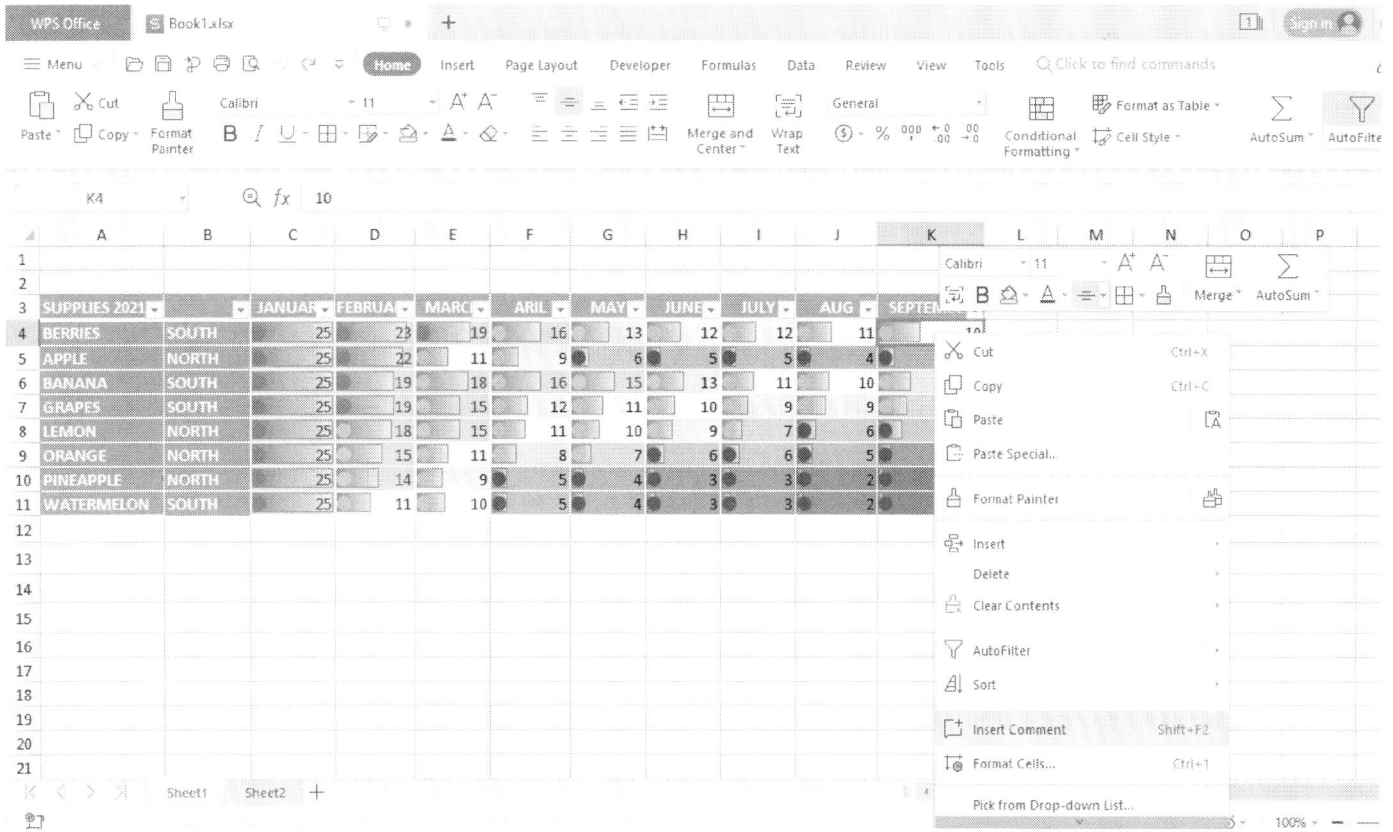

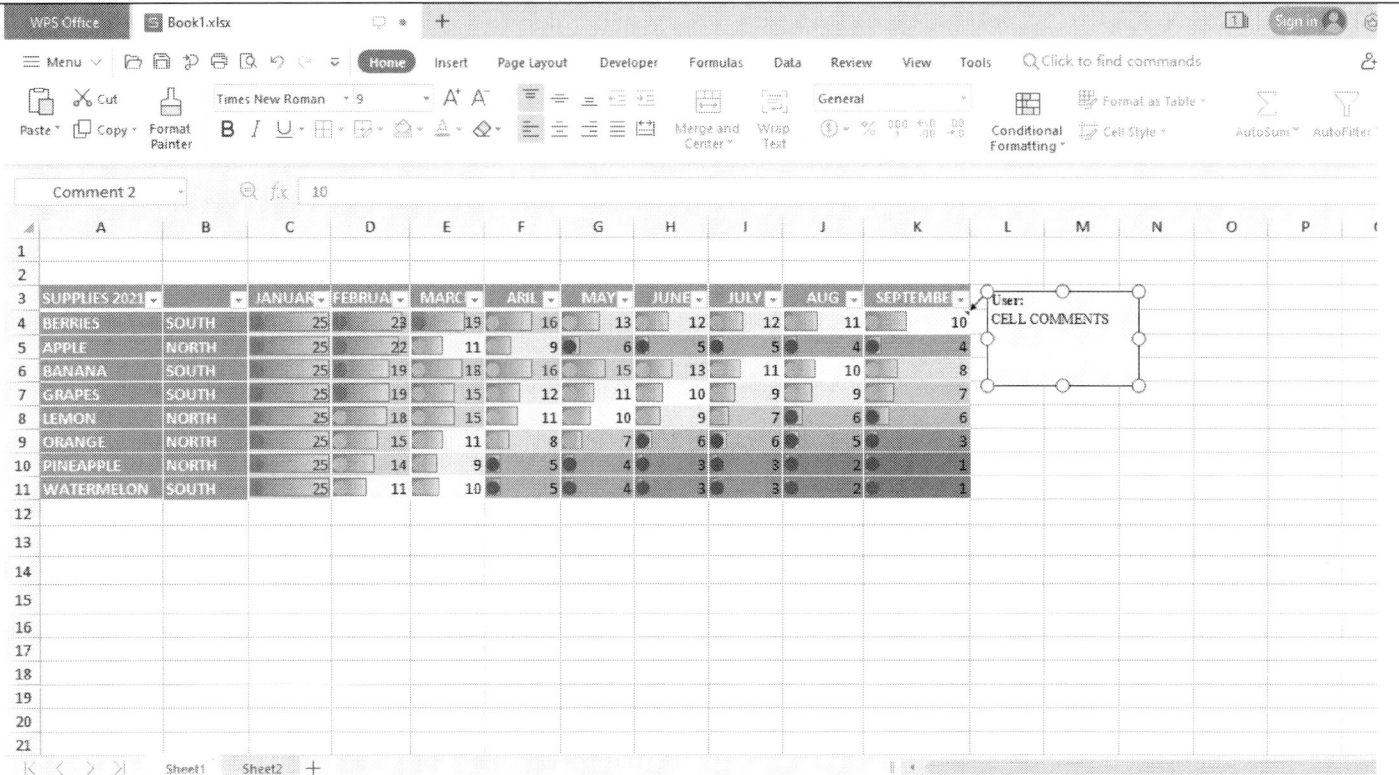

This feature allows you to add a cell-specific comment. These remarks appear when you hover over a cell and vanish when you leave the cell. In data tables, when the comments serve as text notes for other users, words are advantageous.

DRAWING FREEHAND SHAPES

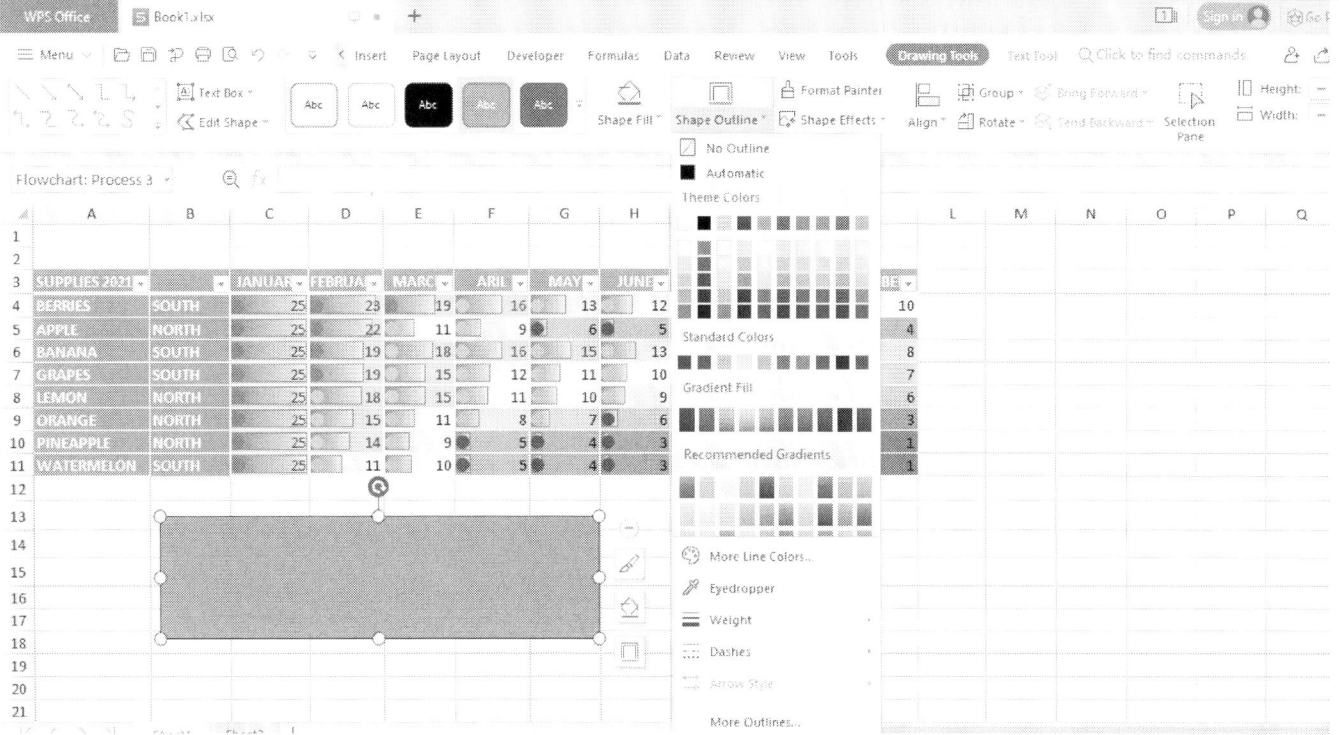

This tool permits the creation of freeform chart designs. These Excel-exclusive patterns can be used to create a variety of appealing designs.

Creating date ranges and dates

This tool enables you to add dates to your graphs. Excel's date functions are intuitive and simple to use. For instance, you can make a graph with many series and add a date to each series in order to observe trends and patterns across various time periods.

Collaborative feature

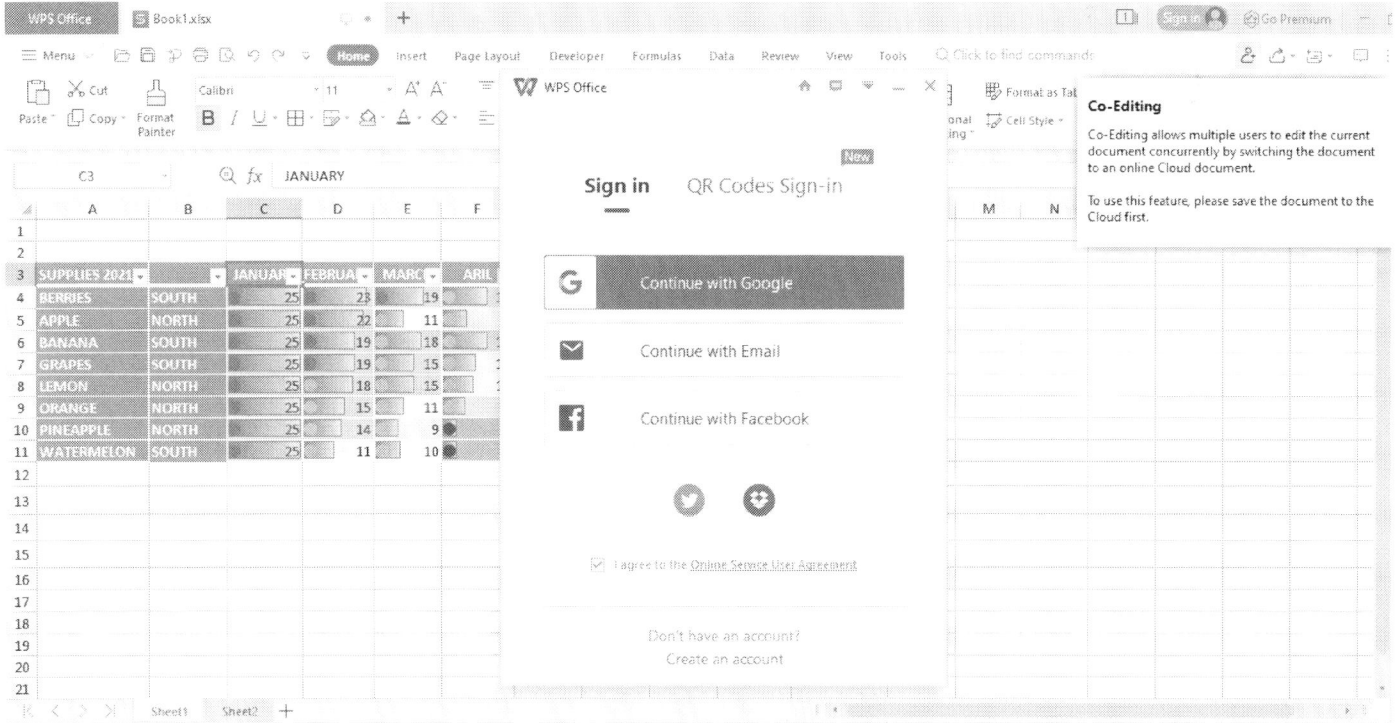

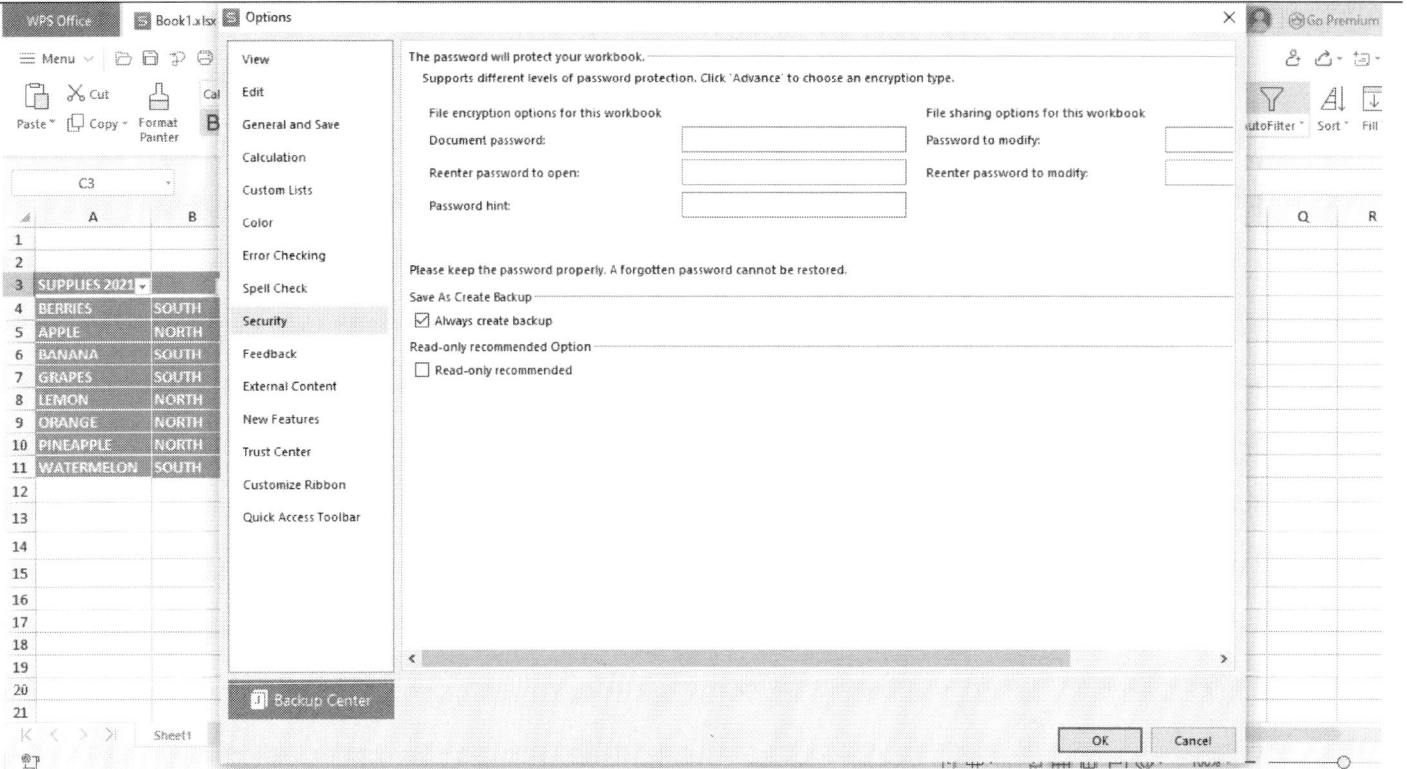

Excel permits the sharing of multiple versions of workbooks with other users, who can then edit the worksheet, save their modifications, and send them back to you. Additionally, you can create password-protected files that restrict other users from making modifications.

CUSTOMIZING RIBBONS

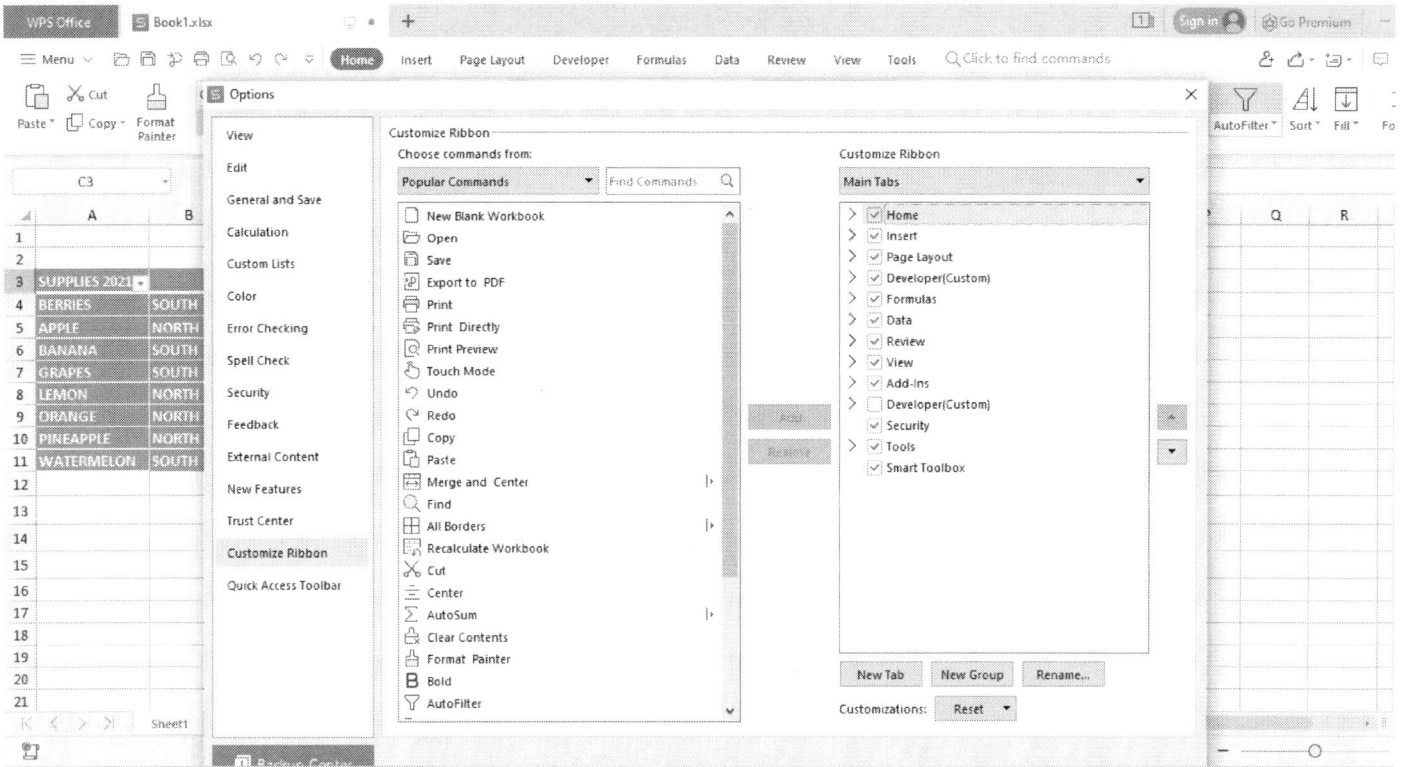

The toolbar that displays at the top of a workbook is called the ribbon. Users can modify ribbons by adding or removing tabs and rearranging them. It can contain a range of commands for usage in your workbook, such as cell formatting and graph insertion.

IMPORTING AND EXPORTING DATA

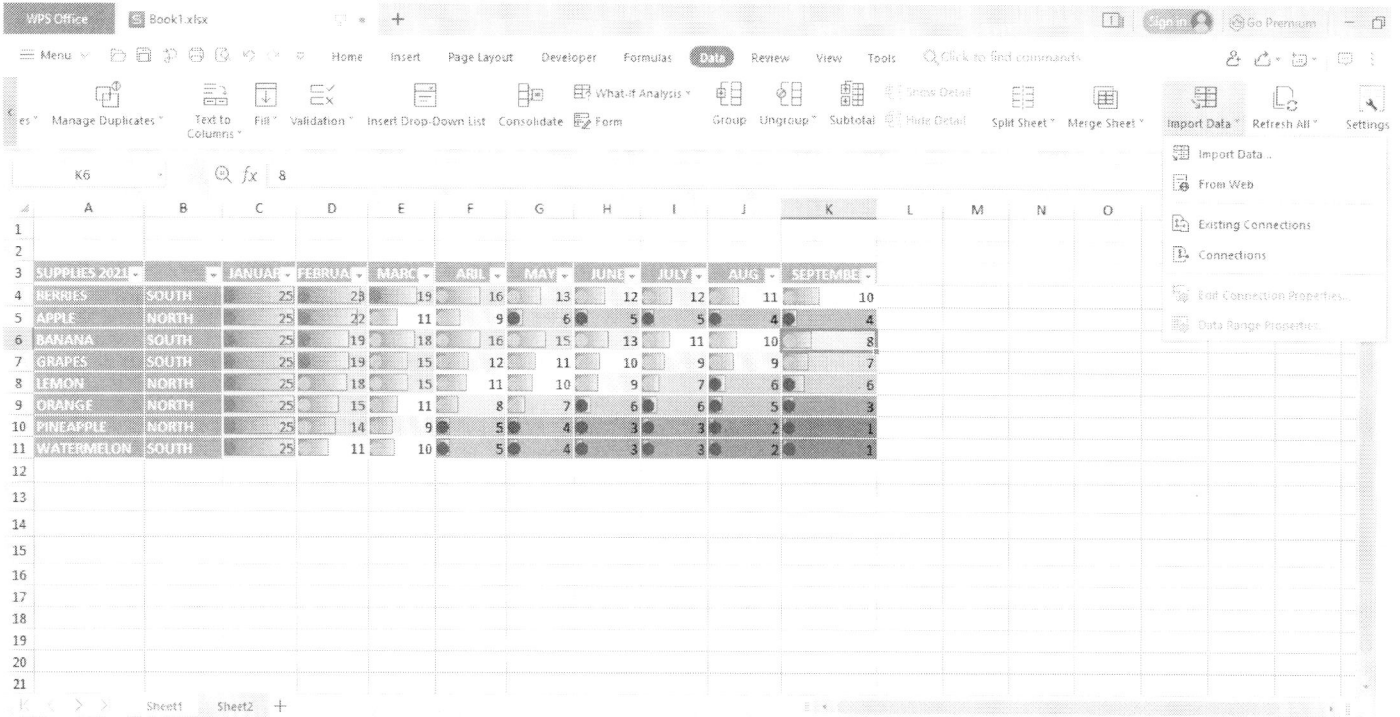

This feature enables you to import data from other sources (such as XML files) and export information into more effective publication formats (such as HTML). You can import other Excel spreadsheets into the one you are currently working on to do computations on this massive collection of data more efficiently. Additionally, you can export information to another workbook so you can work on new projects without losing your present one.

CONVERTING TEXT TO CELLS

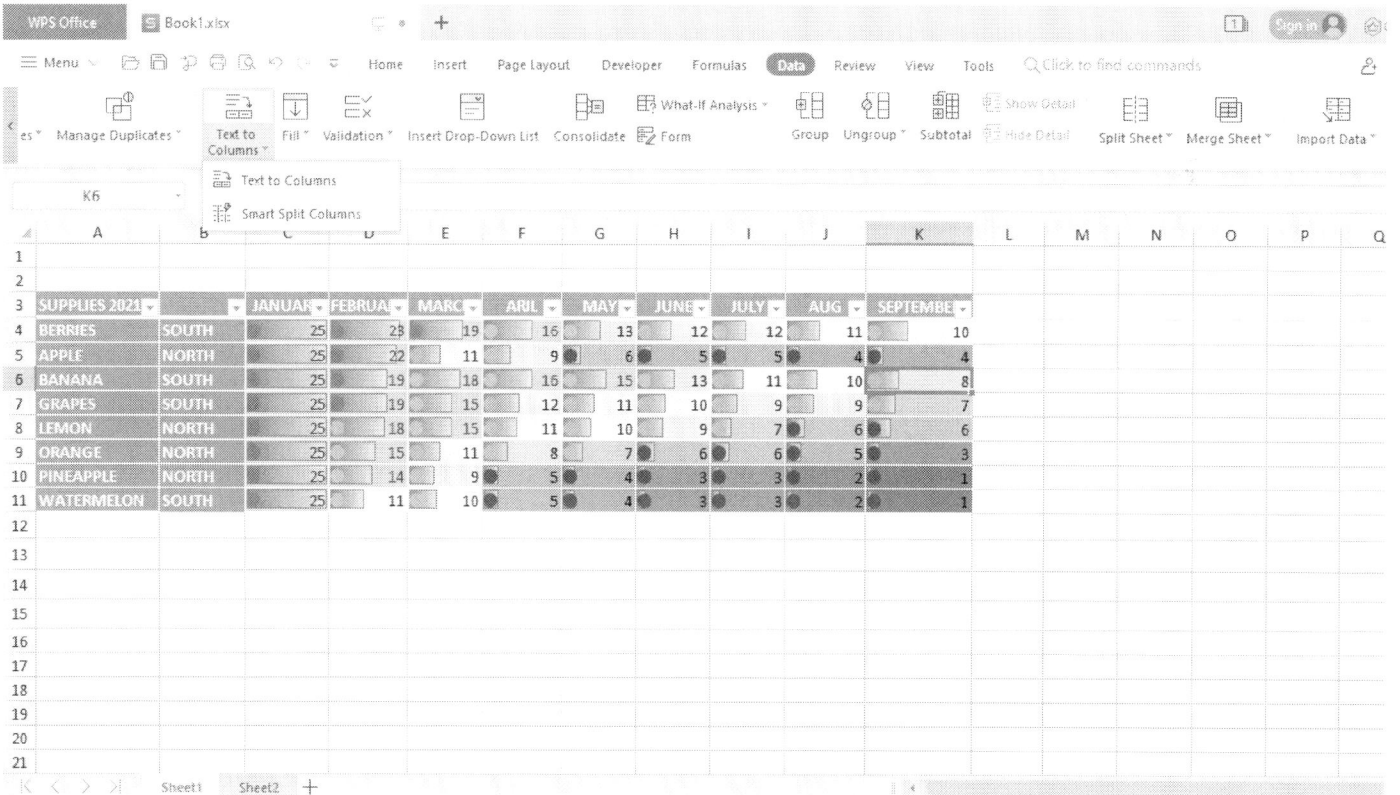

This tool lets you to copy a cell containing text and convert it to one containing numbers, dates, or formulas. This is useful for automating the process of replacing text with different forms of data.

Excel is a potent tool capable of analyzing enormous quantities of data. By building an appropriate workbook, you may evaluate data from many sources and visualize it so that it is accessible and simple to comprehend. With a few clicks, you can make charts and graphs that are visually appealing and clearly illustrate data trends. You may simply arrange and edit your data with this tool to present it in a more comprehensible format. Excel proficiency is a fantastic place to start if you want to visualize your data. However, the best technique to use Excel depends on the individual. Therefore, understanding the pros and cons of this program can be useful while deciding amongst the available options.

In general, if you understand that Excel can provide you with more possibilities for exhibiting your work or allow you to circumvent complex challenges, you should utilize it.

ADDING WATERMARK AND BACKGROUND PICTURES

The addition of a watermark to your data will help prevent unauthorized access. Without a watermark, anyone can utilize your data without your permission.

To add a background image to Excel 2023, you can take the following steps:
1. Click the Page Layout Tab on the top ribbon and select the Background Picture option from it.
2. Click "Browse" and select a picture file from the folder where you saved it in the previous step; then click "Open" and "OK".
3. Click OK.
4. Click the Page Layout Tab on the top ribbon and select the Watermark option from it.
5. 5. The "Excel Custom Watermark" dialogue box will appear in front of you: choose a background picture you have selected earlier and set six parameters for the watermark.
6. 6. Click "OK" when finished to finalize your work on Excel 2023.

Adding Picture in Data Table:

In the same way that you can add a watermark to your data table, you can also add images to your data table to give it a unique appearance and feel. To add images to Excel tables, you must take the following steps:
1. Click the Page Layout Tab on the top ribbon and select the tab "Picture".
2. Click the "Browse" button on the right side and select a picture file you want to add; then click the "Open" button to open it.
3. To place your picture in your Excel data table, you need to click on the table cell where you want to put a picture, then select "Picture" tab on the top and click "Insert Picture", an image that has already been saved is going to appear, it's clear that pictures you have saved from your PC desktop will be shown here automatically.
4. Click the "OK" button to place the picture in your table; then click "OK" on the bottom ribbon.

Setting a background color for an Excel table is crucial. You can set a background color for your Excel tables by following these steps:
1. Click on the Page Layout Tab on the top ribbon and select the Background Color option from it.
2. Select the "Dark or Light" tab, choose a color that suits you and then click "OK".
3. Click the Page Layout Tab on the top ribbon and select the Borders option from it.
4. Select the "Outline" tab, then choose a color that suits you and then click "OK".

Adding Background Pictures with Your Excel Table:

Adding background pictures to your Excel tables with your picture will give a different look to your tables and make your work more colorful.

Excel is a potent tool capable of analyzing vast quantities of data. By creating an appropriate workbook, you can analyze data from various sources and visualize it so that it is accessible and simple to comprehend. With a few clicks, you can generate charts and graphs that are visually appealing and clearly illustrate data trends. You can easily organize and manipulate your data using this tool to present it in a more comprehensible format. Excel proficiency is a good place to start if you want to visualize your data. However, the best way to use Excel depends on the individual. Therefore, understanding the pros and cons of this software can be useful when deciding between the available options.

In general, if you realize that Excel can provide you with more options for displaying your work or allow you to circumvent complex issues, you should utilize it.

Chapter 9. FORMATTING

If you're tired of the same, monotonous Excel grid and labels, it's time to get creative. Various formatting tools can be used to transform a spreadsheet into a work of art, and we will demonstrate how.

CHARACTERS, COLORS, SIZE

Formatting excel is difficult in Excel. However, you can simplify the process by utilizing predefined patterns and styles. Thus, you can apply only the techniques you prefer to your spreadsheet. It is possible to copy and paste characters and designs into other cells without using the styles each time. Each type has a predefined set of formatting options. Styles are meant to save you time by applying the same formatting to an entire spreadsheet. The advantages of storing these styles alongside the text formatting in the same document are twofold. First, those working with multiple documents with similar formatting requirements will be aware of the precise location of each style. And secondly, if you forget the name of a style, it will be easy to recall the one titled "Styles." Styles are applied on top of the existing text formatting, allowing for the simultaneous application of multiple formats to a cell or block of cells. Styles are useful for applying consistent formatting to any document, but they can also be used to format Excel spreadsheets. Excel ships with numerous predefined styles that can be quickly applied to any block of text to format it appropriately. This is the most efficient method for applying consistent formatting to an entire workbook. Fonts and sizes are the most commonly used styles to quickly format a spreadsheet. You can also specify how each style is applied to text in a cell using styles. Suppose you wish to bold the first word in each cell while italicizing the remaining words. Typically, both styles must be applied individually to each word. With styles, however, you only have to choose one of the predefined options that combines these two settings.

To accomplish this, select the data to format. It does not matter whether there is a single or multiple rows of data, as any changes made will affect them all simultaneously. From there, select 'format' and then 'cells.' Then, on the 'home' tab, you will notice various sections. To change the font size, you can either click on the arrow next to the font listed and select a new size from the drop-down menu, or you can click directly on the font size box and enter a new size.

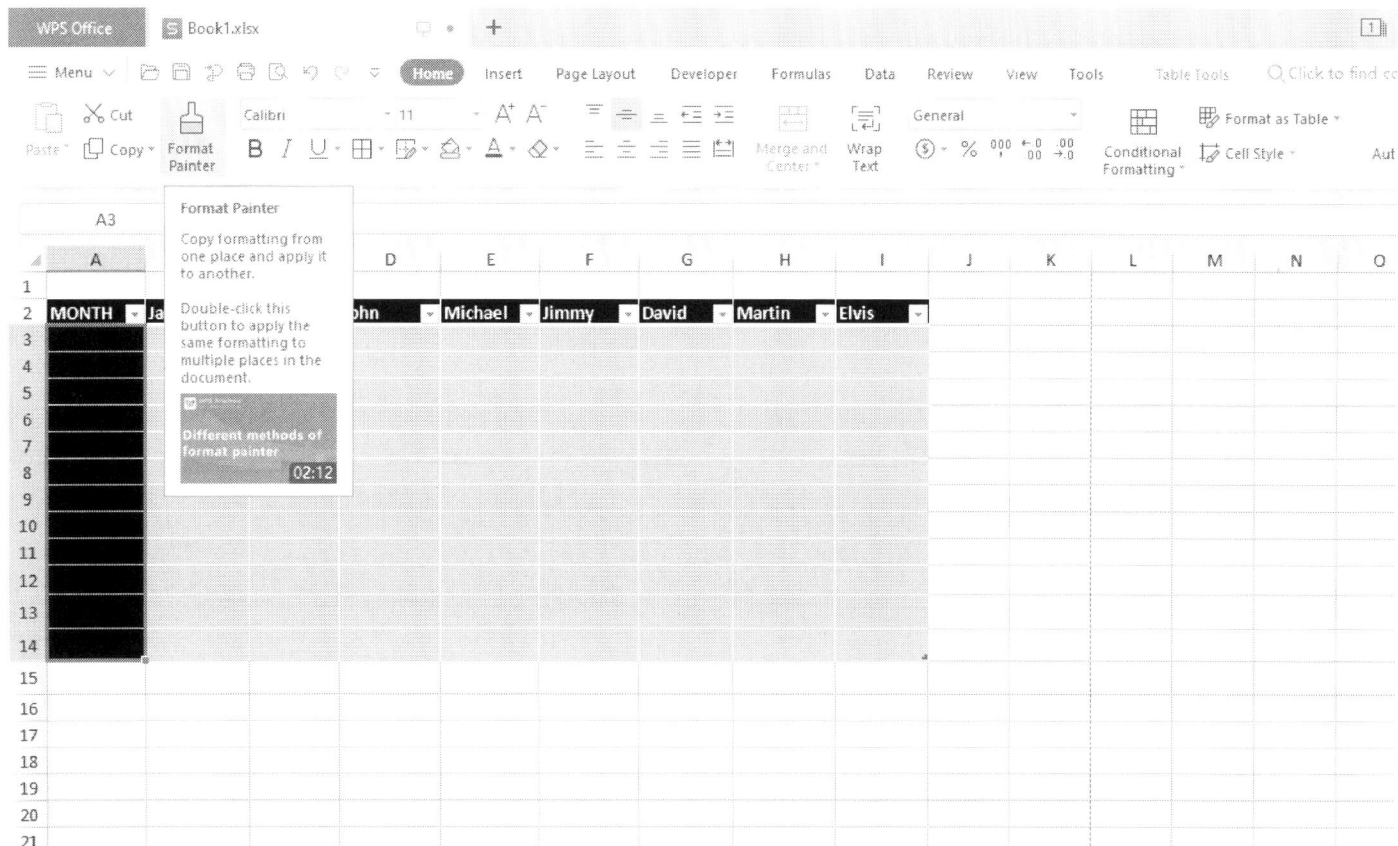

To change the color of your font, you can either click on the arrow next to the font and select a new color from the drop-down menu, or you can click directly on the font color box and enter a new color.

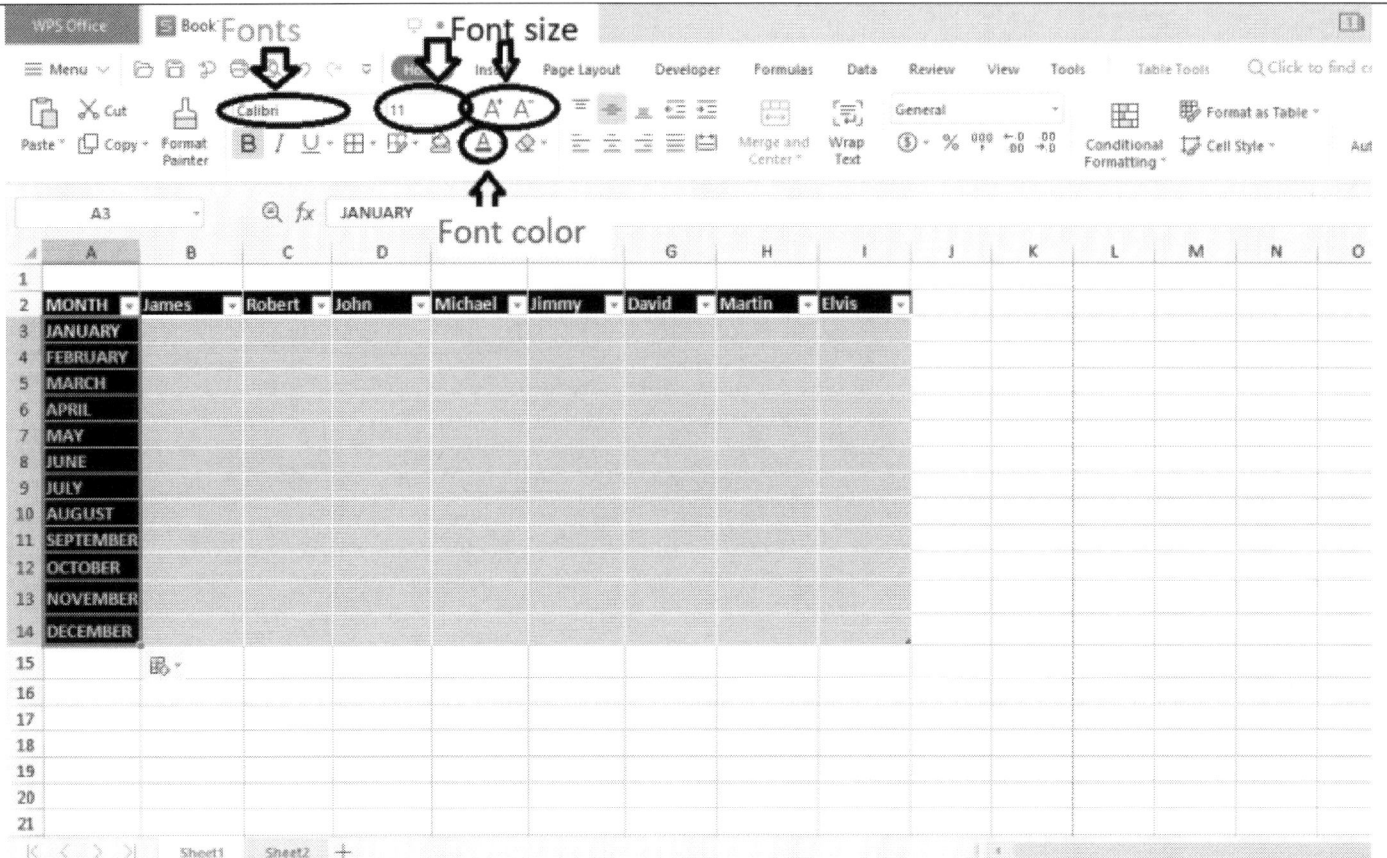

Regardless of the type of formatting you seek, there is a suitable option available. Be creative with your formatting styles, and you will be able to create unique, appealing spreadsheets.

ALIGNMENT, MERGE, WRAP

You can manipulate the cells in Excel to achieve the desired appearance. Alignment Merging and wrapping are comparable, with a few distinctions. First, you should understand that alignment modifies the distance between columns or cells within a column, making your spreadsheet more legible. It allows for left, right, and center alignment. In addition, it allows you to align cells vertically, which will be discussed in the following section. The default alignment option is left, but it can be changed to center or right. If you want to align text and other objects over a single cell, you can merge the cells and wrap the text and other objects. These two actions are not confused with one another because they are grouped as the wrapped group of the alignment group. All three options (Alignment, Merge, and Wrap) are disabled by default. Once enabled, you can align, wrap, or merge any cell using the buttons in the row and column headers' bottom row of cells.

Clicking on a cell and then expanding the alignment button at the bottom of your spreadsheet activates the alignment command. Five options are available: left, right, center, justify, and vertical. The justify option generates two columns as opposed to one. This equalizes the height of the cells, but stacks them on top of one another. To vertically center text on a mobile device, click the icon for vertical alignment and select 'center.' It is convenient when you wish to align columns vertically. This is not always possible; if you require this functionality, use the wrap option instead.

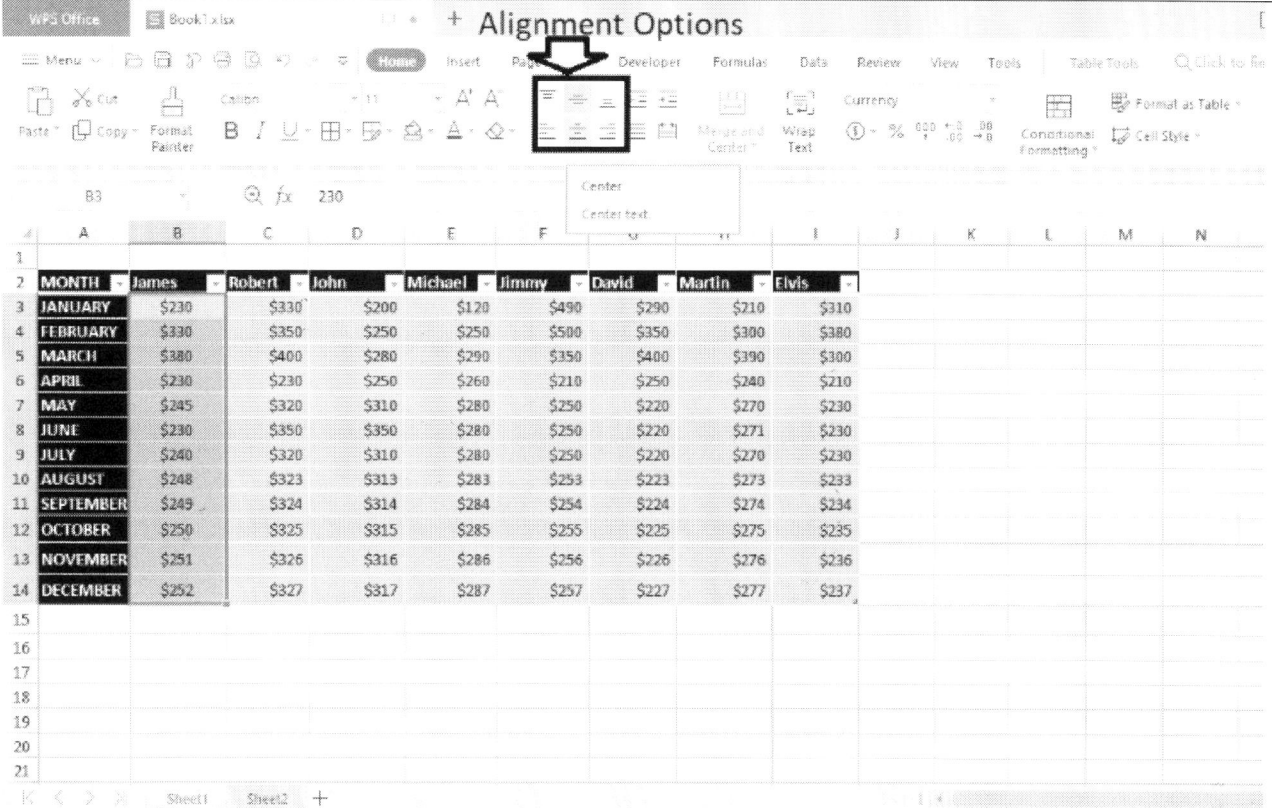

Alignment Options

It is essential to have wrapped text or objects that are not overlapping. Wrap smoothing attempts to automatically adjust column widths when there are too many rows between them, preventing side gaps. You can change the default spacing of 10 characters by adjusting the wrap width. When text or objects are wrapped too closely together, they can appear unsightly. If you need to make a picture's corner, go all the way around it and use wrapping. Also useful if your text spans multiple columns. If your spreadsheet contains numerous wrap lines, they will accumulate at the bottom of the screen and consume valuable space. This can be altered by modifying the wrap margin. The default is 0 characters, but you can also specify a number to prevent the display of a specific number of wrap lines. You can conceal these additional lines using the hide wrap option. The same holds true for merged cells.

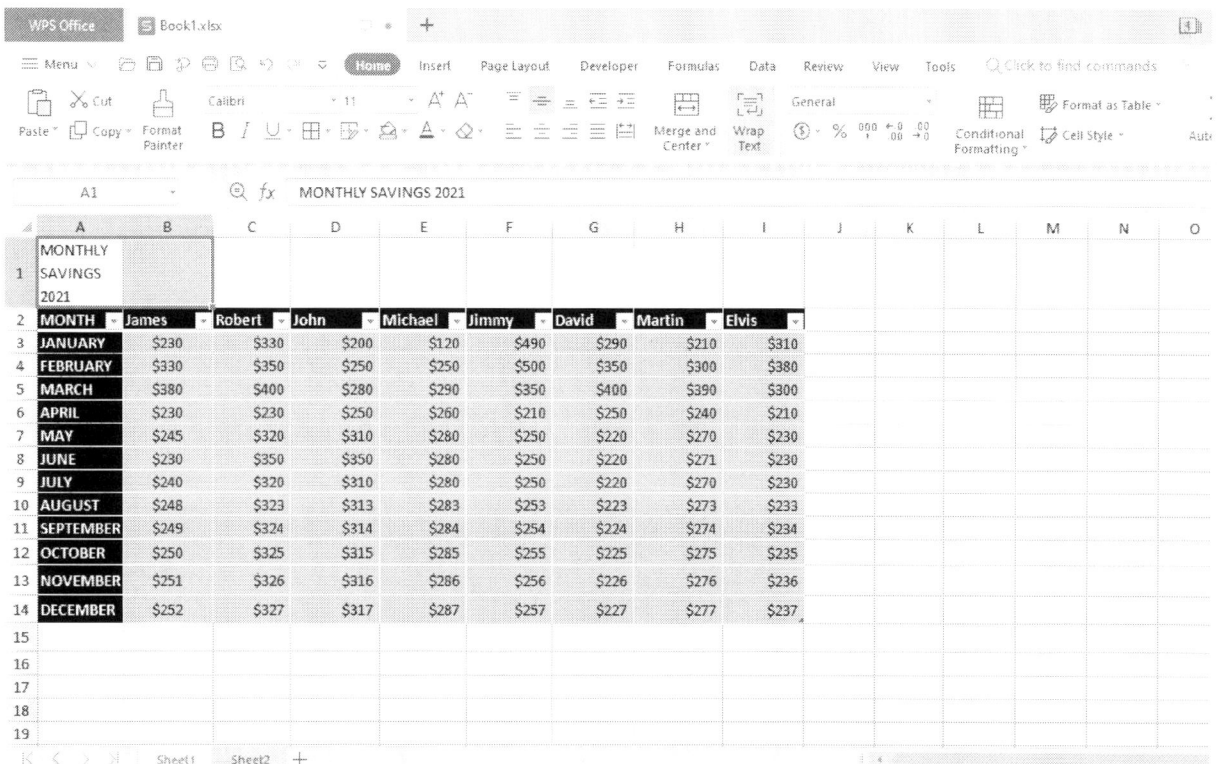

While merged cells and wrapped cells differ slightly, they share certain characteristics. In addition to sitting on top of one another, merged cells have a small space between them that cannot be eliminated. Occasionally, it is necessary to combine cells. Wrap allows you to change the horizontal or vertical orientation of text within a cell. The rotate tool allows you to rotate text and numbers within a cell. This gap is only visible when the spreadsheet is viewed in print mode. You cannot modify the margin of merged cells, but you can reduce it by using the move cells to justify option.

The wrapping and aligning options are similar, but not identical; therefore, let's discuss them separately. Justify is self-explanatory; it simply ensures that the height of each cell is uniform.

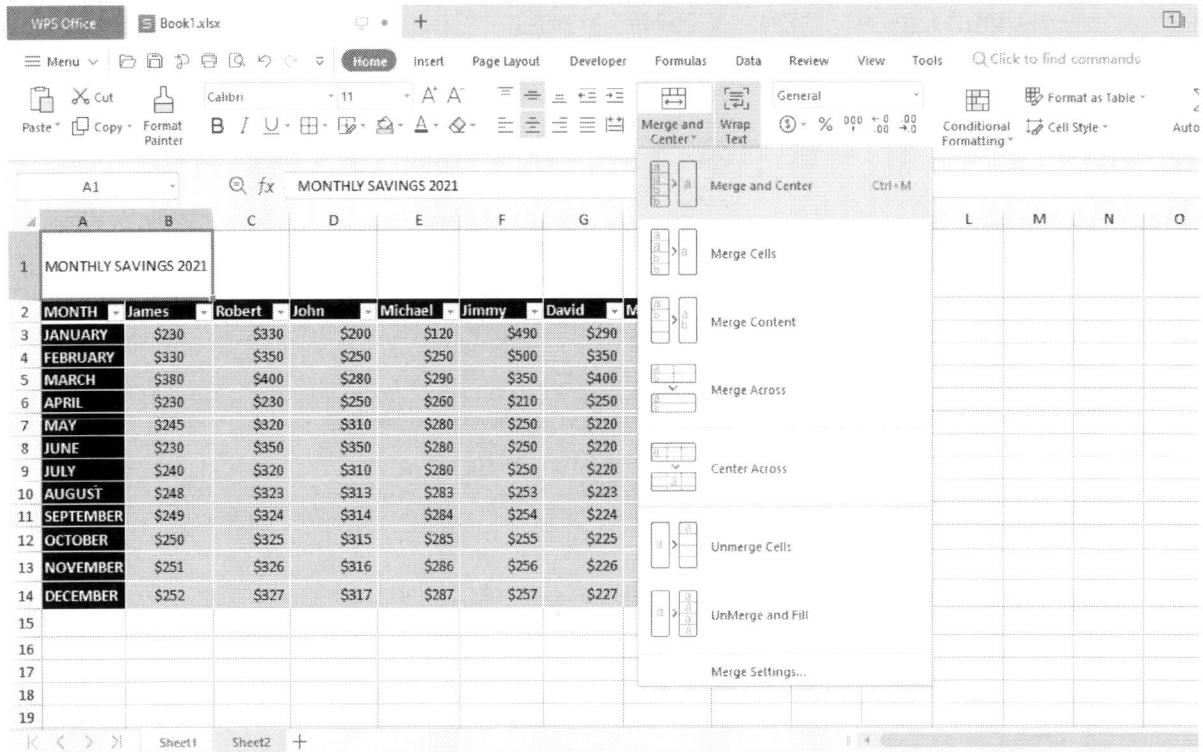

There are numerous ways to improve the readability of your spreadsheets. We have already discussed Excel's built-in alignment, merge, and wrap functions. There are also numerous ways to make your spreadsheet stand out from the competition. Alignment, merge, and wrap are all useful functions for optimizing your spreadsheet. These simple options are more than just ways to make your spreadsheet look more professional; they are also ways to improve it.

ALL CELL DATA TYPES AND COMMON ISSUES

Each year, the world of spreadsheets evolves, and so should the way you format your cells. When including dates in an Excel spreadsheet, many common issues arise, such as displaying numbers as dates. Every few months, there are numerous small updates and new rules that can unexpectedly alter how you should format Excel cells. In this section, we will examine the most common issues you may encounter and the best ways to circumvent them. There is no better time than now to become familiar with Excel's new formatting rules.

First, you must understand that there are two ways to format cells in Excel: Formatting Cells and formatting your data. Formatting your data is generally the method we recommend. Excel is more flexible and gives you greater control over how your data is displayed. However, Formatting Cells is still required in certain circumstances so that you can anticipate what Excel will do with your data when it attempts to format it.

Excel has a unique format for each type of data:

Dates: Short: dd/mm/yy (example: 01/04/2016) Medium: d mmmm, yyyy (example: Jan 4, 2016) Long: dddd, mmmmm yy (example: Wednesday, January 04, 2016)

Time: hh: mm :ss (example: 1 :49 :23 PM)

Numeric: 0,,-,,+,-,.# (example: 4,478.4)

Currency: $#,##0.00 (example: $1,000.5)

Percentage: 0%,#0% (example: 0%,20%)

Fraction: $1/2 = 0.5$, $1/4 = 0.25$

Formatting your data is easy. To include a date in your spreadsheet you need to use either the short / medium / long format. The exact format used depends on how you entered it (if entered as text, like hh:mm by date or mm/dd/yy then the short format is used; if entered as numbers then the medium or long format will be used).

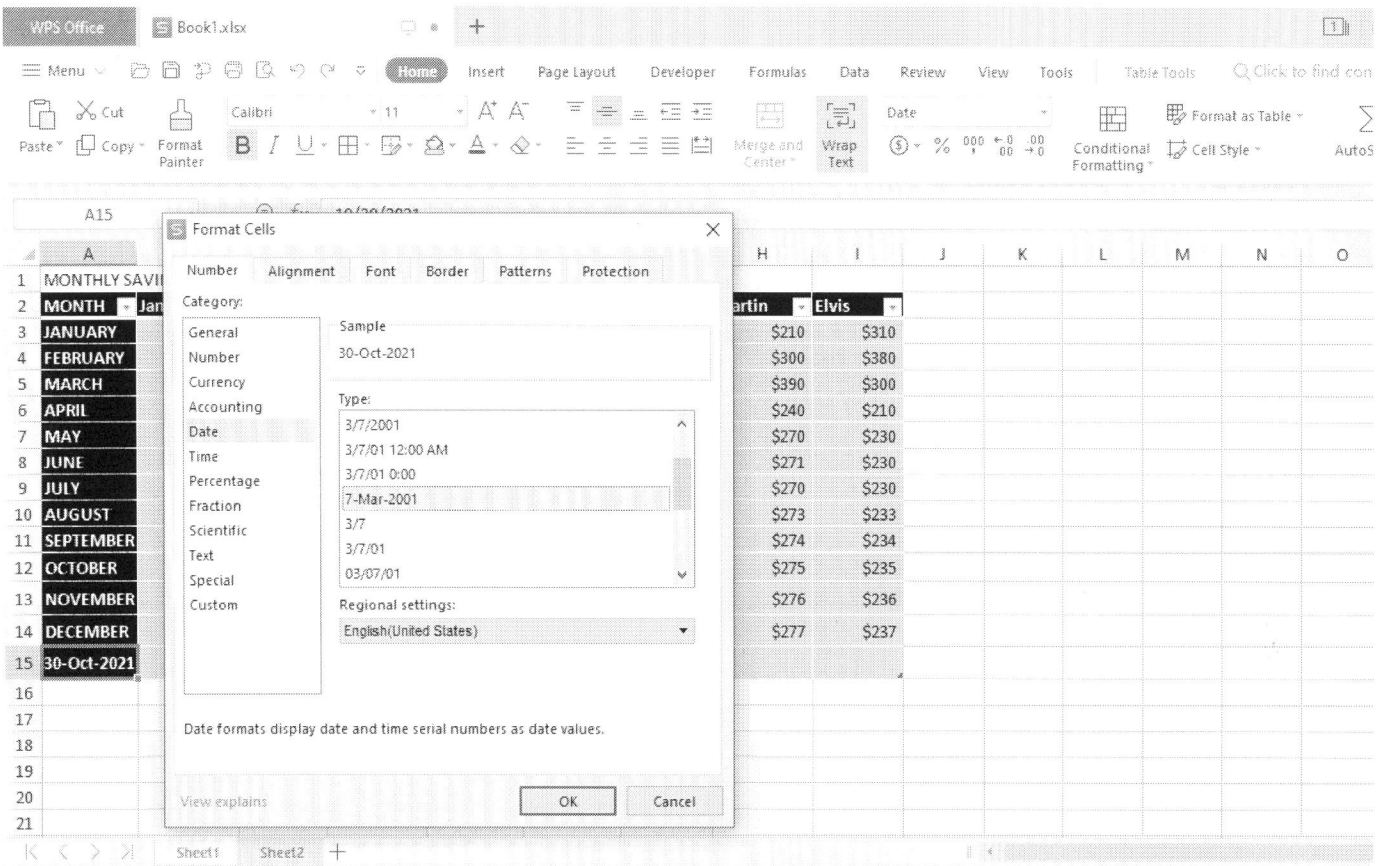

When Excel attempts to format a cell, it examines the cell's contents and makes an educated guess as to which format would make the contents easier to read. Excel will attempt to display data in the format it expects. This is perhaps the most important fact to remember.

CONDITIONAL FORMATTING AND TABLE FORMAT

The majority of spreadsheet applications support conditional formatting. You can filter what data to display or hide when certain conditions are met. Some of these are visually appealing ways to simplify your work without the need for formulas. However, what if you require an infographic? This is where table formatting comes in handy, as it allows multiple data types to be entered into a single column. When entering values, the format of each cell depends on the column's data type.

This section will explain how to combine these two functions to create elegant and informative spreadsheets that are visually appealing and easy to read regardless of the screen size.

1. **Conditional formatting on single columns**

There are 4 conditional formatting functions for single columns called:

Table format function: Used to create unique customized table formats for your data. Highlighting cells matching the criteria is the main purpose of this function.

List format functions: Used to create custom table formats using the same function as the table format one.

List boxes: Used for creating data-heavy displays where list boxes are used for displaying values. List boxes are 2-dimensional. When you use them, you cannot change or reorder columns in your data list or click on individual cells within the list box to edit them directly. If you do not specify any formatting rules, Excel will apply the default formatting rules of your selected data set.

2. **Conditional formatting on multiple columns**

There are 3 conditional formatting functions for multiple columns that allow you to group related cells together. Only 1 of the functions has the option to highlight rows according to specified conditions.

3. Conditional formatting with table format

Conditional formatting with table format is used for creating unique customized table formats for your data. Highlighting cells matching the criteria is the main purpose of this function.

- Click the table format icon in the toolbar or press Ctrl+Alt+L
- Click on one of the following options:

Table Column: to enter values in multiple rows at once.

Table Drop Down list: to enter values in multiple rows at once using a dropdown menu.

Table Widget Boxes: quickly creating conditional formatting rules with different formatting colors based on each data type and cell value combination.

- In the conditional formatting dialog box, specify what you want to be highlighted and additional options such as format color, font size, style, and background color.
- Excel will automatically highlight the cells that meet all the conditions specified. If you want to highlight additional cells that meet some or all your conditions, then select 3-conditions in the dialog box and click on the Plus icon.
- Click OK and see how your data looks like now!

4. Conditional formatting with the list format

Conditional formatting with list format is used for creating custom table formats using the same function as with table format one. Use it to make a stellar data display in your PowerPoint presentations, slide shows, or a PPTX file.

- Click the list style icon in the toolbar or press Ctrl+Alt+L
- Use this dialog box to enter information in your data lists by specifying how you want your data lists to appear. If you use the same format throughout the list, you will need to select only one item for each format type.
- Once you have entered all your formatting rules, check on the Show box near the top of the dialog box so that Excel will highlight each cell that meets all these formatting conditions.
- Click OK and see how your data looks like now!
- In the conditional formatting dialog box, specify what you want to be highlighted and additional options such as format color, font size, style, and background color.

5. Conditional formatting with list boxes

Conditional formatting with list boxes is used to create data-heavy displays where the list boxes are used to display values within each section of the list box. Here's an example:

- Click the Listbox icon in the toolbar or press Ctrl+Alt+L
- Click on one of the following options. The first option has all the conditional formatting rules already set, so you can just click on it, and your data will appear as follows:
- In the conditional formatting dialog box, specify what you want to be highlighted and additional options such as format color, font size, style, and background color.

Conditional formatting is an easy way to give your Excel data sets life by making them more visually appealing. It allows you to highlight specific cells to present data in a clear, understandable way. By using these three functions together, you can create visual art while also skimming the information.

ADD AND REMOVE COLUMNS/CELLS

We all start with a spreadsheet, but sometimes we need to add columns or cells for new data. Here's a quick step to get you started!

How do I add a column?

In Excel 2020, click the "Insert" tab from the Ribbon and select "insert column." You can also right-click where you want the new column to go and click "insert." In either case, choose "right" for vertical spacing or left" for horizontal spacing.

How do I delete a column?

Click the "Insert" or "Manage" tab from the Ribbon, locate the column you want to remove and choose "delete column." You can also right-click where you would like to remove the column and click "remove," or right-click in an empty cell and select "delete."

How do I add a cell?

Locate the row you want to add to, click on the bottom right corner of an unoccupied cell in the row and drag down.

How do I delete a cell?

Right-click on an empty cell where you want to remove a cell and choose "delete." You can also use the "Remove" tab from the Ribbon.

Creating a new worksheet in Excel can be handy, especially when you keep track of multiple projects and keep everything separate. Also, you can add and delete rows and columns as per your needs. In a world where people are constantly hungry for information, the demand for Excel knowledge has never been greater. But being a master of Excel is not as easy as it seems and takes many skills that may come normally to you.

Chapter 10. MERGING CELLS IN EXCEL USING THE MERGE COMMAND

Using the merge command in Excel to merge cells is a helpful way to keep data organized. However, if you do not understand how the merge command operates, you may find yourself working through endless formula strings. This chapter will demonstrate how to use the merge command to keep your data organized.

A cell can be divided into up to three distinct regions. These regions are known as "regions." Each region has a unique name and function. Each region's name is written on its respective cell. Both regions are essential for maintaining data organization. You should separate these regions in this manner to prevent accidentally updating one of the cells. For instance, if you inadvertently change the data in a cell that is part of the title, all the cells below it will be updated when you click the title cell.

Using the section heading to describe each region. As a prefix, the first letter of the heading is used.

Note that if you delete a section heading, the merge command will update your data without adding a new column. This is due to the fact that the commands are intended for merging cells, not for separating columns. Also, if you set up your worksheet without properly separating the regions and then decide to clean it up, you can do so by selecting "clean worksheet" from the "edit" menu.

HOW THE MERGE COMMAND WORKS

When a merge command is executed, the program uses shortcuts to determine which cells belong to which regions. The merge command creates two new columns in this manner. Here's what happens when you execute a merge command:

1. The first thing that happens is that any merged cells are automatically moved to the new column. This way, all merged cells will show up in the same cell after merging.
2. Next, the program counts how many times each region appears. If a range has multiple instances of the same region, it is added to that cell once and then removed.
3. Now, the program looks for any blank cells in your data. These cells are all added to the column of the first instance of a region.
4. If any cells don't have a heading, they will be added directly to this column as well. You can use the "clean worksheet" option to tidy up this data.
5. The last thing that happens is that the cells in your previous columns are shifted down to make room for the new columns. This is done one row at a time, starting with the row with the highest number of heading cells.

Find all cells within a region and select "merge and center" to merge your data. The merge command is also accessible via the Edit menu.

MERGING CELLS USING THE CONTENTS MENU

The contents menu is a convenient method for executing merge commands. If you select the "contents" menu and right-click on a cell within a region, options to merge this cell will appear. You can also change the format of your data using the "contents" menu. All merged cells are bold and underlined by default. You can modify this by selecting the corresponding option in the contents menu or by directly editing your styles.

In today's business world, spreadsheets are an indispensable tool for data analysis. They are utilized in nearly every field and industry due to their ability to collect, sort, and present large amounts of data in an easily readable format.

Many businesses rely on their spreadsheets for accurate, up-to-date information regarding their financial health. As a result, it is difficult to become proficient in creating, working with, and maintaining spreadsheets. This section will provide tips for accomplishing both tasks.

- Before anything else, you must be familiar with the spreadsheet's formulas. These formulas are the building blocks of spreadsheet creation, and they will assist you in learning more advanced techniques.
- To create easily comprehensible spreadsheets, it is essential that your formulas are legible. The formula should ideally be placed directly above the cell it applies to. This makes viewing your spreadsheet easier for anyone in the future.
- If your spreadsheet contains a large amount of data, use the scroll bar to ensure that no vital information is overlooked. Note that the scroll bar must be located above the formula cell.
- Ensure that information entered into a spreadsheet is placed in the correct column. Excel may not place it in the correct column if the column menu is not used.
- If you want to enter information in the same column, you can use the "equal sign" as a shortcut.
- The "delete" button is used to delete data from your spreadsheet and repeatedly enter keys.

- Use the "Insert" button to add data to your spreadsheet. If your formula incorporates text from another source, the text will be inserted into the appropriate cell.
- Your spreadsheet is formatted using the "format as" option. This option is compatible with "format rows" and "format columns."
- The "sort" option sorts the data based on the column or row selected. You have the option to sort by column or row, ascending or descending.
- When you are finished with a cell, the "delete" key will delete an empty cell. If it contains information, it will not be removed.
- The "enter" key is used to accept the value of a cell and advance to the next cell.
- If your spreadsheet has become too crowded and you are unable to move past a certain cell, click "zoom" and then "zoom-out." This will allow you to view a row or column in its entirety.
- Use the arrow keys to move up and down within a column.
- To return to the default settings, click the "Reset" button, which will restore your current settings to their initial state.
- To move from point A to point B, use the arrow keys (up and down) followed by the enter key, which will place you precisely in the next cell. You can now set through your data in the specified column or row.

When working with a spreadsheet, various data formats are required. The "format" button allows you to modify the data's presentation. The font type, font color, and border color are modifiable. In addition, the format button can be used to sort and merge data. These options are intended to simplify the process of keeping your data organized. Therefore, the next time you update your data, you can use a merge command instead of endless formula strings.

Chapter 11. INSERTING

The option to insert a table into a spreadsheet is among the new features of Excel 2021. Data is organized in rows and columns using tables.

To insert a table, place the cursor in cell A1 and select Insert > Table... from the menu. This will open a dialog box where you can specify the table's dimensions, including the number of rows, columns, etc.

When attempting to insert a table into a spreadsheet, one of the most frequent Excel errors is that the table is inserted in the wrong cell. To insert a table into the incorrect cell, either choose an empty cell or enable editing options. For instance, if you are inserting a table that spans two or more rows, it is suggested that you insert the table into a column of the same row as the table you wish to place.

These simple steps will assist you in avoiding these errors and creating a table of professional quality.

1. First, select the area you want to be a table.
2. Then create a table by going to Insert > Table... from the menu bar.
3. A dialog box will appear where you can specify the number of rows and columns.
4. Click OK and you will see your table!

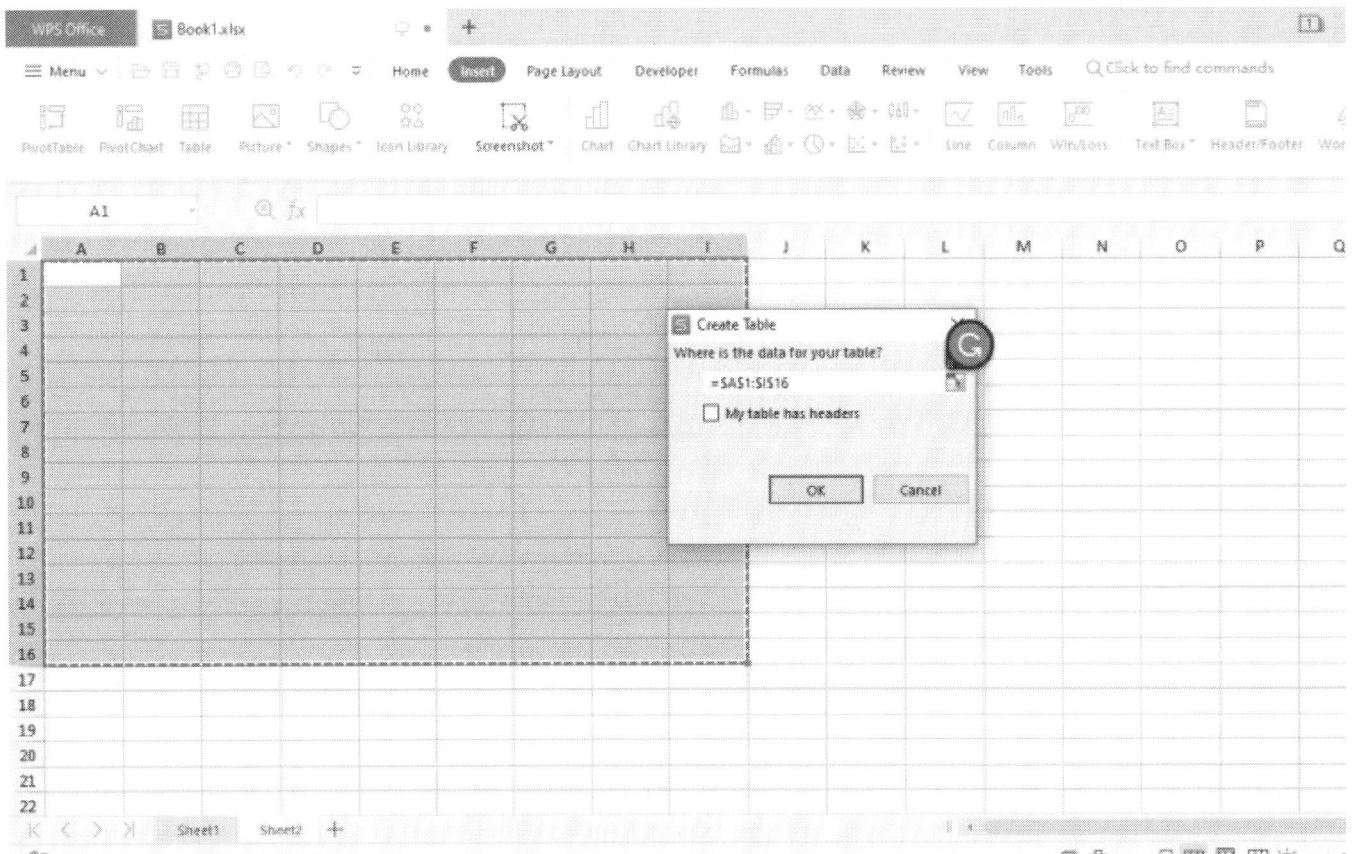

PIVOT TABLE

Excel's "pivot table" is essentially a data summarizer, despite its fancy name. Pivot tables are designed to summarize data in an Excel workbook so that you can explore subsets of your data without exporting it to another application or modifying your worksheet.

A pivot table summarizes raw data in two primary ways: by displaying summary totals for each field and by decomposing these totals into counts of unique values for each field.

The Pivot Table is an excellent data visualization tool, but extracting insights from it often requires patience and skill! In your workbook, you will find a collection of Excel Pivot tables constructed from the raw data in your workbook. The fundamental steps are listed below.

Step 1: Create a Pivot table.

The beginning step is to create a Pivot table to view the data in your workbook. You can make the pivot table from the ribbon menu click "DATA" > "PivotTable."

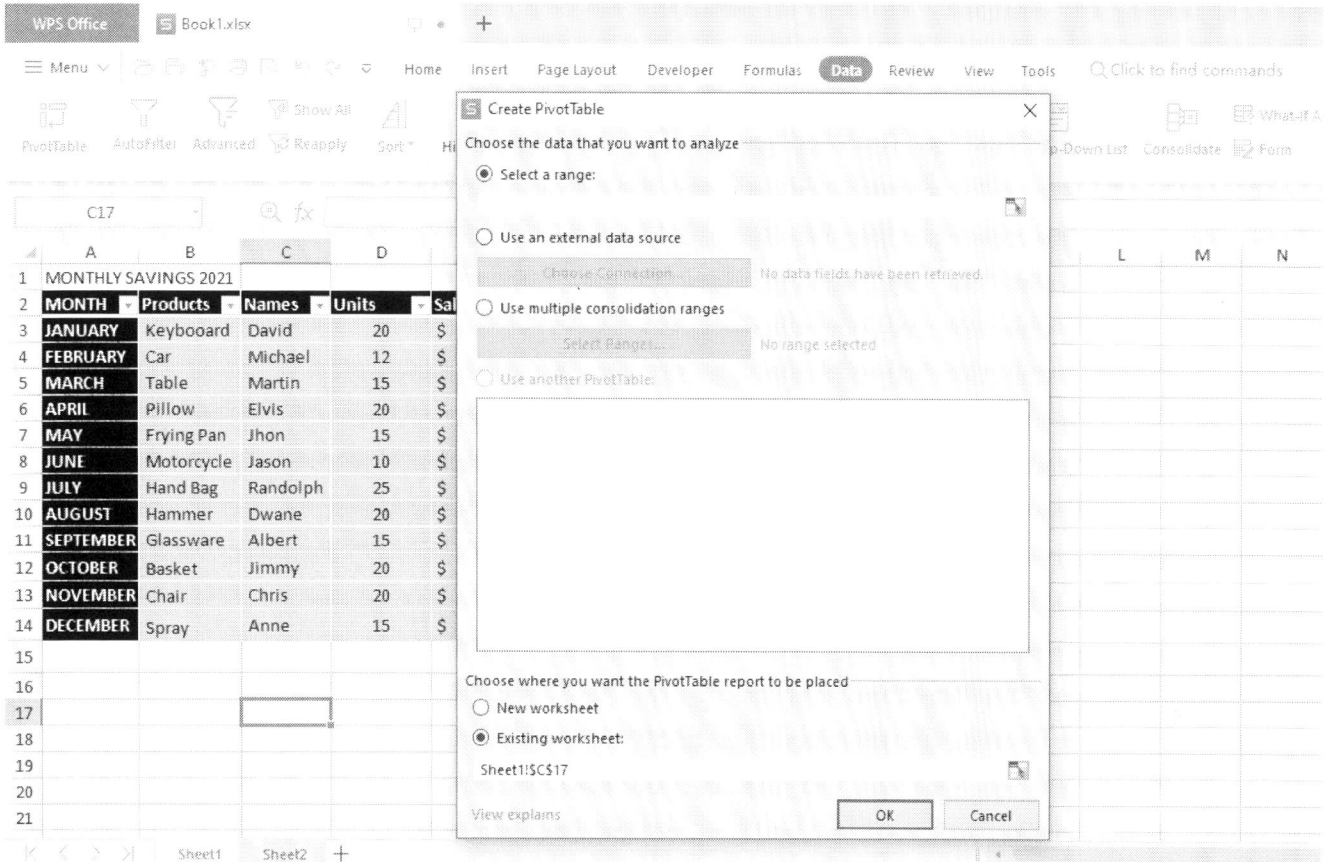

Step 2: Create a Pivot table from a range of cells.

In the next step, you would select the range of data that you want to summarize in your pivot table. This can either be fit by dragging the cursor.

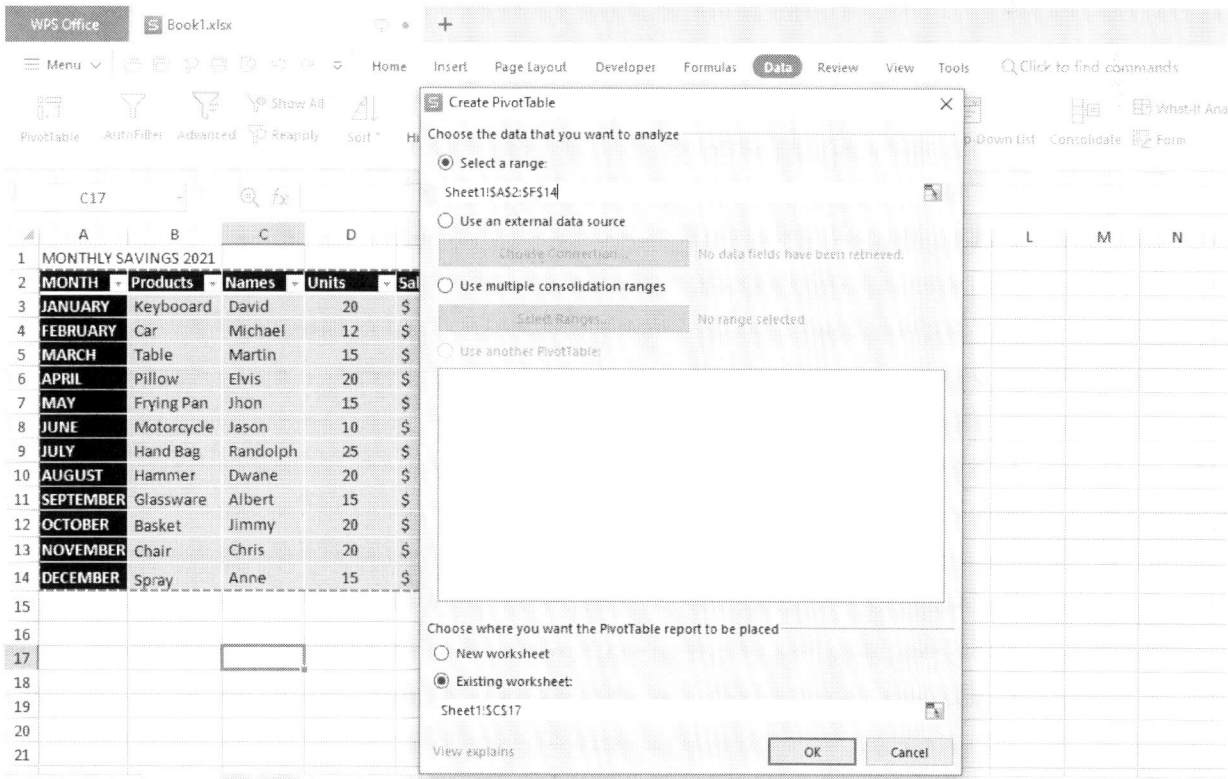

Step 3: Select and define the sort column.

Then, you would select the column in which you wish to view information and click the arrow within that column. This will highlight the column and condense all of the data into a single line. In this step, you must choose the sort order because the Pivot table needs to know what type of data is being sorted in order to process it correctly.

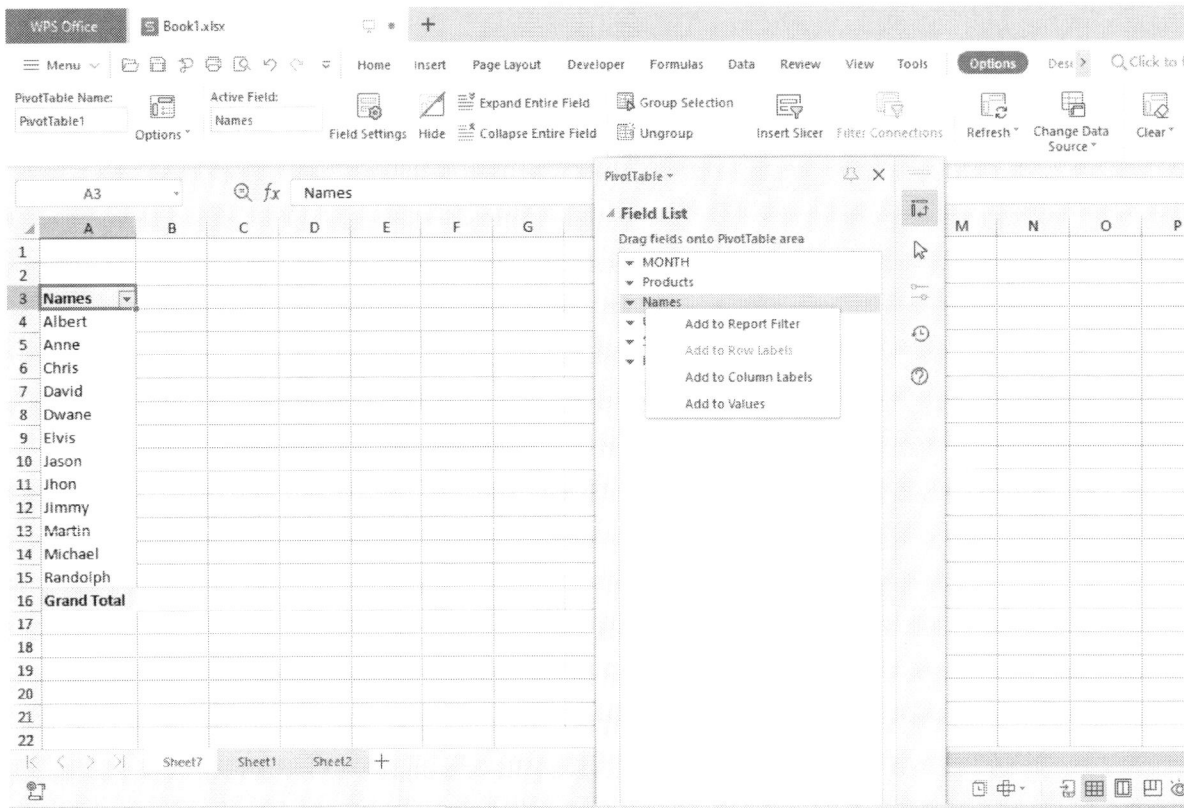

Step 4: Define a summary field that will help you visualize your data quickly.

Repeat the previous step to select the other columns, and you will have a Pivot table that allows you to see your data in aggregate. There are also summaries from various fields that can assist you in comprehending what is occurring with your data.

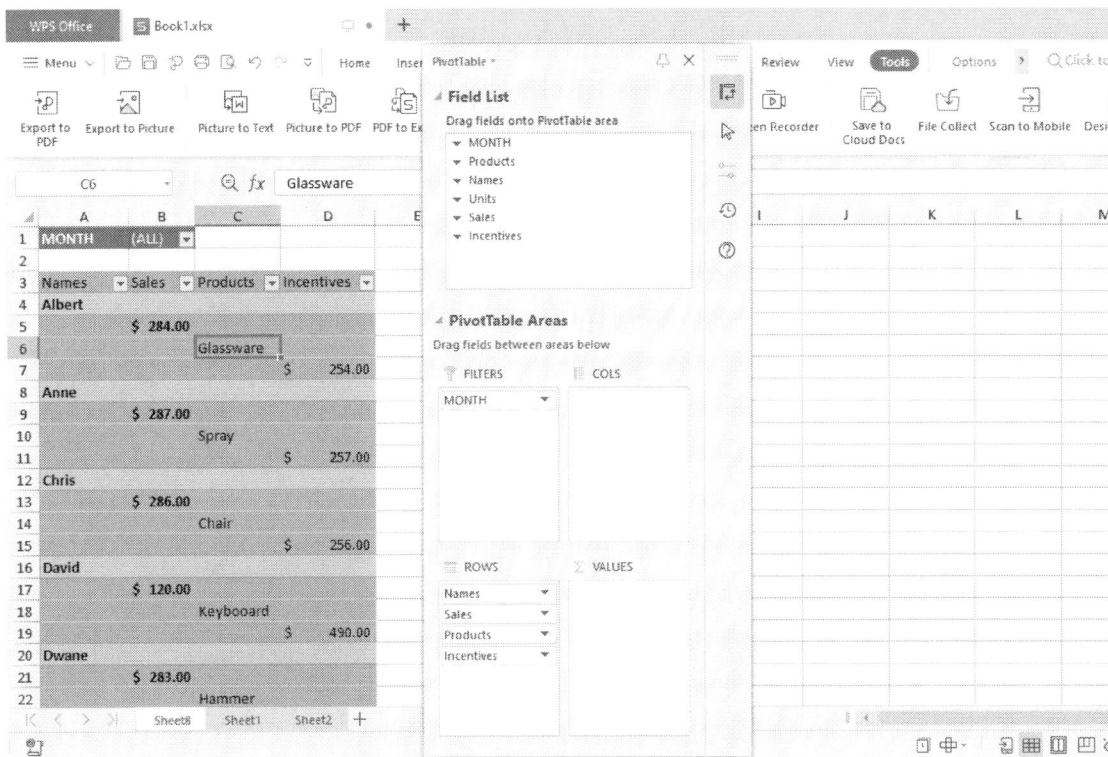

ILLUSTRATION

Adding illustration in Excel is the process of adding an image to a spreadsheet. It can be useful when attempting to represent data or make text more readable.

Excel's insert tab allows for the insertion of images. Wordart, text boxes, shapes, and images are all types of illustrations that can be inserted into a spreadsheet. Using the shapes tool in Excel, you can create your own illustration.

Using shapes

When you click the shapes icon on the Insert tab, a list of all available shapes will appear. Drop any shape into your spreadsheet.

Once a shape has been added, you can select it and adjust its position using the control handles.

You can also alter the size of the shape by clicking the resize handle in the top-right corner of the shape. By adjusting the size of shapes in a spreadsheet, you can increase or decrease the surrounding white space.

To change the color of a shape, you can select it with the mouse and then click the box icon at the right end of the control handle. The customization section will appear. Select More fill options in the upper-left corner and then click Fill options. A new configuration window will appear. Click the color fill button and select any color to alter the default color.

A simple Excel illustration is created.

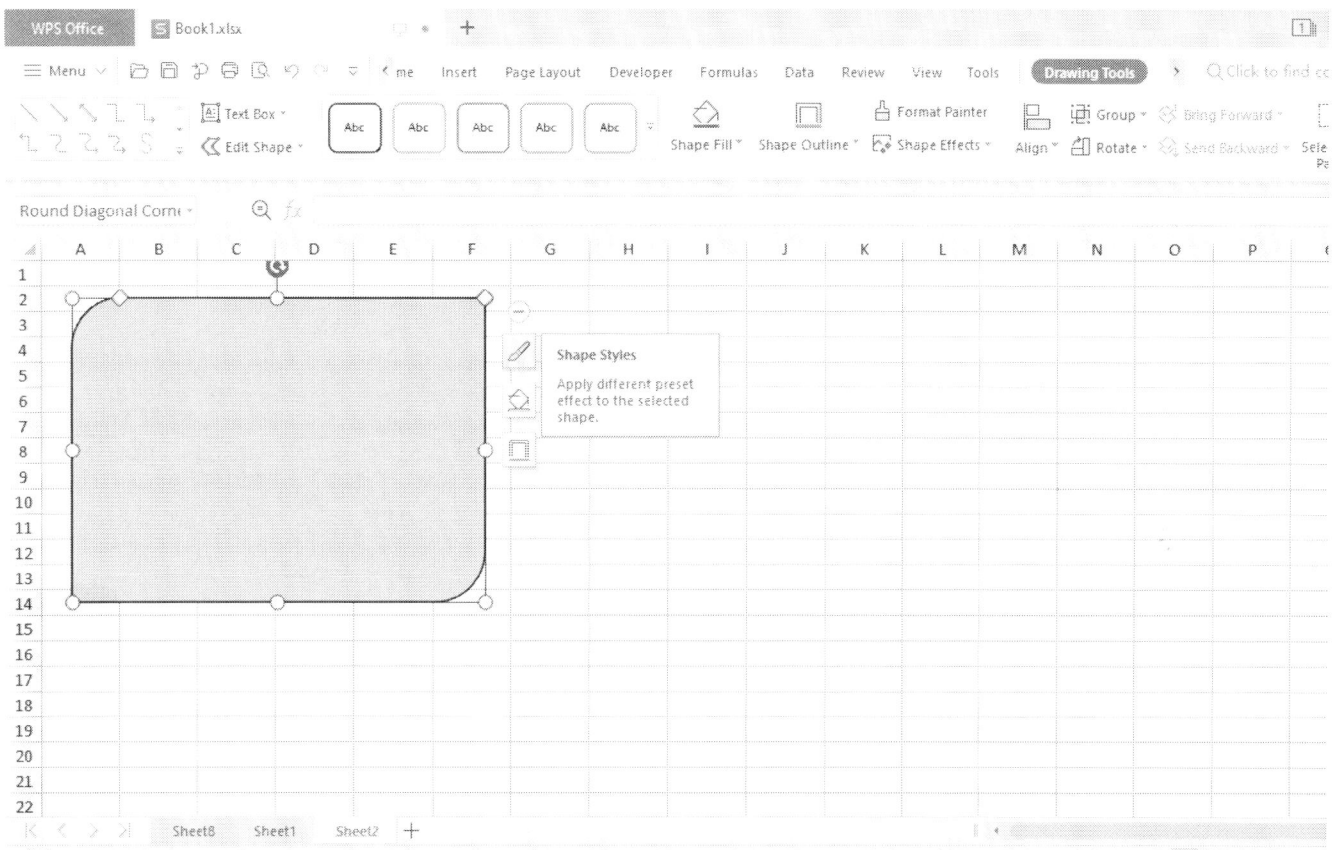

Using textbox

Use the textbox option if you wish to include text in your illustration. Textbox is located directly next to wordart on the Insert tab. It allows you to add text, an image, or both to a box and resize it as needed. The box can be placed anywhere on the spreadsheet.

After adding a textbox, selecting it with the mouse will reveal the box's control handles. With these handles, you can alter the size, position, and color of the box.

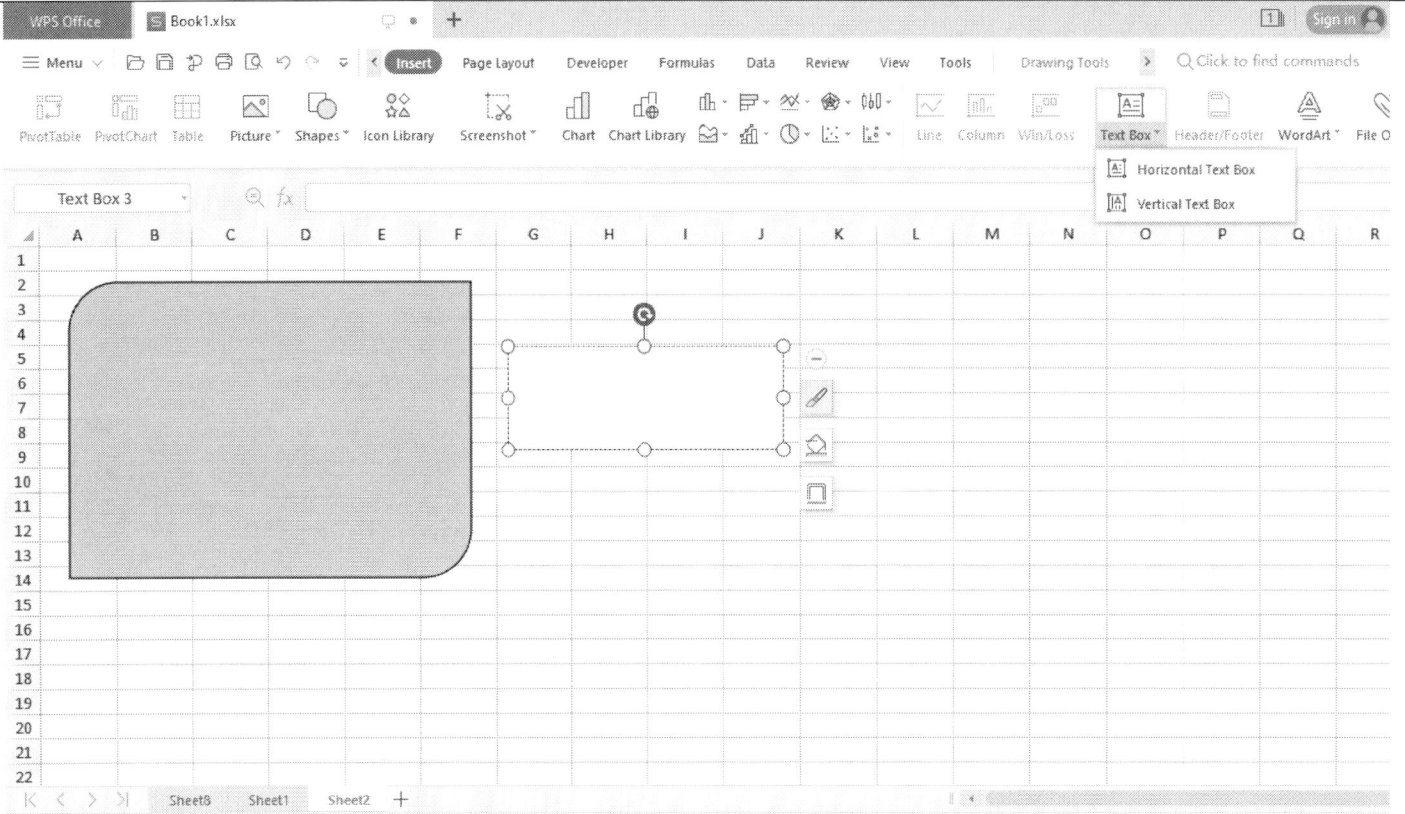

Using wordart

Wordart is an image created in Microsoft Word that can be used to illustrate your data. The Wordart option on the Insert tab will insert a word art image into your spreadsheet. After selecting this option, a list of available wordarts will appear. Choose the word art to insert it into your spreadsheet.

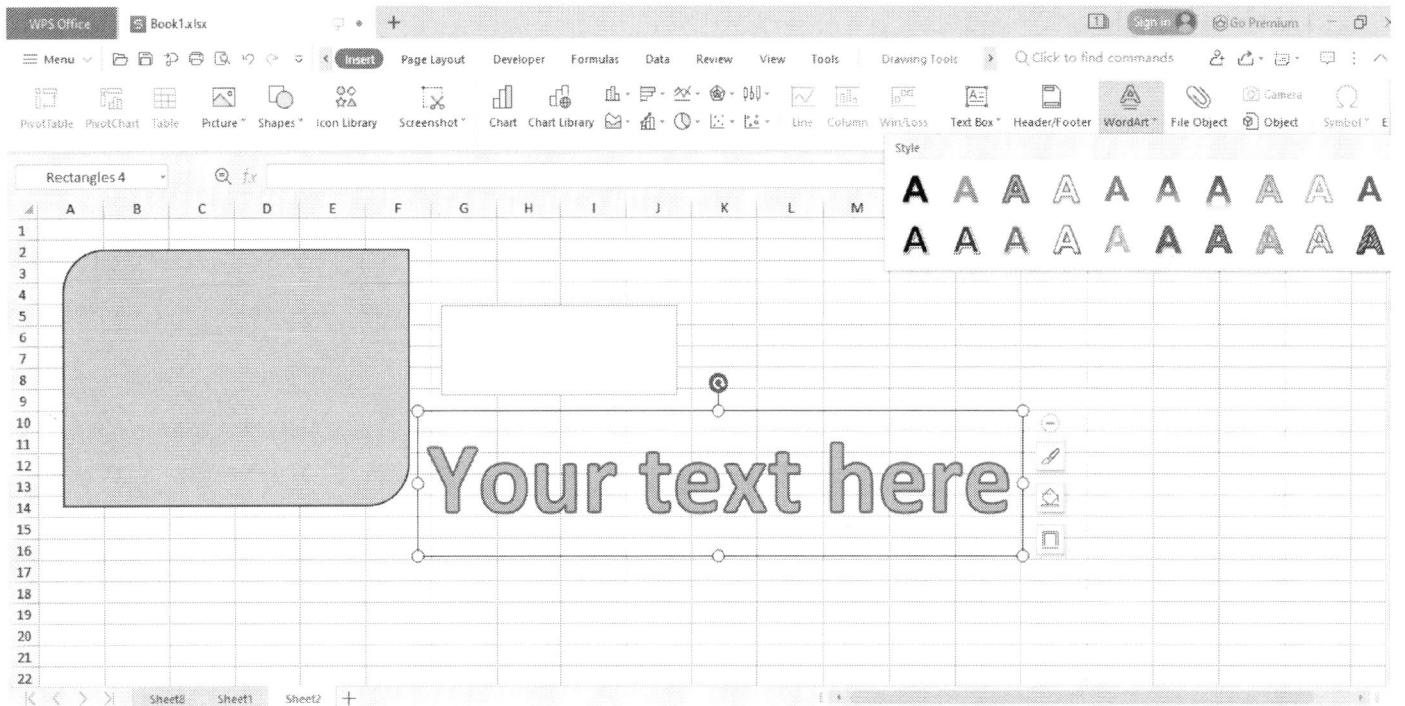

Using Pictures

Using the insert tab, you can also insert images from your computer or other devices into Excel. Simply click the Pictures option under the Insert tab and select images from your computer or other device to display in your spreadsheet. After selecting images, they will be inserted into your spreadsheet.

You can also add an image from a specific website or attachment, as depicted in the image below.

To add a picture to a specific cell, you must first select the cell with the mouse and then select the pictures option from the Insert tab. It will supply you with various placeholders. Choose the desired placeholder and click the image download link in your browser.

Excel was used to create a simple illustration using the clip art, text box, and shapes tools.

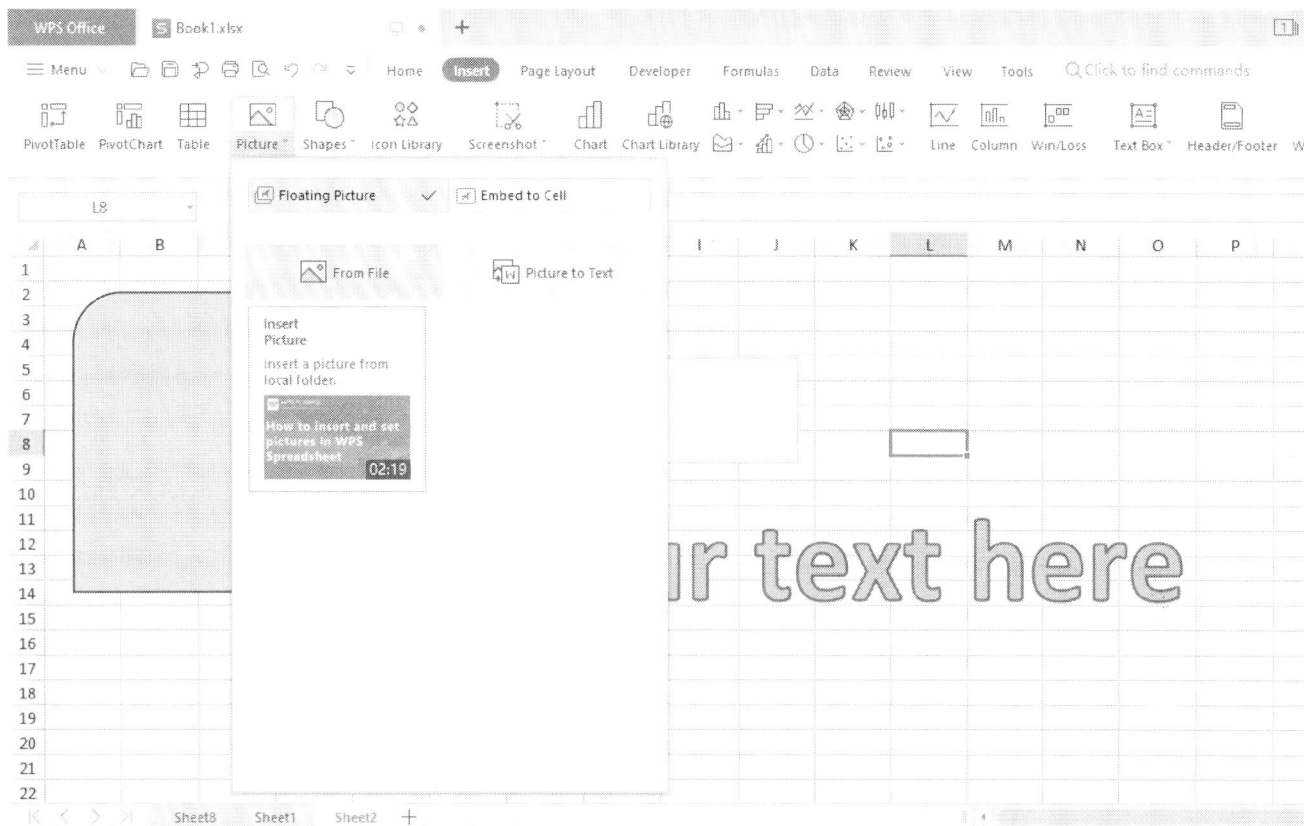

This is useful for creating diagrams and even drawings. It is user-friendly and ideal for children who are learning about shapes and how to modify them independently. Illustration in Excel can be a useful tool for designers who wish to create more visually appealing spreadsheets.

CHARTS

If you are using Excel for your report, the best type of graph to use is a chart. Utilized to visualize numerical data, charts are graphical representations of statistical information. Excel provides special chart types by default and allows you to modify their visual appearance in a number of ways. The colors, titles, and labels of charts can be modified. Depending on the data you have collected, there are a variety of charts that you may wish to include in your spreadsheet. You can also create your own chart or download one from a website. Here is a list of additional types of Charts:

Column Chart: This is utilized when displaying the relative change in a series of data, such as sales or cost, for example.

Line chart: This is used to illustrate various changes in your data over time.

Pie Chart: Is used when displaying parts of whole like percentages or shares.

Bar Charts: Are used when you want to represent a series of values for each category.

Area chart: Is used to show changes in your data over a period, whether it is a rising or falling line.

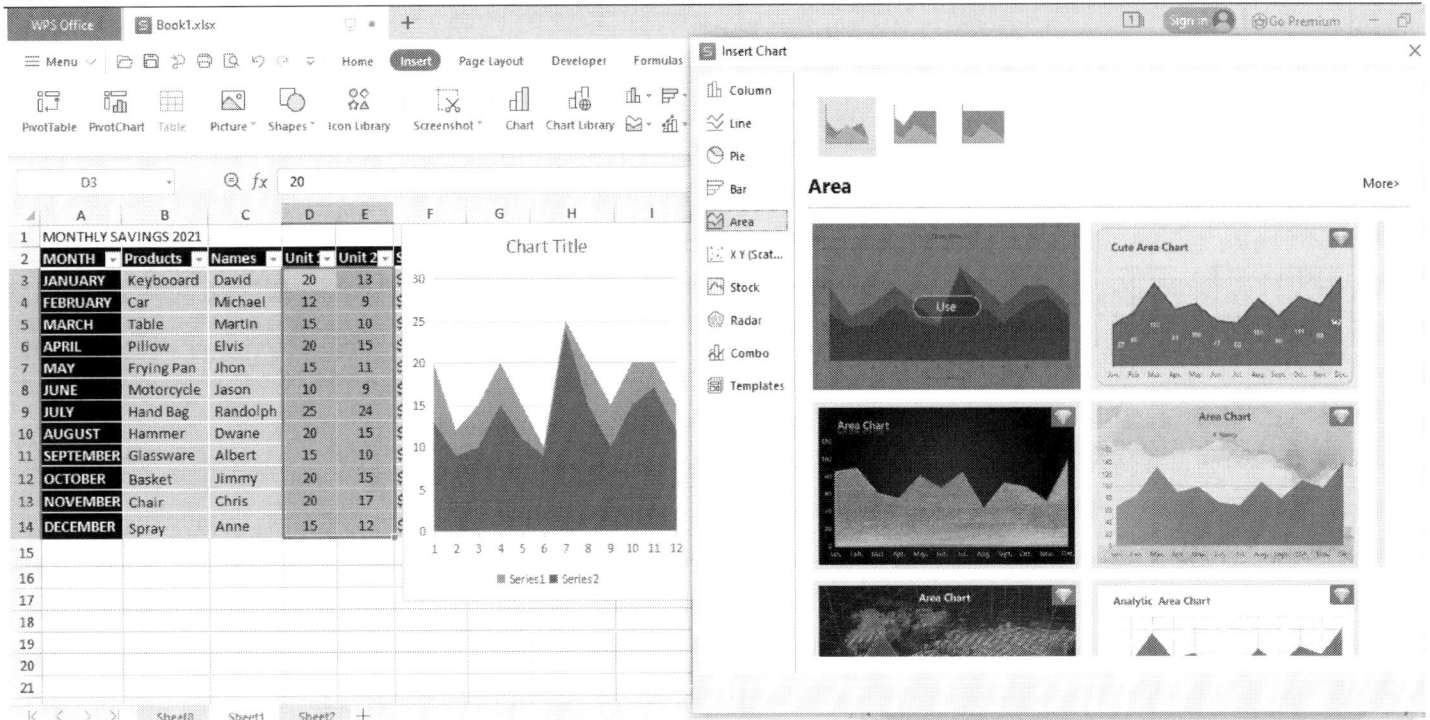

Scatter chart: Is used to show the relationship between two or more variables.

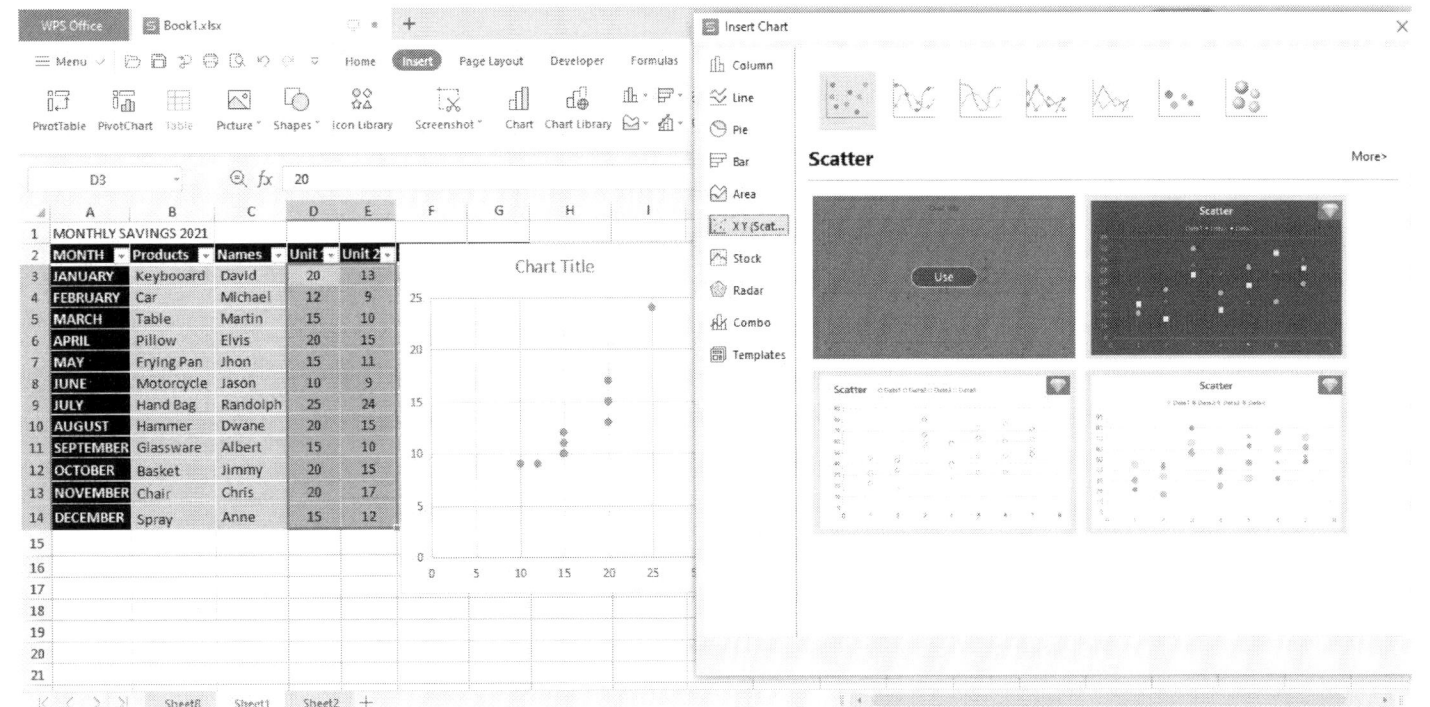

Stock chart: This type of chart is used by new traders to show their potential for a certain stock in the stock markets.

Radar Chart: For presenting changes in your data in a single dimension.

Combo Chart: Is also called time series chart. It is a combination of two different types of charts. It can be used to show changes in data over a period.

One of the cool things about them is that you can control the appearance of your data down to the smallest detail. Excel contains so many different types of charts. Customization of all chart elements, including background, title, data, and axes, is a feature shared by all of these programs.

LINKS AND COMMENTS

Links and comments in Excel workbooks are the most common means of enhancing the interactivity of a spreadsheet. This could be a collaboration tool, additional information on an entity, or comments about the data in your spreadsheet. However, as you add more links to your workbooks, they can become unwieldy and disorganized. This entails a method for enhancing the readability of Excel workbook links. How to improve the formatting of the internal links that comprise a dashboard or report. This section will describe how to format the display of internal links to make them easier to read and navigate throughout an Excel workbook. Before we proceed, let's discuss how to display external links and why internal links are sometimes required.

External links in Excel workbooks typically serve as references to external information or values. This is not always the case, however: a workbook can also contain an internal link. Typically, these are used as references between worksheets that function as navigational aids. For instance, you can have one worksheet containing all of your product names and another containing all of the relevant information. In this case, you can provide the user with a navigational aid by establishing an internal link between the two sheets. However, if the user clicks on this link, they will simply return to the same sheet, regardless of how far they are from the desired location on your dashboard. This may appear to be a problem, but it can be useful when working with a simple set of worksheets. You can have a worksheet containing all of the products, followed by a worksheet where users navigate to find product descriptions. Then, you can use an internal link within the initial sheet to return to the product description sheet.

Links and comments in Excel workbooks are the most common means of enhancing the interactivity of a spreadsheet. Links can provide additional information on a subject or lead the reader to a different workbook. The author can leave notes for someone else, such as an editor or colleague, without interrupting their writing flow. These are only two methods for facilitating user interaction with workbooks.

Comment length is limited to 80 characters and formatting is prohibited. They can be added using the command insert comment. The comments will be visible to anyone who opens the workbook, unless they have been disabled via the view tab of the Excel Options dialog box. While editing the workbook, comments are visible in the comments window.

How to add comments to an excel workbook:

1. Select the cell you want to place the comment in...
2. Use the ribbon's insert tab and click comments
3. Fill-in the comment
4. Apply any formatting or additional information

Links are useful when a reader needs additional information on a topic or wants to navigate between pages. If a worksheet is moved, renamed, or deleted, the links will change automatically. You cannot add links to cells that contain merged cells or table elements. Add links on the insert tab under links.

Links can be added individually or within a hyperlink. Similar to a link, a hyperlink creates a clickable connection to an external file, such as another excel workbook or an online web page.

How to add links and hyperlinks in an excel workbook:

1. Select the cell you want to place the link/hyperlink in...
2. Use the ribbon's insert tab, and click links or hyperlinks
3. Select your link/hyperlink from the submenu.
4. Fill-in the link parameters.
5. Click OK

The only difference between comments and links is that comments appear in the comments window. Links may be assigned a hotkey, but comments do not. You can add links and comments using keyboard shortcuts under the insert comment and insert link commands. Links can contain up to 255 characters and formatting. They can be added with the command insert link. Similar to comments, links are visible to anyone who opens the workbook unless they have disabled links in the view tab of the excel options dialog box.

How to add a link to an excel workbook

1. Click the tab called "Insert" at the top.
2. Click "Hyperlink".
3. Click "Text link".
4. Click one of the following:

Paste text from your spreadsheet in an email or in a document

Paste a hyperlink to any site you want on your spreadsheet

Type it yourself! that's right, type anything you want, even emoji! and then click "OK"

Thus, users can share their perspectives on the subject, and other readers can gain a deeper understanding of the information presented. Additionally, if you wish to advertise your company name or a link within your workbook while maintaining anonymity, this function is ideal for you.

Chapter 12. UNDERSTANDING THE PIVOT TABLE

In versions 7.0 and later, Microsoft added additional application features to the spreadsheet, including pivot tables. Pivot tables are one of the most powerful features available in Excel, but they operate in a slightly different manner than you might expect. Here are some tips on how to master the pivot table feature of the world's most popular spreadsheet application. This chapter will take your Excel skills to the next level by teaching you how to create a pivot table! After reading this section, you will be able to create pivot tables using the commands provided. This chapter will take your Excel skills to the next level by teaching you how to create a pivot table! After reading this section, you will be able to create pivot tables using the commands provided.

WHAT IS A PIVOT TABLE?

A Pivot table is a worksheet function that displays the data from multiple rows and columns in a way that makes it easy to see how your totals are broken down by various variables. The term "pivot table" is derived from the fact that you can view your data as if it were mounted on the front of a car, with each number stored on a different component. You can then turn the vehicle in any direction and read the numbers that appear on the "side" of the table.

By default, Excel Pivot tables are configured to display values from two fields, such as "sales" and "cost of goods sold," that you select in a separate area of your spreadsheet, such as "sales" and "cost of goods sold." If a third field, such as "month," is present in the data you are examining, Pivot tables will display sales totals for each month. If you have a fourth field, such as "market share," it will display all sales and profits for the third, fourth, fifth, and sixth "market segments."

While it's true that Pivot tables display how your data is segmented in multiple ways and can include multiple information fields, the Pivot table's primary benefit is that it allows you to focus on a single piece of data without having to absorb all the available information. This can save a great deal of time when examining a large number of numbers.

WHY USE PIVOT TABLES?

For example, pivot tables are useful when you want to compare different measures and present different results based on the measures. Suppose you wish to determine which product has performed well in terms of sales. You may wish to compare sales revenue and product count to determine which product is performing better. You could also compare the number of sales to the profit to determine which product is performing best on the market.

The pivot table feature is useful because it allows you to input various measurements, calculate them, and summarize them under various categories.

Even if you do not need to compare different measures, there are many advantages to using pivot tables for other purposes.

HOW DO WE USE PIVOT TABLES?

In the pivot table, the measure, such as sales revenue or number of products, is specified. Then, you can specify unique measurements for each product and immediately receive the result. Then, you can compare the various metrics to determine the direction of your sales. You can also determine the average from a few measurements and compare it to the average from the previous year to determine how much your sales have grown.

Chapter 13.   MASTERING THE DIFFERENT PARTS OF A PIVOT TABLE

There are two main components in creating Pivot tables:

- Defining fields or Field List
- Creating a table or Pivot Table Areas

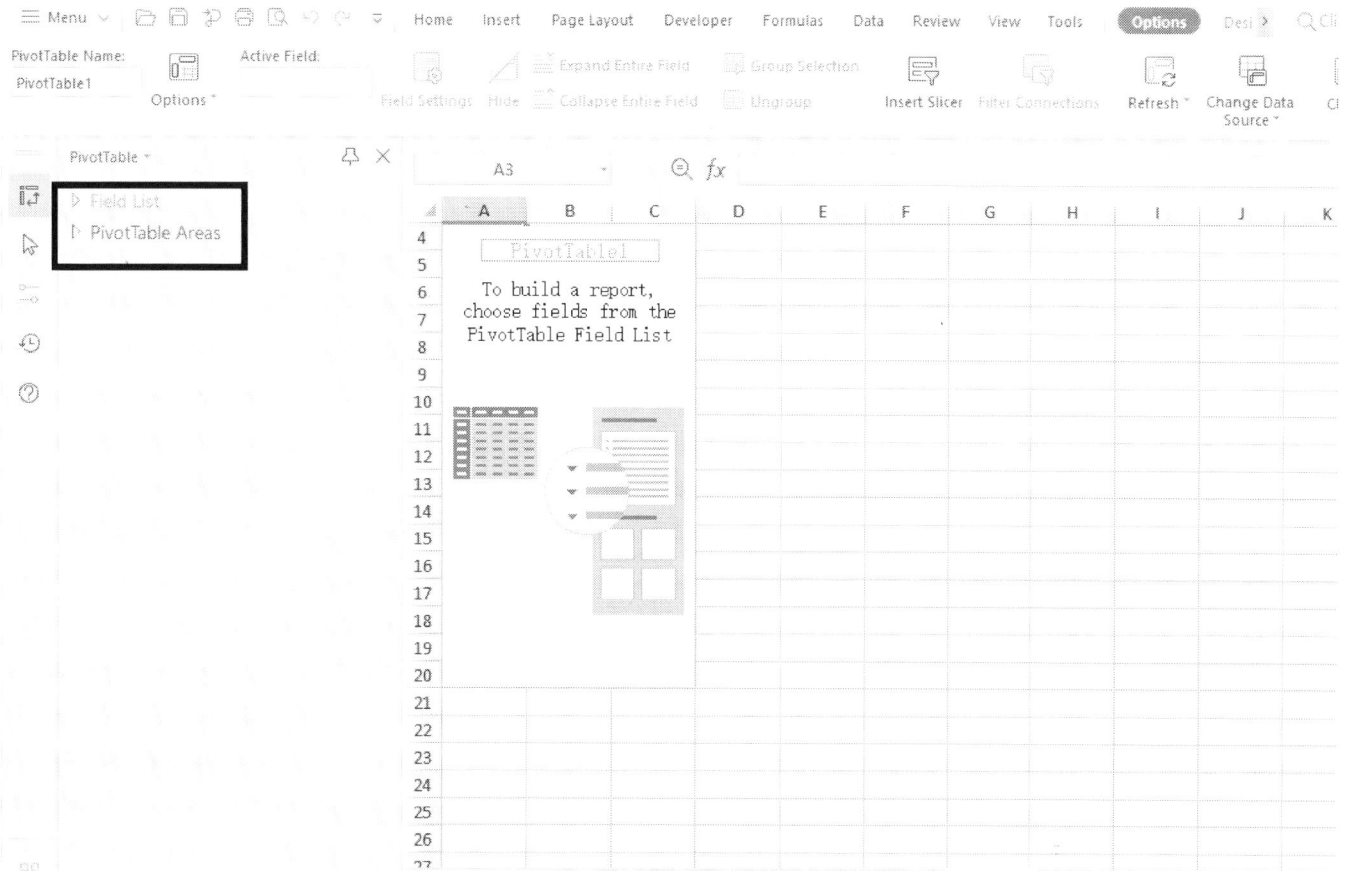

Two reasons make it essential to comprehend pivot tables and define fields:

1. It describes its nature.
2. It explains how to import information into a Pivot table.

You must be familiar with Pivot tables in order to comprehend this section. The first thing to keep in mind is that the Pivot table will be automatically sorted by the field you select. For example, if you select a date field and then sort by another date field, the Pivot table will be automatically sorted by the date column.

The second thing to keep in mind is that you can define as many fields as you like for your Pivot table. This permits us to generate a unique Pivot table for each data category or topic.

FIELD LIST

The Pivot field list consists of the small icons at the bottom of each column. The little arrows on the left side of each column indicate which column is which. Depending on your intentions, the Icon will alter accordingly. You can add or remove data fields from this list by clicking and dragging the corresponding icon. If you click the icon to highlight it, a drop-down menu will appear from which you can choose the data that column should contain.

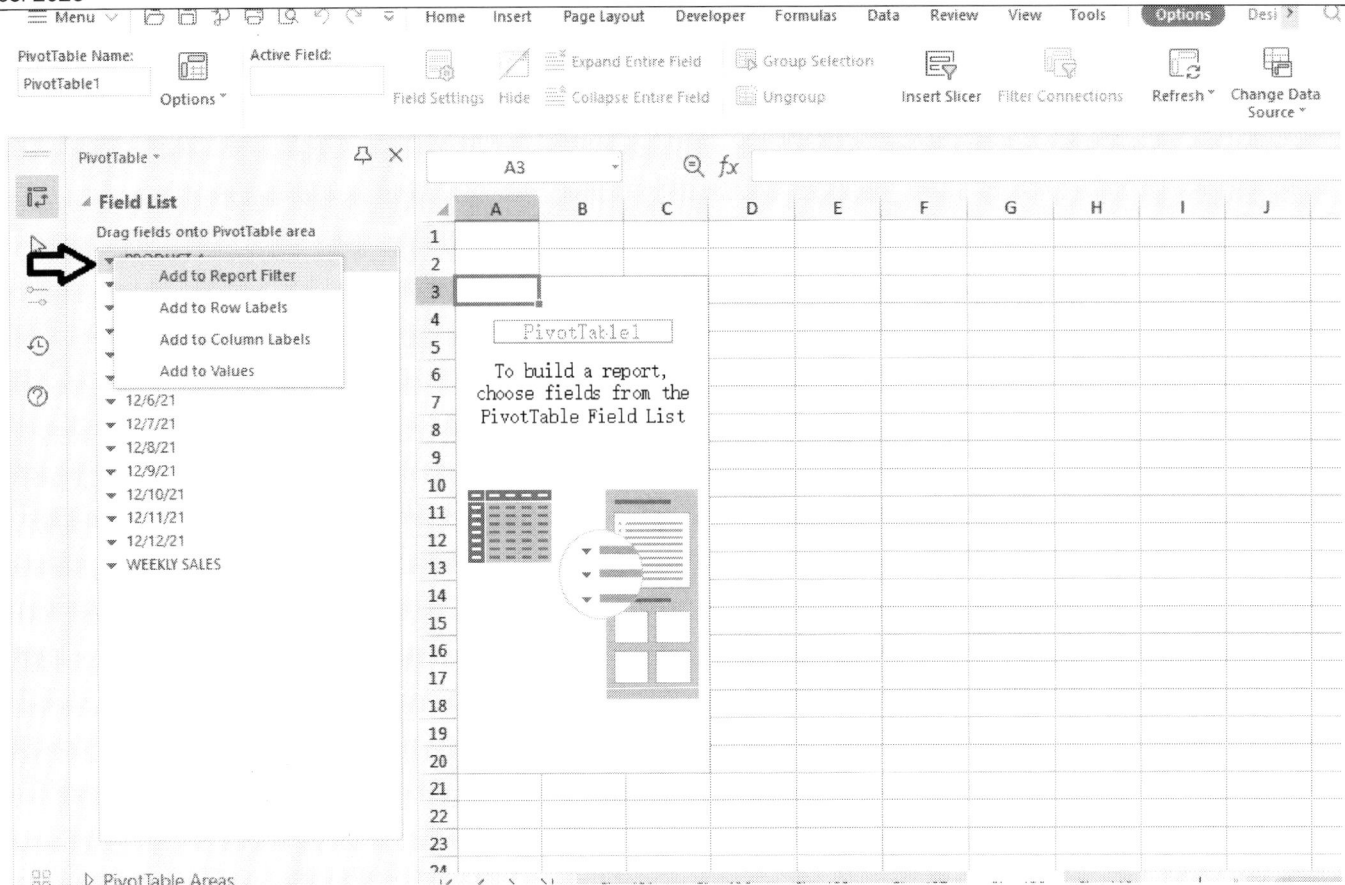

There are multiple ways to access the list of Pivot fields.

1) From a Field list column, you can select the field by clicking on the arrow next to the field's name.

2) It is also possible to drag a field from the main screen to the Pivot field list.

PIVOT TABLE AREA

The Pivot table is where all of the data selected from the Pivot field list is assembled into a table. The Pivot table contains headings for each of the categories, as well as the order in which each field for that category is arranged beneath those headings.

A pivot table consists of four components: the Filter area, Rows, Columns, and Values.

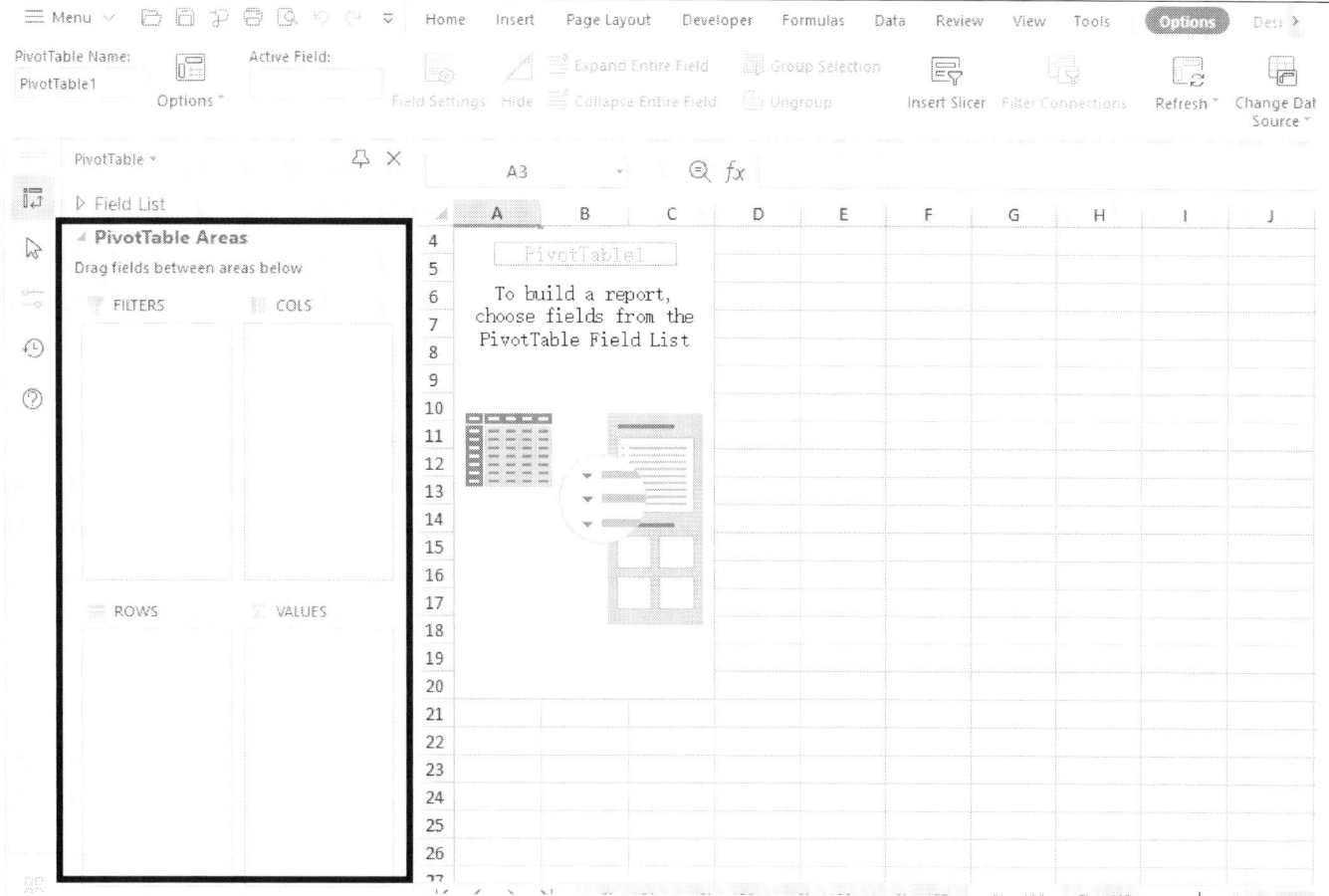

THE FILTER AREA

This area is used to apply a condition to the data and appears on the right side of the table. Clicking the Product A filter in the first pivot table, for instance, enables the selection of a different Product range. The drop-down menu in Excel's formula bar allows for automatic data filtering.

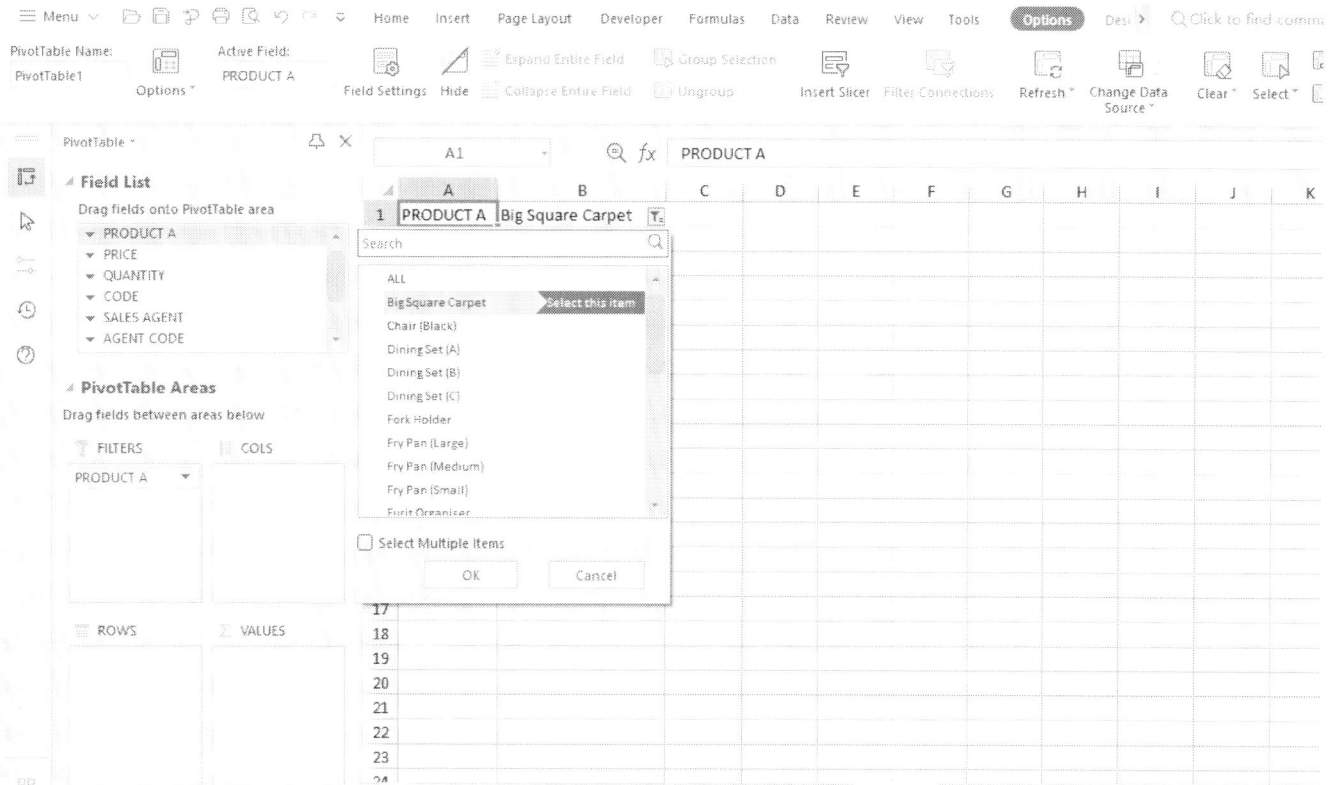

THE ROWS AREA

The Rows section of an Excel spreadsheet displays the original data from which the pivot table was derived. For instance, the first column in the rows section contains the names of each Sales Agent for the Product.

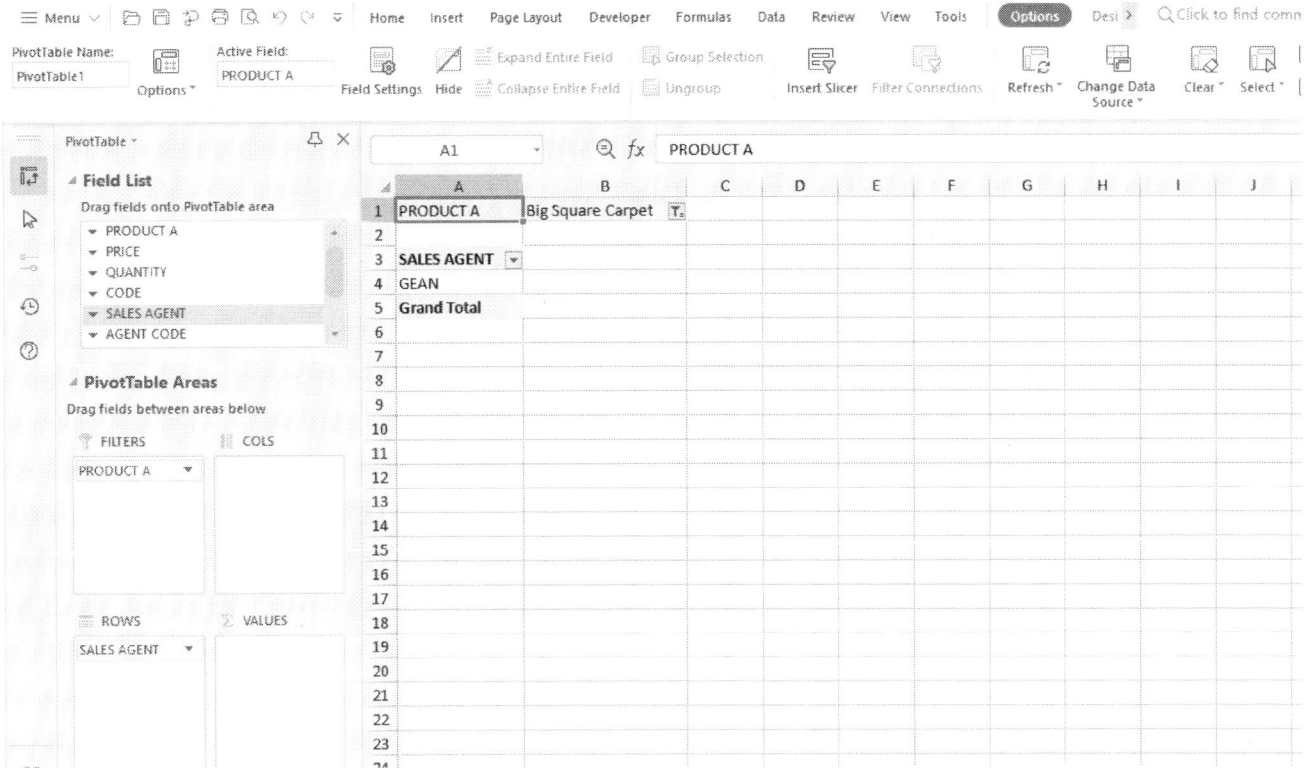

In above example, the name of "GEAN" appears under the row, it's because she's the sales agent of the said Product.

Now, let's filter the Product and select "ALL".

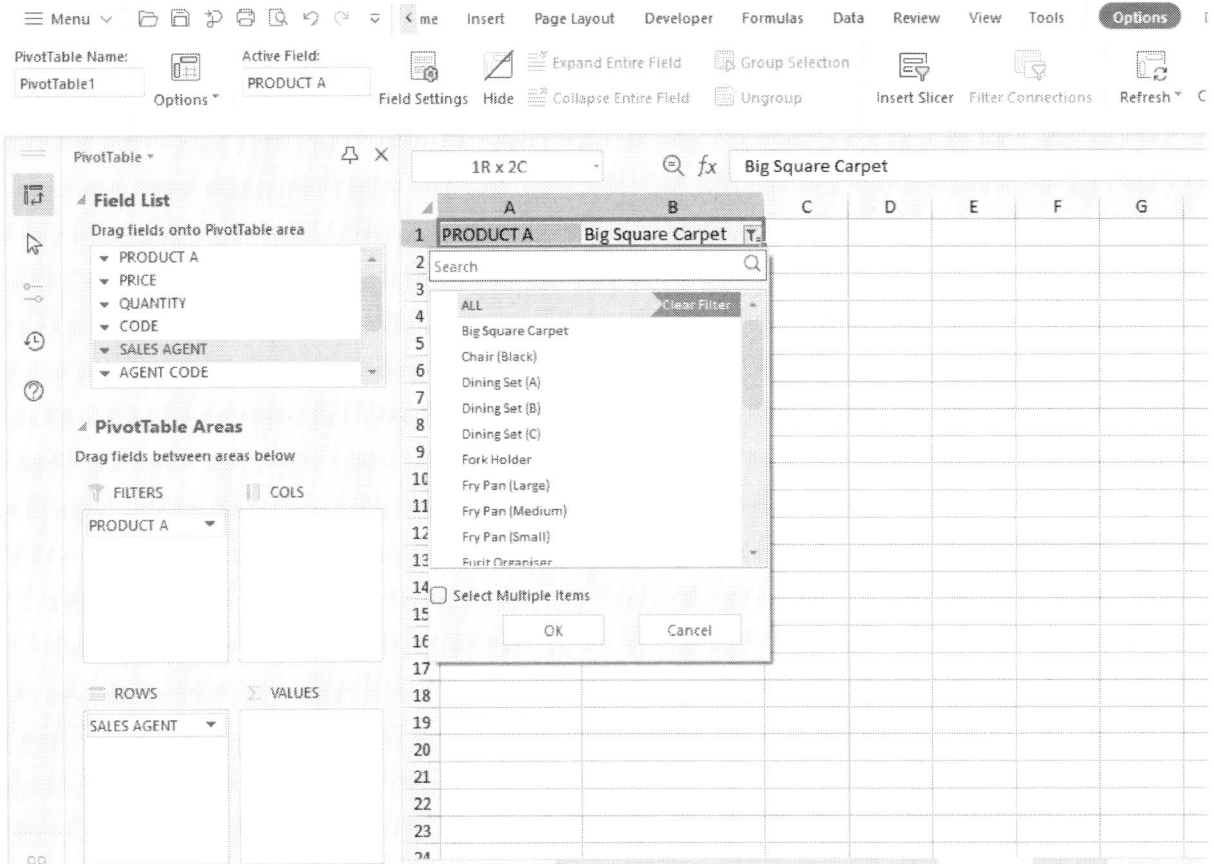

This is how it looks like:

As you can see, all the name of the agents from the Product Range appears in our Pivot table. This is how to get information into your Pivot table.

THE COLUMNS AREA

The columns of the pivot table are organized to display the data that is most relevant to you. For example, the columns in the second pivot table are arranged to display the Sales Code.

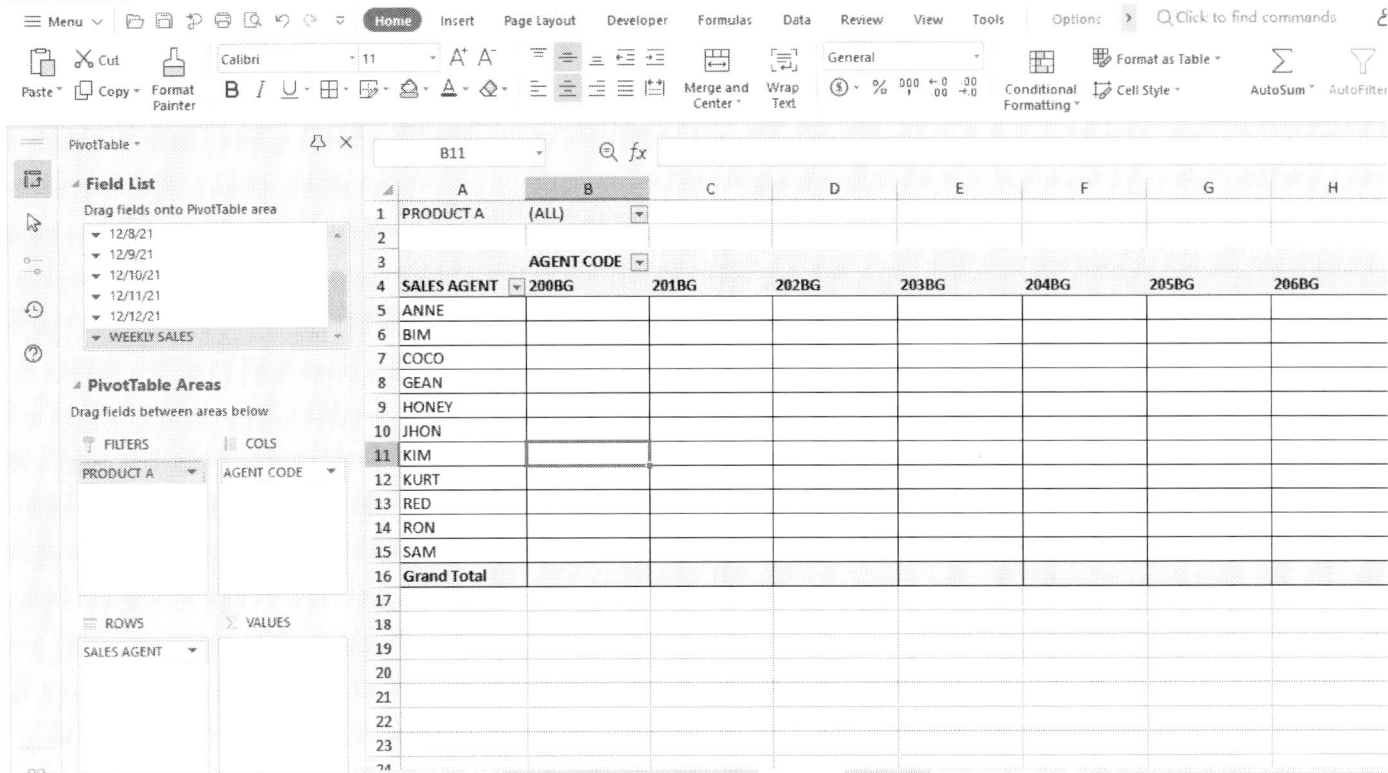

THE VALUES AREA

The Values Area is located at the bottom of a Pivot table and contains summary calculations created from the source data. The Values Area can be used to manipulate and analyze your worksheet data further.

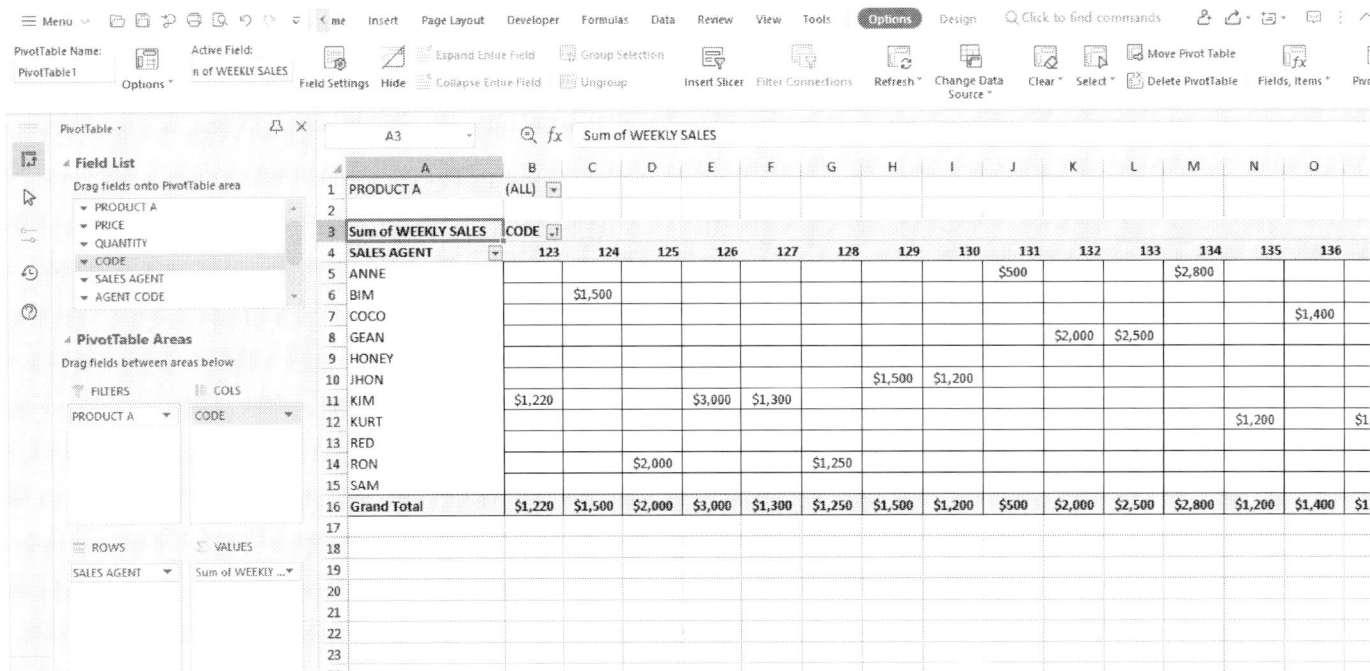

This is how your Pivot Table looks like.

USING THE COMMANDS TO ACCOMPLISH A PIVOT TABLE

Unlike other spreadsheets, pivot tables are not limited by row and column dimensions. Additionally, they can have a value field with multiple dimensions.

To determine which cells in column A will be evaluated for values, you must however specify the settings for the value field and the value label. To accomplish this, select the design tab at the top of your pivot table and then click on the value field settings icon below the fields.

You will then see the subsequent options:

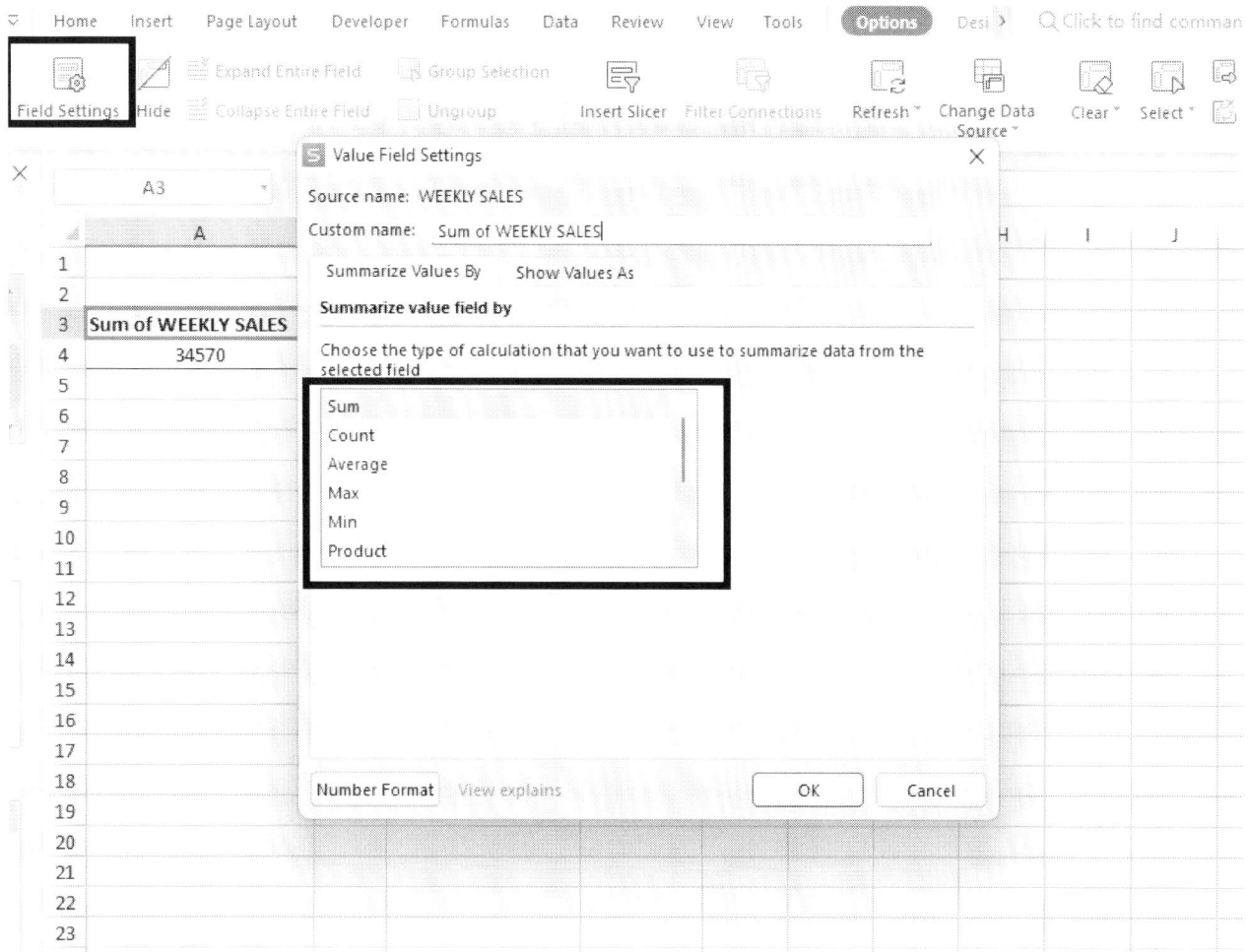

There are 11 different operations that you can choose from. Depending on your requirement, these are SUM, COUNT, AVERAGE, MAX, MIN, PRODUCT, COUNT NUMBERS, STDDEV, STDDEVP, VAR and VARP.

Sum: This operation will summarize the values in a field or column as a numerical value.

Count: This operation will count the number of values in a column or field and put it into another column.

Average: This operation will calculate the average of values from a specified row or column and place it in another cell.

Max: This operation will display the maximum value from a specified row or column and place it in another cell.

Min: This operation falls on the minimum value from a specified row or column and place it in another cell.

Product: Used to calculate the product of numbers that are found in different columns or rows, this option is selected if you want to multiply all the numbers that you have on your spreadsheet.

Count Numbers: This operation will count the number of numbers in a column or row and put into another column. This is functional if you want to display only a certain number of numbers both in your cell and on your pivot table.

STDev: is applied to calculate the standard deviation, which is a measure of how far the average value of a data set differs from the mean value.

STDVEP: This operation turns out when you have calculated the standard deviation, this will calculate the value of standard deviation and place it into another field.

VAR: This operation calculates the variance from numbers in different columns or rows, this calculation falls on the variance of the data.

VARP: This value returns the variance of numbers of the population. This is usually used in the context of being a function that is performed on a population.

What is the value field setting used for?

The main purpose of the value field setting is to extract the details that you need from all the values in a row or column. These includes:

- Summarizing data in a column or row as a whole
- Allowing you to filter out only one column or row in your pivot table
- Calculating the average and standard deviation of data in cells

The value field setting determines which operation is executed when using the extract function to extract values. As stated previously, there are various types of value field settings; we will examine all Values.

For instance, you wish to determine the Agent's weekly profit from product sales. Typically, the entire table is analyzed to determine which product was the most popular. Rather than searching for each individual column and row, it is much simpler to create a pivot table to analyze sales by product.

To get started with it, here's what we do:

1. Make sure you have a clear data with Headings on each column and no empty rows or columns in the center of your data set and set your data is set as table.

PRODUCT A	PRICE	QUANTITY	CODE	SALES AGENT	AGENT CODE	6-Dec-2021	7-Dec-2021	8-Dec-2021	9-Dec-2021	10-Dec-2021	11-Dec-2021	12-Dec-2021	WEEKLY SALES
Round Table	$35	200	123	KIM	200BG	13	3	5	6	11	20	25	1220
Chair (Black)	$50	200	124	BIM	201BG	5	30	10	12	10	21	20	1500
Round Rug	$50	200	125	RON	202BG	17	30	15	45	9	25	22	2000
Dining Set (A)	$100	150	126	KIM	203BG	10	30	14	12	19	26	20	3000
Dining Set (B)	$120	150	127	KIM	204BG	15	40	27	11	16	13	25	1300
Dining Set (C)	$130	150	128	RON	205BG	20	23	30	17	15	14	23	1250
Wood Table (A)	$100	150	129	JHON	206BG	25	13	28	18	14	19	27	1500
Wood Table (B)	$150	150	130	JHON	207BG	40	23	13	23	12	12	13	1200
Wood Table (C)	$180	150	131	ANNE	208BG	30	25	14	24	13	10	14	500
Round Carpet	$50	250	132	GEAN	209BG	30	27	7	25	32	13	17	2000
Big Square Carpet	$75	250	133	GEAN	210BG	25	18	17	22	33	32	15	2500
Knife Organiser	$25	200	134	ANNE	211BG	20	29	37	27	17	34	35	2800
Spoon Holder	$25	200	135	KURT	212BG	25	12	39	28	12	35	33	1200
Fork Holder	$25	200	136	COCO	213BG	60	15	23	19	25	15	23	1400
Grocery Racks (3 ply)	$120	300	137	KURT	214BG	65	19	25	30	39	32	27	1500
Grocery Racks (4 ply)	$140	300	138	RED	215BG	55	10	22	31	32	23	12	1200
Grocery Racks (5 ply)	$160	300	139	RED	216BG	35	22	21	12	30	24	12	3500
Furit Organiser	$80	150	140	SAM	217BG	30	25	12	13	13	43	11	1200
Shoe Organiser	$80	150	141	RED	218BG	20	18	14	15	14	33	11	1200
Fry Pan (Small)	$80	200	142	SAM	219BG	25	22	18	35	15	12	15	1200

2. Rename your table so you won't get confused.

3. Go on the data tab and click Pivot Table, A window will pop up. You'll be asked to choose a location where it will be saved and then hit OK.

Excel will create your pivot table for you like this:

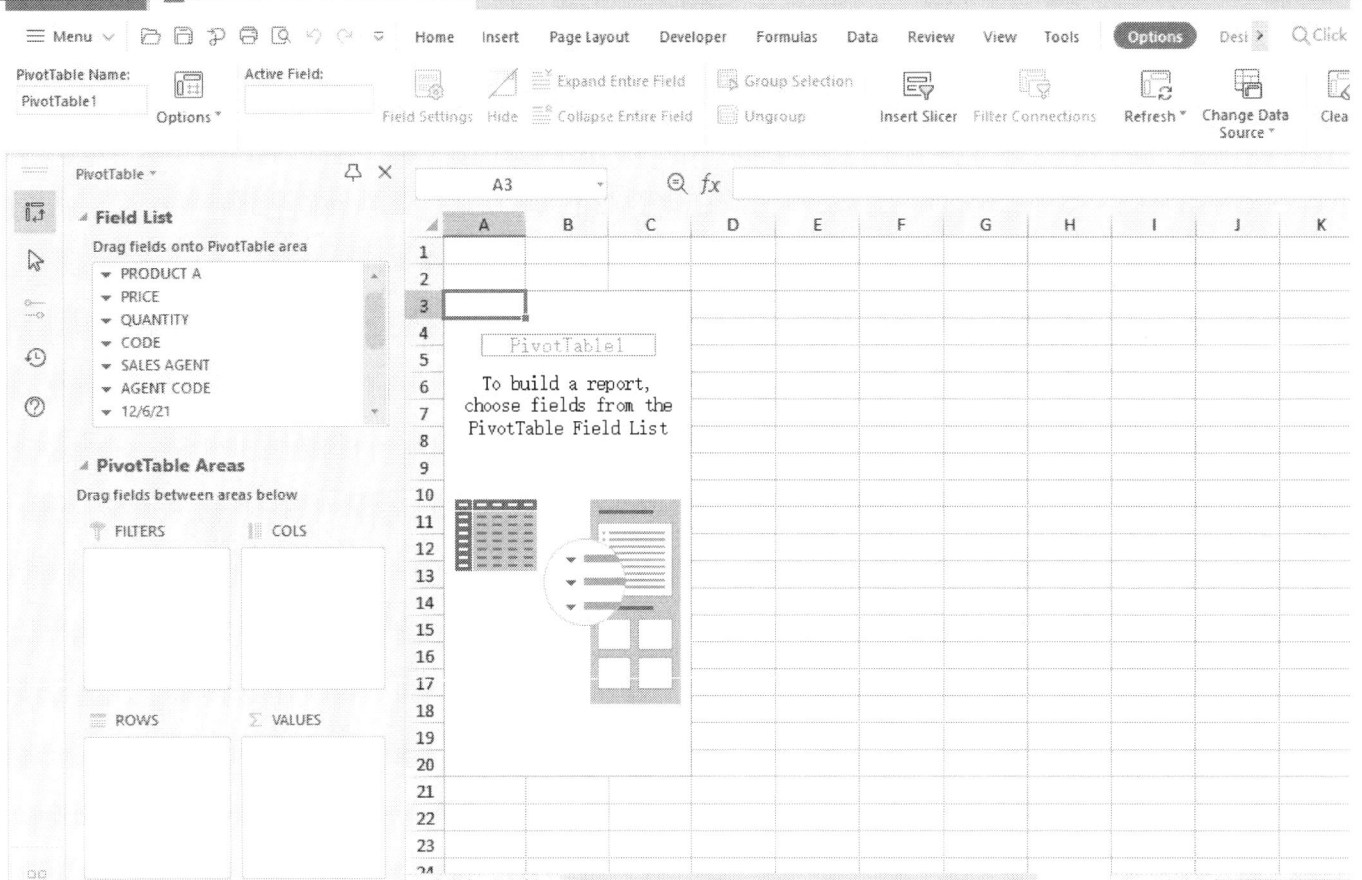

A blank pivot table appears on your worksheet. This is your work area where you will define all your fields and how they are broken down into individual items for analysis.

4. After you see your pivot table. Select any cell in the pivot table and click on Fields, you'll see a drop down list of options to organize your data set into columns.

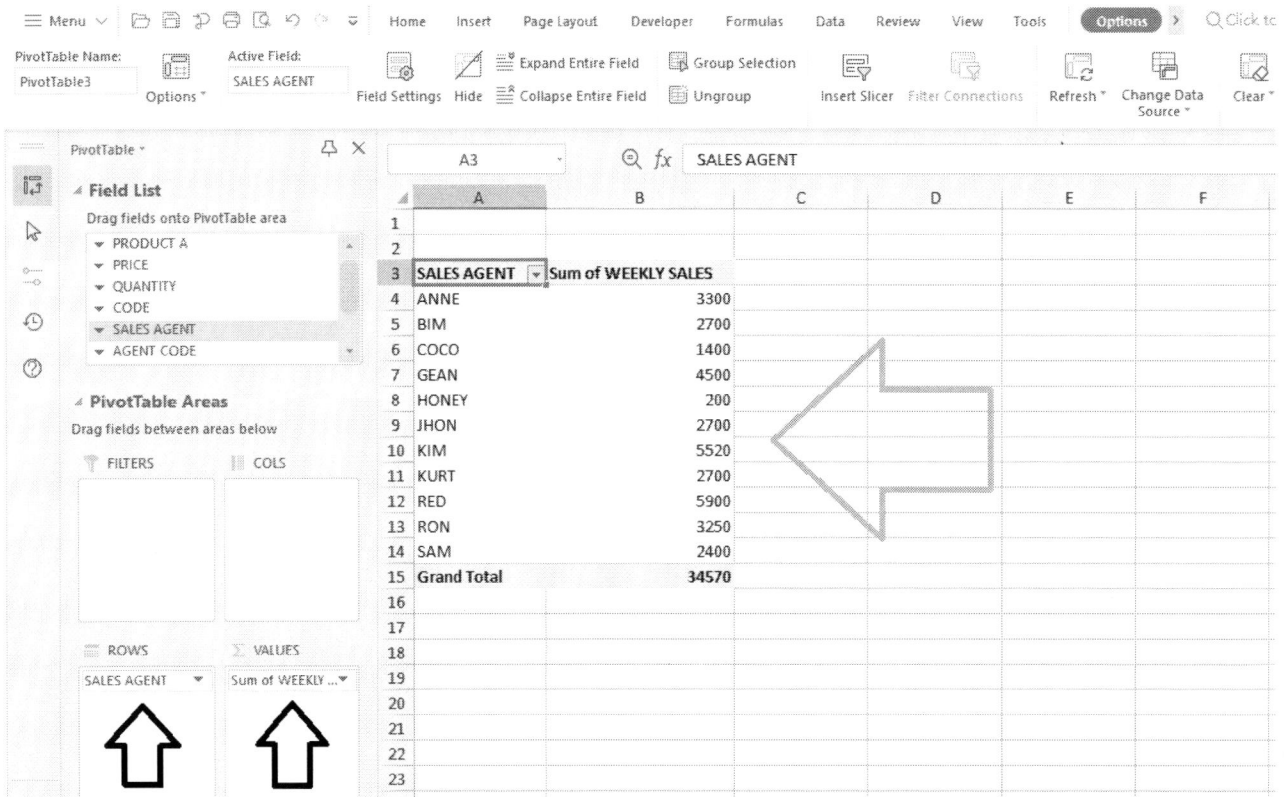

SUM VALUE

This operation will produce a numerical sum of the values in a field or column. In this example, we will enter the Sales Agent into the 'Row' field and the Weekly Sales into the 'Value' field. How Does the Sum Value Work?

Another example of using the Sum Value is to determine how many Products a particular Agent sold each day.

To implement this, you must set the data on each table. Let's accomplish this by placing the Sales Agent on Filters and setting the Dates in the Value area.

There you go, we got how many products that Agent Kim has sold every day.

Let's check out the other agents by filtering the name. Let's choose ANNE with the products under her department.

To check whether our table is correct, let's look in our data source. To do this, just double click the result value and you will be directed into a new spreadsheet showing the summarize data.

COUNT VALUE

The count operation will count the number of values in a column or field and store the result in a new column. For instance, we have a row for sales agents, but we only want to see the total number of products associated with their department.

Place the Product table in the Value Field Settings window and set the Field Settings to Count Value.

e Name:		Active Field:			Expand Entire Field	Group Selection							Move Piv
le3	Options ˅	um of PRODUCT A	Field Settings	Hide	Collapse Entire Field	Ungroup	Insert Slicer	Filter Connections	Refresh ˅	Change Data Source ˅	Clear ˅	Select ˅	Delete Pi

PivotTable ˅

◢ **Field List**

Drag fields onto PivotTable area

- ˅ PRODUCT A
- ˅ PRICE
- ˅ QUANTITY
- ˅ CODE
- ˅ SALES AGENT
- ˅ AGENT CODE
- ˅ 6-Dec-2021

◢ **PivotTable Areas**

Drag fields between areas below

🔽 FILTERS	▥ COLS

▦ ROWS	Σ VALUES
SALES AGENT ˅	Sum of PRODU... ˅

	A
B4	
1	
2	
3	
4	SALES AGENT
5	ANNE
6	BIM
7	COCO
8	GEAN
9	HONEY
10	JHON
11	KIM
12	KURT
13	RED
14	RON
15	SAM
16	Grand Total
17	
18	
19	
20	
21	
22	
23	
24	

Value Field Settings ✕

Source name: PRODUCT A

Custom name: Count of PRODUCT A

Summarize Values By   Show Values As

Summarize value field by

Choose the type of calculation that you want to use to summarize data from the selected field

- Sum
- Count
- Average
- Max
- Min
- Product

Number Format   View explains   OK   Cancel

E	F

The table should look like this:

ble Name:		Active Field:			Expand Entire Field	Group Selection				
able3	Options ˅	unt of PRODUCT A	Field Settings	Hide	Collapse Entire Field	Ungroup	Insert Slicer	Filter Connections	Refresh ˅	Change Da Source ˅

PivotTable ˅

◢ **Field List**

Drag fields onto PivotTable area

- ˅ PRODUCT A
- ˅ PRICE
- ˅ QUANTITY
- ˅ CODE
- ˅ SALES AGENT
- ˅ AGENT CODE
- ˅ 6-Dec-2021

◢ **PivotTable Areas**

Drag fields between areas below

🔽 FILTERS	▥ COLS

▦ ROWS	Σ VALUES
SALES AGENT ˅	Count of PROD... ˅

B4   🔍 fx   Count of PRODUCT A

	A	B	C	D	E
1					
2					
3					
4	SALES AGENT 🔽	Count of PRODUCT A			
5	ANNE	2			
6	BIM	2			
7	COCO	1			
8	GEAN	2			
9	HONEY	1			
10	JHON	2			
11	KIM	3			
12	KURT	2			
13	RED	3			
14	RON	2			
15	SAM	2			
16	Grand Total	22			
17					
18					
19					
20					
21					
22					
23					

What if we would also like to know what kind of Products under their department? To do this, just simply add your Product data in Row.

This explains that Agent Anne has two kinds of products under her department.

AVERAGE VALUE

This operation will calculate the average of values in a row or column and place it into another field. For example, the average price of each product under their department.

MAX VALUE

This operation will display the row or column's maximum value and place it in another cell. For example, you will have daily sales information. Each day's sales can be calculated and recorded, but rather than summing the numbers, we're only interested in the highest selling quantity per day. Simply click 'Max' value under 'Value Field Settings' to accomplish this. Then, you will notice in your pivot table that the total sales maximum is placed in a separate cell.

Max of 6-Dec-2021	Max of 7-Dec-2021	Max of 8-Dec-2021	Max of 9-Dec-2021	Max of 10-Dec-2021	Max of 11-Dec-2021	Max of 12-Dec-2021
65	45	39	45	39	43	35

Max of 6-Dec-2021
Value: 65
Column: Max of 6-Dec-2021

MIN VALUE

This operation determines the minimum value in a specified row or column and places it in another cell. Similarly to Max, but instead of displaying the maximum value from a specified row or column and placing it in another cell, we want to find the minimum value from a specified row or column and place it in another cell. We simply click on Min value under 'Value Field Settings', and the obtained data will be placed in another cell.

SALES AGENT	Min of 6-Dec-2021	Min of 7-Dec-2021	Min of 8-Dec-2021	Min of 9-Dec-2021	Min of 10-Dec-2021	Min of 11-Dec-2021	Min of 12-Dec-2021
ANNE	20	25	14	24	13	10	14
BIM	5	30	10	12	10	11	17
COCO	60	15	23	19	25	15	23
GEAN	25	18	7	22	32	13	15
HONEY	11	11	23	21	13	19	18
JHON	25	13	18	18	12	12	13
KIM	10	3	5	6	11	13	20
KURT	25	12	25	28	12	32	27
RED	20	10	14	12	14	23	11
RON	17	23	15	17	9	14	22
SAM	25	22	12	13	13	12	11
Grand Total	5	3	5	6	9	10	11

Min of 6-Dec-2021
Value: 5
Row: Grand Total
Column: Min of 6-Dec-2021

PRODUCT VALUE

This operation will calculate the product of numbers found in different columns or rows; select this option if you wish to multiply all of the numbers in your spreadsheet.

COUNT NUMBERS VALUE

This operation will count the numbers in a column or row and place them in a new column. For instance, there is a column for the product and a list of all salespeople assigned to each product. You can calculate the total number of salespeople on this list and place the result in a separate column.

STDDEV VALUE

StdDev is utilized to compute the standard deviation, which is a measurement of how far the average value of a data set deviates from the mean. In other words, it is used to determine whether your numbers are normally distributed.

For instance, you have weekly sales data and wish to calculate the standard deviation. Calculate the average value of your weekly sales and a second set of weekly sales values to determine the standard deviation. Then, you will see the result of standard deviation for your weekly sales in your pivot table.

STDDEVP

This operation is performed after the standard deviation has been calculated; it provides an additional option for displaying the standard deviation on all or a subset of rows or columns.

VAR VALUE

VAR: This operation computes the variance between numbers in different columns or rows; this calculation pertains to the data variance. To determine the variance of your weekly sales, for instance.

VARP VALUE

This value returns the population's number distribution variance. This term is typically employed in the context of a function performed on a population.

EXCEL TIPS FOR PIVOT TABLES

Here are some Excel Pivot table tips that will help you make the most of your data.

1. Be truthful with yourself. If you have incomplete data, you should exclude it from your pivot table. This will prevent inaccurate calculations, which could lead to interpretation problems in the future.
2. 2.Include only relevant information in a Pivot table. Excel will evaluate different numbers depending on which variables are included in the table.
3. Don't forget where your data resides! If your data are located in a different location, be sure to inform Excel of its location.
4. Use consistent column headings to maintain the efficiency of your pivot table. Use the same naming convention for each column, if possible, to make it easier to see their relationship. This is useful if you wish to export your Pivot data.
5. Don't overlook summary functions and the various options available for them. These are excellent methods for simplifying your numbers and determining the direction of your business.

Chapter 14.   Enhancing your Pivot Table Presentations

If you're familiar with Microsoft Excel's Pivot Tables, you'll know how crucial it is to make your tables as clear and concise as possible. Time and practice are required to develop a technique for maximizing the effectiveness of your pivot tables. We are all aware of the importance of pivot tables. A pivot table is analogous to a summary table that divides your data into one or more new columns. They facilitate the identification of data trends, the discovery of patterns, the simplification of complex calculations, and the exploration of data in countless ways.

How to use a Subtotals option on pivot table

Excel pivot tables are an excellent tool for summarizing, organizing, and analyzing data. SUBTOTAL is a function that can be used to break down your data. Here is an example of a pivot table with subtotals. It displays all of the data in columns along with the subtotals for each column.

SALES AGENT	PRODUCT A	Sum of 6-Dec-2021	Sum of 7-Dec-2021	Sum of 8-Dec-2021	Sum of 9-Dec-2021	Sum of 10-Dec-2021	Sum of 11-Dec-2021	Sum of 12-Dec-2021
ANNE		50.00	54.00	51.00	51.00	30.00	44.00	49.00
ANNE	Knife Organiser	20.00	29.00	37.00	27.00	17.00	34.00	35.00
ANNE	Wood Table (C)	30.00	25.00	14.00	24.00	13.00	10.00	14.00
BIM		15.00	75.00	39.00	43.00	26.00	32.00	37.00
BIM	Chair (Black)	5.00	30.00	10.00	12.00	10.00	21.00	20.00
BIM	Fry Pan (Medium)	10.00	45.00	29.00	31.00	16.00	11.00	17.00
COCO		75.00	55.00	50.00	30.00	41.00	28.00	48.00
COCO	Dining Set (B)	15.00	40.00	27.00	11.00	16.00	13.00	25.00
COCO	Fork Holder	60.00	15.00	23.00	19.00	25.00	15.00	23.00
GEAN		55.00	45.00	24.00	47.00	65.00	45.00	32.00
GEAN	Big Square Carpet	25.00	18.00	17.00	22.00	33.00	32.00	15.00
GEAN	Round Carpet	30.00	27.00	7.00	25.00	32.00	13.00	17.00
HONEY		66.00	21.00	45.00	52.00	45.00	42.00	30.00
HONEY	Fry Pan (Large)	11.00	11.00	23.00	21.00	13.00	19.00	18.00
HONEY	Grocery Racks (4 ply)	55.00	10.00	22.00	31.00	32.00	23.00	12.00
JHON		65.00	36.00	46.00	41.00	26.00	31.00	40.00
JHON	Wood Table (A)	25.00	13.00	28.00	18.00	14.00	19.00	27.00
JHON	Wood Table (B)	40.00	23.00	18.00	23.00	12.00	12.00	13.00
KIM		23.00	33.00	19.00	18.00	30.00	46.00	45.00
KIM	Dining Set (A)	10.00	30.00	14.00	12.00	19.00	26.00	20.00
KIM	Round Table	13.00	3.00	5.00	6.00	11.00	20.00	25.00
KURT		90.00	31.00	64.00	58.00	51.00	67.00	60.00
KURT	Grocery Racks (3 ply)	65.00	19.00	25.00	30.00	39.00	32.00	27.00
KURT	Spoon Holder	25.00	12.00	39.00	28.00	12.00	35.00	33.00

The pivot table option "Do not show subtotals"

Even though the SUBTOTAL function is useful, you may not always want the subtotals displayed in a pivot table. In this instance, we do not want subtotals for the Sales Agent field to be displayed. To do so, click the Subtotals drop-down arrow and select the option "Do not show subtotals."

	SALES AGENT	PRODUCT A	Sum of 6-Dec-2021	Sum of 7-Dec-2021	Sum of 8-Dec-2021	Sum of 9-Dec-2021	Sum of 10-Dec-2021	Sum of 11-Dec-2021	Sum of 12-Dec-2021
5	ANNE								
6	ANNE	Knife Organiser	20.00	29.00	37.00	27.00	17.00	34.00	35.00
7	ANNE	Wood Table (C)	30.00	25.00	14.00	24.00	13.00	10.00	14.00
8	BIM								
9	BIM	Chair (Black)	5.00	30.00	10.00	12.00	10.00	21.00	20.00
10	BIM	Fry Pan (Medium)	10.00	45.00	29.00	31.00	16.00	11.00	17.00
11	COCO								
12	COCO	Dining Set (B)	15.00	40.00	27.00	11.00	16.00	13.00	25.00
13	COCO	Fork Holder	60.00	15.00	23.00	19.00	25.00	15.00	23.00
14	GEAN								
15	GEAN	Big Square Carpet	25.00	18.00	17.00	22.00	33.00	32.00	15.00
16	GEAN	Round Carpet	30.00	27.00	7.00	25.00	32.00	13.00	17.00
17	HONEY								
18	HONEY	Fry Pan (Large)	11.00	11.00	23.00	21.00	13.00	19.00	18.00
19	HONEY	Grocery Racks (4 ply)	55.00	10.00	22.00	31.00	32.00	23.00	12.00
20	JHON								
21	JHON	Wood Table (A)	25.00	13.00	28.00	18.00	14.00	19.00	27.00
22	JHON	Wood Table (B)	40.00	23.00	18.00	23.00	12.00	12.00	13.00
23	KIM								
24	KIM	Dining Set (A)	10.00	30.00	14.00	12.00	19.00	26.00	20.00
25	KIM	Round Table	13.00	3.00	5.00	6.00	11.00	20.00	25.00
26	KURT								
27	KURT	Grocery Racks (3 ply)	65.00	19.00	25.00	30.00	39.00	32.00	27.00
28	KURT	Spoon Holder	25.00	12.00	39.00	28.00	12.00	35.00	33.00
29	RED								

'Show Subtotal at Bottom of Group'

If you find the subtotal bar too much of an eye sore, you can hide it altogether by choosing Show Subtotal at Bottom of Group.

	SALES AGENT	PRODUCT A	Sum of 6-Dec-2021	Sum of 7-Dec-2021	Sum of 8-Dec-2021	Sum of 9-Dec-2021	Sum of 10-Dec-2021	Sum of 11-Dec-2021	Sum of 12-Dec-2021
5	ANNE								
6	ANNE	Knife Organiser	20.00	29.00	37.00	27.00	17.00	34.00	35.00
7	ANNE	Wood Table (C)	30.00	25.00	14.00	24.00	13.00	10.00	14.00
8	ANNE Total		50.00	54.00	51.00	51.00	30.00	44.00	49.00
9	BIM								
10	BIM	Chair (Black)	5.00	30.00	10.00	12.00	10.00	21.00	20.00
11	BIM	Fry Pan (Medium)	10.00	45.00	29.00	31.00	16.00	11.00	17.00
12	BIM Total		15.00	75.00	39.00	43.00	26.00	32.00	37.00
13	COCO								
14	COCO	Dining Set (B)	15.00	40.00	27.00	11.00	16.00	13.00	25.00
15	COCO	Fork Holder	60.00	15.00	23.00	19.00	25.00	15.00	23.00
16	COCO Total		75.00	55.00	50.00	30.00	41.00	28.00	48.00
17	GEAN								
18	GEAN	Big Square Carpet	25.00	18.00	17.00	22.00	33.00	32.00	15.00
19	GEAN	Round Carpet	30.00	27.00	7.00	25.00	32.00	13.00	17.00
20	GEAN Total		55.00	45.00	24.00	47.00	65.00	45.00	32.00
21	HONEY								
22	HONEY	Fry Pan (Large)	11.00	11.00	23.00	21.00	13.00	19.00	18.00
23	HONEY	Grocery Racks (4 ply)	55.00	10.00	22.00	31.00	32.00	23.00	12.00
24	HONEY Total		66.00	21.00	45.00	52.00	45.00	42.00	30.00
25	JHON								
26	JHON	Wood Table (A)	25.00	13.00	28.00	18.00	14.00	19.00	27.00
27	JHON	Wood Table (B)	40.00	23.00	18.00	23.00	12.00	12.00	13.00
28	JHON Total		65.00	36.00	46.00	41.00	26.00	31.00	40.00
29	KIM								

'Show Subtotal at Top of Group'

You can see the subtotal at the top of each grouping instead of putting it at the bottom.

≡ Menu ∨ 🗅 🗅 🗗 🖨 🔍 🖒 ⤢ ▽   Home   Insert   Page Layout   Developer   Formulas   Data   Review   View   Tools   Options   Desi ›   🔍 Click to find commands   ⊘

Subtotals ⋮ Grand Totals ⋮ Report Layout ⋮ Blank Rows ⋮ ☑ Row Header ☐ Banded Rows   ☑ Column Header ☐ Banded Columns

Do Not Show Subtotals

Show all Subtotals at Bottom of Group

Show all Subtotals at Top of Group

fx ANNE

	A	B	C	D	E	F	G	H	I
			Sum of 6-Dec-2021	Sum of 7-Dec-2021	Sum of 8-Dec-2021	Sum of 9-Dec-2021	Sum of 10-Dec-2021	Sum of 11-Dec-2021	Sum of 12-Dec-2021
5	ANNE		50.00	54.00	51.00	51.00	30.00	44.00	49.00
6	ANNE	Knife Organiser	20.00	29.00	37.00	27.00	17.00	34.00	35.00
7	ANNE	Wood Table (C)	30.00	25.00	14.00	24.00	13.00	10.00	14.00
8	BIM		15.00	75.00	39.00	43.00	26.00	32.00	37.00
9	BIM	Chair (Black)	5.00	30.00	10.00	12.00	10.00	21.00	20.00
10	BIM	Fry Pan (Medium)	10.00	45.00	29.00	31.00	16.00	11.00	17.00
11	COCO		75.00	55.00	50.00	30.00	41.00	28.00	48.00
12	COCO	Dining Set (B)	15.00	40.00	27.00	11.00	16.00	13.00	25.00
13	COCO	Fork Holder	60.00	15.00	23.00	19.00	25.00	15.00	23.00
14	GEAN		55.00	45.00	24.00	47.00	65.00	45.00	32.00
15	GEAN	Big Square Carpet	25.00	18.00	17.00	22.00	33.00	32.00	15.00
16	GEAN	Round Carpet	30.00	27.00	7.00	25.00	32.00	13.00	17.00
17	HONEY		66.00	21.00	45.00	52.00	45.00	42.00	30.00
18	HONEY	Fry Pan (Large)	11.00	11.00	23.00	21.00	13.00	19.00	18.00
19	HONEY	Grocery Racks (4 ply)	55.00	10.00	22.00	31.00	32.00	23.00	12.00
20	JHON		65.00	36.00	46.00	41.00	26.00	31.00	40.00
21	JHON	Wood Table (A)	25.00	13.00	28.00	18.00	14.00	19.00	27.00
22	JHON	Wood Table (B)	40.00	23.00	18.00	23.00	12.00	12.00	13.00
23	KIM		23.00	33.00	19.00	18.00	30.00	46.00	45.00
24	KIM	Dining Set (A)	10.00	30.00	14.00	12.00	19.00	26.00	20.00
25	KIM	Round Table	13.00	3.00	5.00	6.00	11.00	20.00	25.00
26	KURT		90.00	31.00	64.00	58.00	51.00	67.00	60.00
27	KURT	Grocery Racks (3 ply)	65.00	19.00	25.00	30.00	39.00	32.00	27.00
28	KURT	Spoon Holder	25.00	12.00	39.00	28.00	12.00	35.00	33.00
29	RED		55.00	40.00	35.00	27.00	44.00	57.00	23.00

HOW TO USE GRAND TOTAL OPTION ON PIVOT TABLE

Once you have subtotals in your pivot table, you can also show grand totals. That way, it's easier to see all the data briefly.

You can hide the total by clicking 'Off for Rows and Columns' on the menu.

≡ Menu ∨ 🗅 🗅 🗗 🖨 🔍 🖒 ⤢ ▽   Home   Insert   Page Layout   Developer   Formulas   Data   Review   View   Tools   Options   Desi ›   🔍 Click to find commands   ⊘ ⬆

Subtotals ⋮ Grand Totals ⋮ Report Layout ⋮ Blank Rows ⋮ ☑ Row Header ☐ Banded Rows   ☑ Column Header ☐ Banded Columns

On for Rows and Columns

Off for Rows and Columns

On for Rows Only

On for Columns Only

ANNE

	A	B	C	D	E	F	G	H	I
16			30.00	27.00	7.00	25.00	32.00	13.00	17.00
17									
18	HONEY	Fry Pan (Large)	11.00	11.00	23.00	21.00	13.00	19.00	18.00
19	HONEY	Grocery Racks (4 ply)	55.00	10.00	22.00	31.00	32.00	23.00	12.00
20	JHON								
21	JHON	Wood Table (A)	25.00	13.00	28.00	18.00	14.00	19.00	27.00
22	JHON	Wood Table (B)	40.00	23.00	18.00	23.00	12.00	12.00	13.00
23	KIM								
24	KIM	Dining Set (A)	10.00	30.00	14.00	12.00	19.00	26.00	20.00
25	KIM	Round Table	13.00	3.00	5.00	6.00	11.00	20.00	25.00
26	KURT								
27	KURT	Grocery Racks (3 ply)	65.00	19.00	25.00	30.00	39.00	32.00	27.00
28	KURT	Spoon Holder	25.00	12.00	39.00	28.00	12.00	35.00	33.00
29	RED								
30	RED	Grocery Racks (5 ply)	35.00	22.00	21.00	12.00	30.00	24.00	12.00
31	RED	Shoe Organiser	20.00	18.00	14.00	15.00	14.00	33.00	11.00
32	RON								
33	RON	Dining Set (C)	20.00	23.00	30.00	17.00	15.00	14.00	23.00
34	RON	Round Rug	17.00	30.00	15.00	45.00	9.00	25.00	22.00
35	SAM								
36	SAM	Fry Pan (Small)	25.00	22.00	18.00	35.00	15.00	12.00	15.00
37	SAM	Furit Organiser	30.00	25.00	12.00	13.00	13.00	43.00	11.00
38	TOTAL		586.00	490.00	448.00	477.00	410.00	486.00	435.00
39									
40									

HOW TO USE REPORT LAY OUT:

The Report Layout option allows the user to modify the pivot table's layout format and structure. It contains five sections: display in compact form, display in outline form, display in tabular form, repeat all item labels, and do not repeat all item labels.

When a user wants to compare data in different formats or alter the structure of the pivot table, changing these layouts is useful.

Show in condensed Form

If a user selects Show in compact form in the report layout, the pivot table will be displayed in a simple format. Only the summary and total of value items will be displayed.

Show in outline Form

This option will display a pivot table in detailed format. It will show all the labels and values of the report in a separate column.

Show in tabular Form

Select this option if you wish to view the pivot table in tabular format. Each row will be represented by a separate column, and each column will be represented by a separate row, in tabular format.

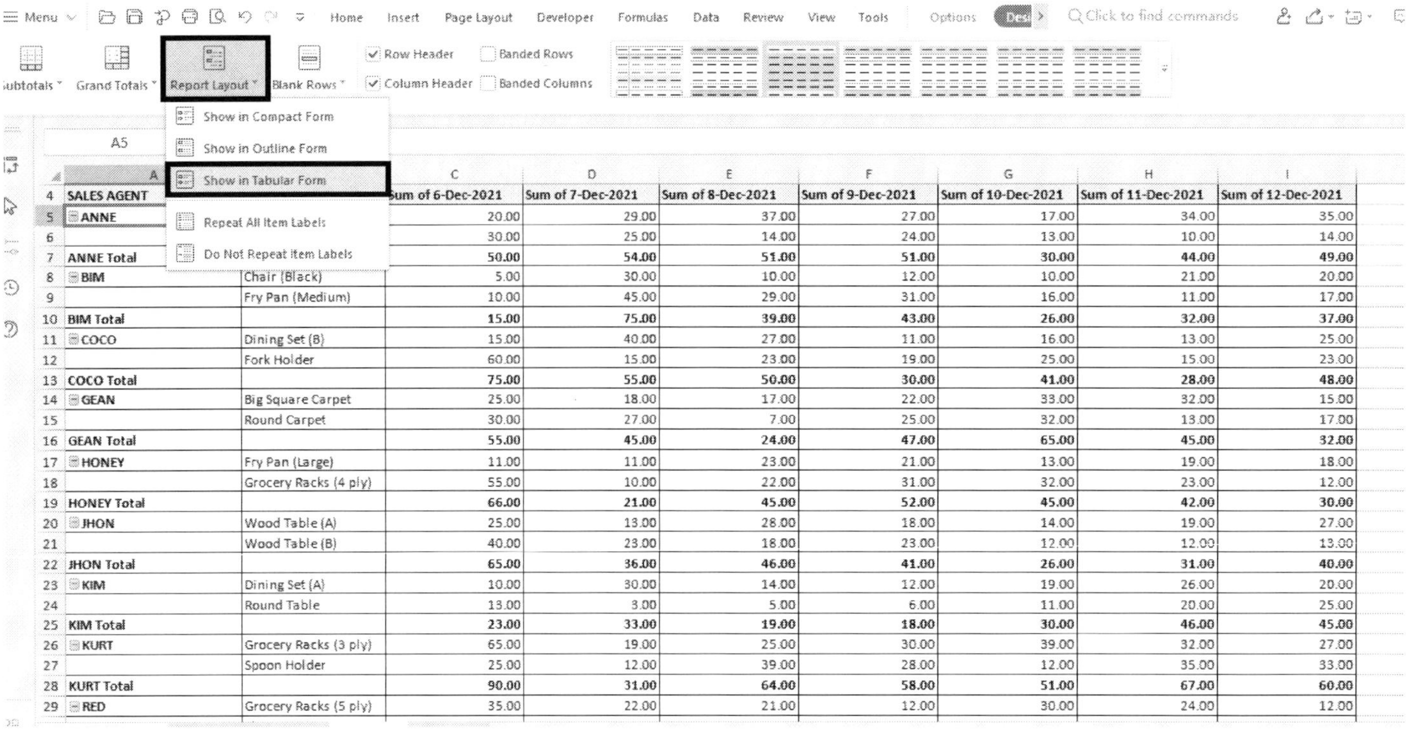

Show All Item Labels

Choose this option to display the item labels in the report layout. Even though the items are grouped under a single section, they will all be represented with their respective labels.

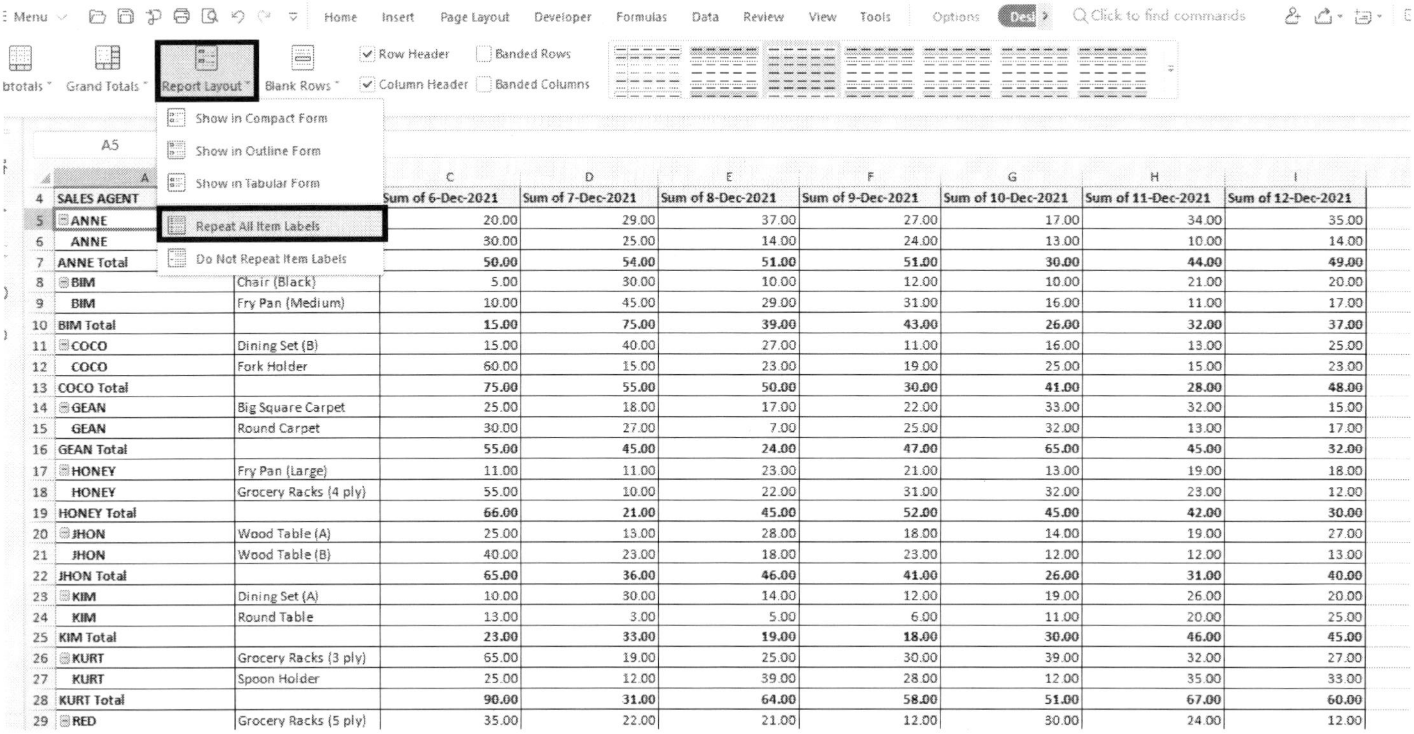

Do No Repeat Item Labels

This option is useful when a user wants to hide certain items from being repeated.

Buttons +,-

These buttons allow you to hide or show the some of the data in your field.

To hide this button, click on the "Options<Buttons+,-".

SALES AGENT	PRODUCT A	Sum of 6-Dec-2021	Sum of 7-Dec-2021	Sum of 8-Dec-2021	Sum of 9-Dec-2021	Sum of 10-Dec-2021	Sum of 11-Dec-2021	Sum of 12-Dec-2021
ANNE	Knife Organiser	20.00	29.00	37.00	27.00	17.00	34.00	35.00
	Wood Table (C)	30.00	25.00	14.00	24.00	13.00	10.00	14.00
ANNE Total		50.00	54.00	51.00	51.00	30.00	44.00	49.00
BIM	Chair (Black)	5.00	30.00	10.00	12.00	10.00	21.00	20.00
	Fry Pan (Medium)	10.00	45.00	29.00	31.00	16.00	11.00	17.00
BIM Total		15.00	75.00	39.00	43.00	26.00	32.00	37.00
COCO		75.00	55.00	50.00	30.00	41.00	28.00	48.00
GEAN	Big Square Carpet	25.00	18.00	17.00	22.00	33.00	32.00	15.00
	Round Carpet	30.00	27.00	7.00	25.00	32.00	13.00	17.00
GEAN Total		55.00	45.00	24.00	47.00	65.00	45.00	32.00
HONEY	Fry Pan (Large)	11.00	11.00	23.00	21.00	13.00	19.00	18.00
	Grocery Racks (4 ply)	55.00	10.00	22.00	31.00	32.00	23.00	12.00
HONEY Total		66.00	21.00	45.00	52.00	45.00	42.00	30.00
JHON	Wood Table (A)	25.00	13.00	28.00	18.00	14.00	19.00	27.00
	Wood Table (B)	40.00	23.00	18.00	23.00	12.00	12.00	13.00
JHON Total		65.00	36.00	46.00	41.00	26.00	31.00	40.00
KIM	Dining Set (A)	10.00	30.00	14.00	12.00	19.00	26.00	20.00
	Round Table	13.00	3.00	5.00	6.00	11.00	20.00	25.00
KIM Total		23.00	33.00	19.00	18.00	30.00	46.00	45.00
KURT	Grocery Racks (3 ply)	65.00	19.00	25.00	30.00	39.00	32.00	27.00
	Spoon Holder	25.00	12.00	39.00	28.00	12.00	35.00	33.00
KURT Total		90.00	31.00	64.00	58.00	51.00	67.00	60.00
RED	Grocery Racks (5 ply)	35.00	22.00	21.00	12.00	30.00	24.00	12.00
	Shoe Organiser	20.00	18.00	14.00	15.00	14.00	33.00	11.00

Now, you're good to go to create your Pivot Table!

PIVOT CHART AND PIVOT CHART OPTIONS

To create a pivot chart in Excel, click the Pivot Chart button on the Create tab. Depending on what is selected in the Data Field list at the top of the window, different options will appear.

If you have a data-summarizing table, you can generate a pivot chart in a single step.

Large data sets are frequently summarized and trends are identified using pivot charts. In addition, they are a useful method for creating multiple charts from the same data set, with each chart illustrating a different aspect of the story. The pivot Charts depicted below were generated using the same table.

The pivot chart displays data in a more compact format and depicts relationships between data sets with greater precision.

The primary advantage of using a Pivot Chart over a standard chart is that Pivot Charts offer an interactive solution that can be tailored to your analysis requirements.

When you have a large amount of data and want to focus on subsets of it, pivot charts are particularly useful.

To create a Pivot Chart, navigate to your table and click the arrow at the top of the field you wish to include in your chart.

Create Pivot Chart is accessible via the Insert tab and automatically generates a chart from your data. Click on the Pivot Chart to reveal the Chart Tools menu. You can modify the layout of your chart, add a chart title, change the style of your chart, and decide whether or not to display items in the Field List. The Pivot Chart will display the data in your Field List automatically. Group headings are included alongside their respective items. If you have multiple summary levels, they will be arranged in the Field List according to their order. Excel calculates automatically a value for each member of the series when applicable.

There are several things you can do to improve the efficiency of your Pivot Charts. Change the chart type, for instance, to display the data in a different format. You may need to specify a chart's title and other elements, such as legend items. You may also wish to alter your Pivot Chart's layout. In addition to modifying the chart type, you can also modify the field list that appears on the chart. Changing the chart's size is one of the possible actions. You can also select the amount of data to display based on your analysis requirements.

Excel includes three standard charts, which will be displayed when you click Layout at the top of the Pivot Chart Tools window. You can modify the chart's sorting and layout to meet your needs. The purpose of a pivot chart is to illustrate data relationships. Using pivot charts, you can identify trends or changes over time by modifying the measure or percentage columns.

INSERT SLICER

Creating a slicer with a pivot table is an additional option. A slicer is a column of spreadsheet cells that can be used to drill down into the pivot table's data. You can add slicers before or after the pivot table in any report location. Slicers are an innovative method of interacting with pivot table data. You can filter and explore your data in entirely new ways using slicers.

To add slicer to the pivot table, select Insert Slicer.

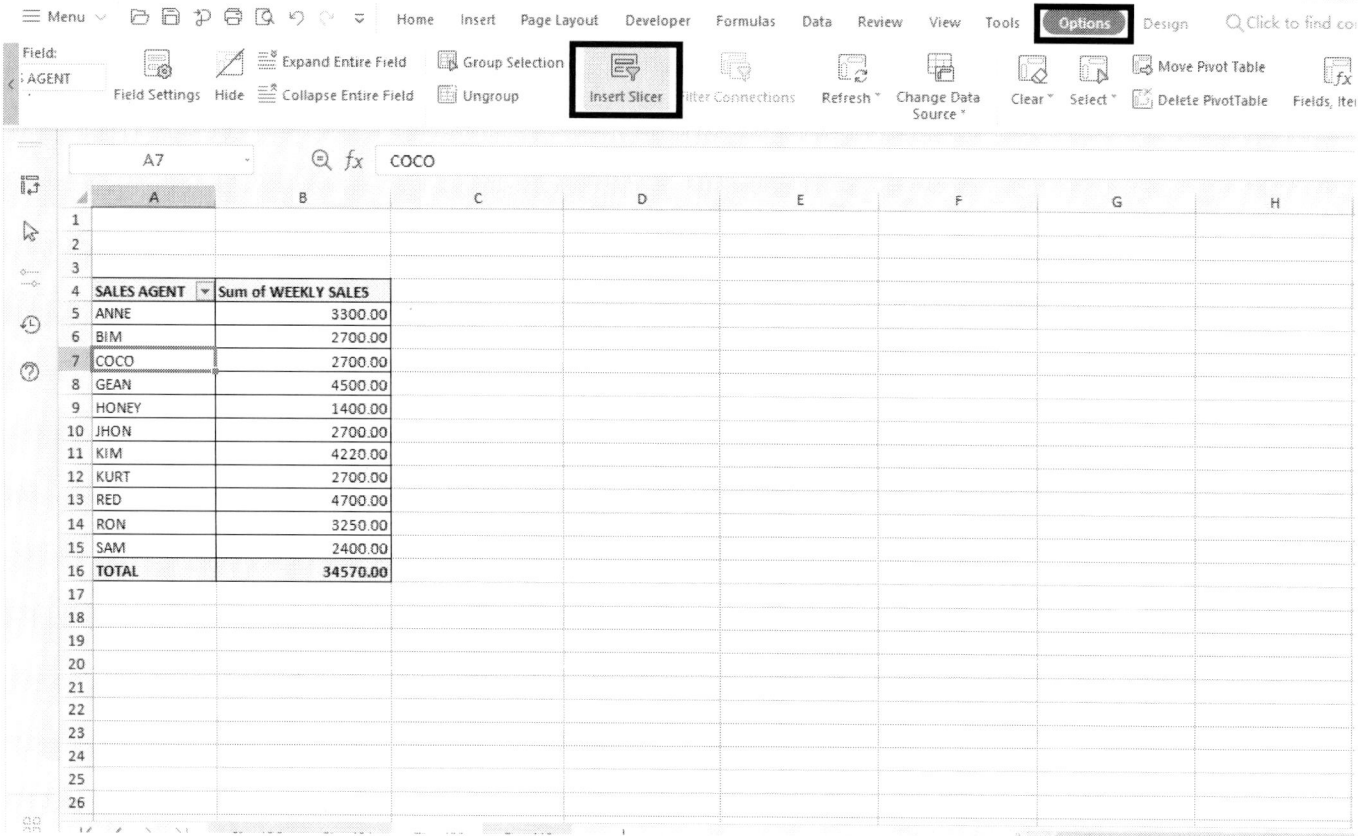

Now enter the values of slicer in the combo box then click OK button.

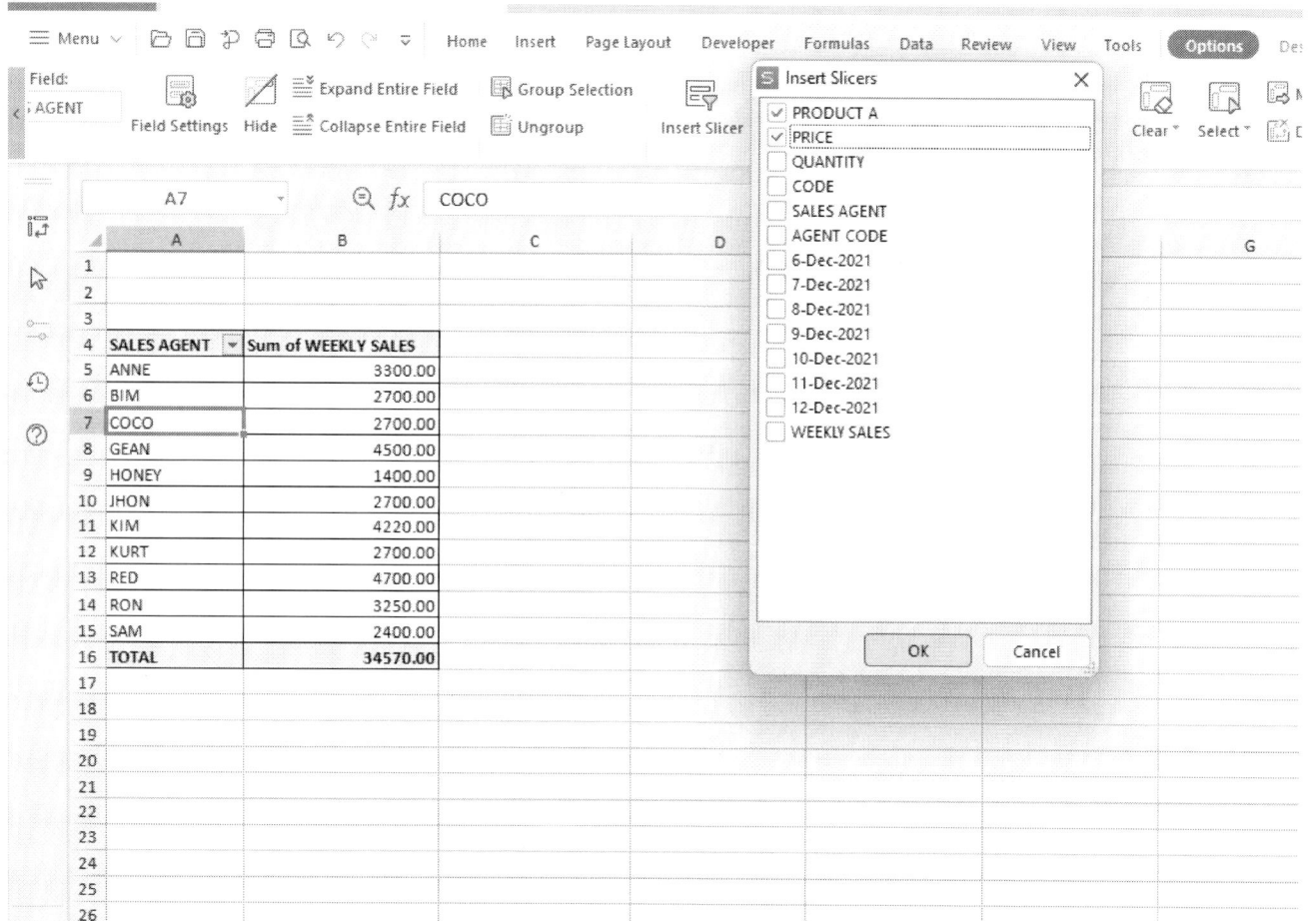

A new button will appear with name of selected pivot table on it.

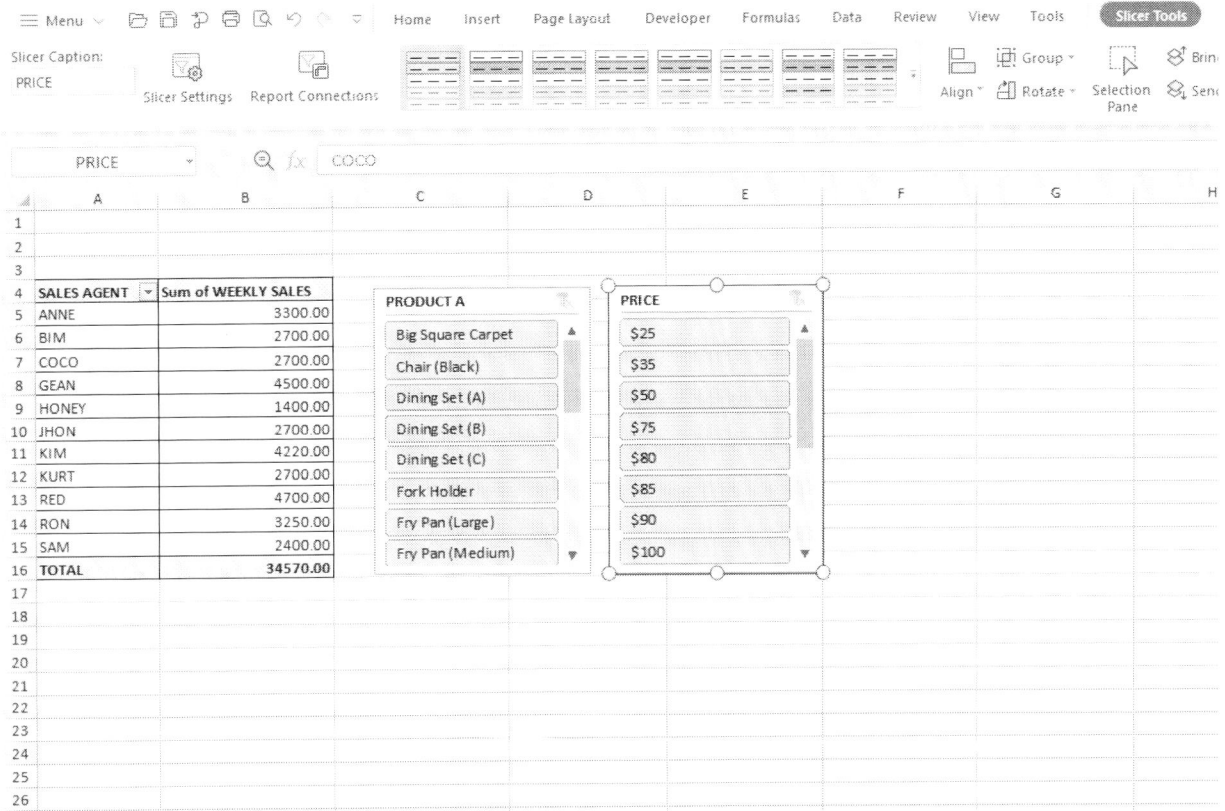

Now you can use these columns as if it is an additional data column in your pivot table.

SELECTION PANE

Selection pane allows you to find or hide a single object in the pivot table. In this case, if you select an item and you want to hide it, select selection pane and click on Hide Button.

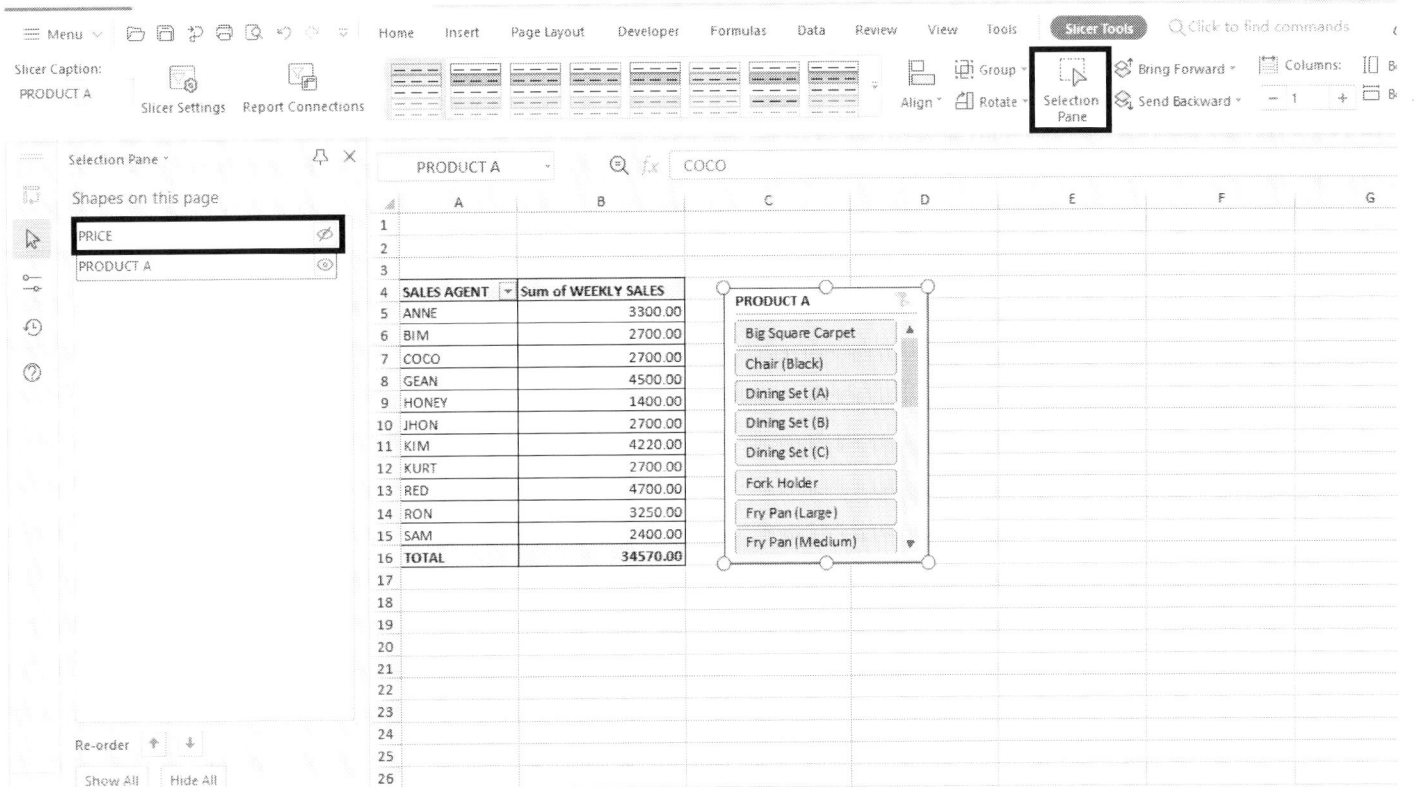

Slicer allows you to easily find the data you are looking for without having to scroll through the pivot table.

For example, if you want to find data which is related with the product, you can click the data and it will automatically show the result.

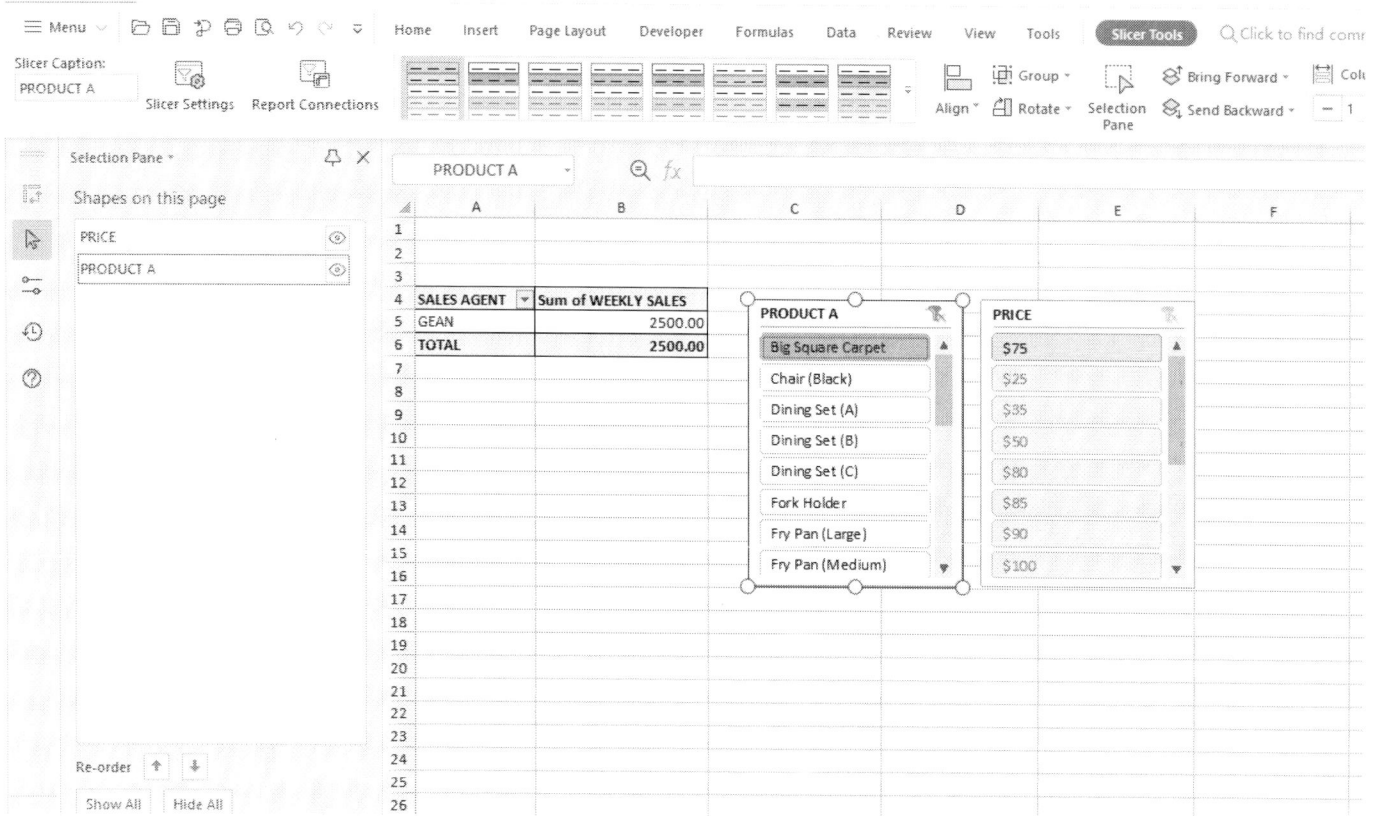

This displays the price and Sales Agent for the product in question.

Frequently, your pivot table will be a summary of the additional options selected by various individuals; therefore, you will need to customize the table with colors or icons that reflect these selections.

Despite the fact that Pivot Tables offer a tremendous amount of power and functionality, sometimes simple enhancements can make your work even simpler.

Chapter 15.   GETTING TO KNOW FORMULAS

Formulas are Excel's central feature. You should learn how to write spreadsheet formulas that perform calculations, combine values, and reference cells.

Types of Formulas

There are three types of calculation formulas available in Excel: arithmetic, financial, and lookup. Each of these formulas has a unique function key.

ARITHMETIC FORMULAS

Using arithmetic formulas to calculate and determine the outcomes of mathematical operations with numbers. Simple math functions and standard arithmetic operators (such as +, -, *, and /) are the most frequently used arithmetic formulas in Excel. You can also find these functions in the calculator of your word processor.

FINANCIAL FORMULAS

Using money values, such as interest rates and percentages, financial formulas calculate financial transactions. To learn how to write financial formulas in Excel, you must understand how to use certain financial formulas within formulas that operate on these values.

LOOK-UP FORMULAS

Look-up formulas are utilized to locate information such as the size or year of a company's financial statement or the price of gasoline in five states. INDEX, MATCH, and IFERROR are the Excel lookup formulas you'll use most frequently. These functions determine the outcomes of data location in a range or table.

How to Work with Formulas

You may type a formula into a cell or copy it from another cell. These steps will demonstrate how to enter data and formulas into a cell.

1. Enter data in a cell by typing.
2. To enter a formula, click in the cell, and then type = (equal sign).
3. In the formula bar, type the formula's components (arguments), such as values and operators.
4. Press "Enter" to finish.
5. To see your formula result in the cell, go to the cell and click "Formula." The Formula bar displays your formula and its result.

Before you learn how to write formulas, you should be aware of the following things:

DEFINING FUNCTIONS IN EXCEL

A function is a collection of instructions that performs a calculation or action on the cell values. The formula contained within parentheses is referred to as an argument. Any number of arguments may be passed to a function, but the number and types of these arguments depend on the function.

There are two types of functions that can be created in Excel: user-defined (formulas) and built-in (built-in functions).

USER-DEFINED FUNCTIONS

A user-defined function is a piece of code created by the user. Visual Basic for Applications (VBA), the programming language for Excel and other Office applications, is used to write the code. Then, you execute the VBA macro to view the function's output in the worksheet.

BUILT-IN FUNCTIONS

Built-in functions are Excel formulas that perform a variety of cell-based operations. Some perform complex tasks, such as looking up data in a table, while the majority of them are simple mathematical formulas.

The following are characteristics of built-in functions:

- They are applicable to any worksheet.
- They are simple to use and comprehend.

- They are transferable between workbooks.
- They have "built-in" error checking, so if you make a mistake in your function, Excel displays a warning dialog box and halts function execution.
- Excel does not permit the creation of new built-in functions. You can only use the available ones or add them to a customized toolbar later.
- Their names consist of the initial letters of the function.
- They perform the same actions in all versions of Excel.
- They utilize a set of specified arguments and may include functions that return values.
- Depending on the type of function, one or more arguments may be used.

UNDERSTANDING ARGUMENTS

The values enclosed by parentheses in a formula constitute a function's arguments. The function uses the arguments to calculate its results. When creating a function, you must specify all required arguments, but you can typically omit any optional arguments you do not need.

Example of arguments:

=sum(A1:B10)

=Sum(Number1, …)

In the formula above, the arguments are used as follows:

Number1 - this argument is the input range, which can be an array formula. For example, if you want to sum cells A1 through A10, you will input =sum(A1:A10). These arguments are the other input ranges for your formula.

The output will be a single cell with the value of each range (the sum of column C) added together (sum of B column).

=Date(year,month,date)

In the formula above, the first argument is the date to find, and the second argument is the year, month, and date.

=FV(rate, nper, pmt, pv, [fnce])

In the formula above, the following arguments are specified: rate — this argument is used to set the interest rate for this payment. nper — this argument sets the number of payments. pmt — this argument is used to set the amount of each payment. pv —this argument sets the current unpaid balance. [fnce] – if you do not specify an optional argument, you must use brackets ([]) to indicate that it is an optional one.

=if(logical_test,value_if_true,[value_if_false])

In the formula above, the following arguments are:

x: The result of the logical test can be either "true" or "false."

value_if_x: The value the formula returns when the variable x is true. If it evaluates to false, then that argument will not appear in the formula.

#N/A: This means that there is no such value for this argument.

REASONS FOR USING FORMULAS IN EXCEL

Excel formulas can be employed for a variety of purposes. The first reason is that you can see the results of a calculation or action on your worksheet. This can help you make more informed decisions and maintain control over your worksheet's actions.

The second reason is that you may want to perform calculations with variables, such as the number of sales or the daily sales, so that you can change these numbers without modifying all of your formulas.

Calculations can aid in the management of multiple worksheets within a workbook, which is the third benefit. In a business bookkeeping application, you may be required to enter information about your vendors, customers, and employees, for example. If you do so in one worksheet, you must verify and update the corresponding data in all other worksheets. After entering data into the first worksheet, you can easily update these values using functions, and all other customer, sales, and employee records will be updated automatically.

The fourth reason is if you wish to create your own functions by combining multiple Excel features. For instance, you can create an Excel formula to perform a calculation on the date of the New Year and to add a custom date field to your worksheet.

Even if you do not use formulas in Excel, formulas and comments are displayed every time you save your workbook, which is useful for programmers and document maintainers.

IMPORTANT THINGS TO KNOW ABOUT FUNCTIONS

There are five important things that I want to share with you:

1. Functions can be very long, so be careful about what you enter in the cell. The function enclosed in parentheses is called the function's argument or argument. For example, the formula =COUNTA(A:B:D) refers to the range A:B:D.

2. Functions can also include text (words). If you select a cell that contains the formula and then copy it to another cell, Excel pastes that text instead of replacing it with numbers within the formula.

3. If you create a formula with incorrect spelling or syntax, Excel displays a #NAME? error in the cell. The formula works only when you correct the error.

4. The question mark (?) is called a wildcard because it represents any value. When Excel replaces the question mark with a value, it performs calculations on that value according to what you specified in your function formula.

5. If you press F4 on a cell that contains a formula, Excel displays the results of your function and its arguments. This is called "displaying the formula." You can also press F4 to display information about your function in the formula bar.

Chapter 16. FORMULAS

Excel is, as you may already know, the most popular spreadsheet application available. The vast majority of businesses, universities, and individuals use it. It has become one of the most widely used applications in the world due to its adaptability. Therefore, many users seek assistance when inserting formulas into their spreadsheets to obtain an output or manipulate data.

As a spreadsheet application, Excel also permits the creation of formulas and the use of functions that can be used to compute new cell values. You can perform complex calculations such as calculating averages, sums, and various types of statistics with these tools. Using functions, you can also create formulas that combine multiple inputs and display the result in a single cell. This section will provide an overview of these features and how they can benefit your work.

Excel also enables you to further manipulate your work data through the use of various formatting options. These include utilizing multiple colors, fonts, and borders to create more impressive results.

You can also enter arithmetic operations in cells using functions instead of formulas.

The result is displayed in the referencing cell, which is another cell (C2 in this case).

Let's look at an example when we want to calculate the age of all employees in our database. First, you would need to create a table: NAME AND DATE OF BIRTH. Our formula is simply:

=datedif(b2,today(),"Y") , in this formula , the letter "Y" stands for how many years old the person is.

Excel is not an easy program to learn for beginners and can be quite confusing and difficult on average. Nonetheless, it is a good program that is widely used around the world and has many advantages.

Excel's IF-formula allows you to calculate the value of an investment at any given time, which is useful for calculating profit or loss.

This is one of the most important Excel formulas to learn because it is universally applicable and allows you to calculate profit or loss at any time. To determine whether a cell is empty, you use the "not equal to" operator (>) with an empty string (""). If cell C2 is not empty, the formula returns "Yes," otherwise it returns "No":

You will learn a simple and common Excel formula that is often overlooked by those learning the program.

Excel's most common formulas

SUM

=SUM(D3:D14)

Calculates the total of cells D3 through D14

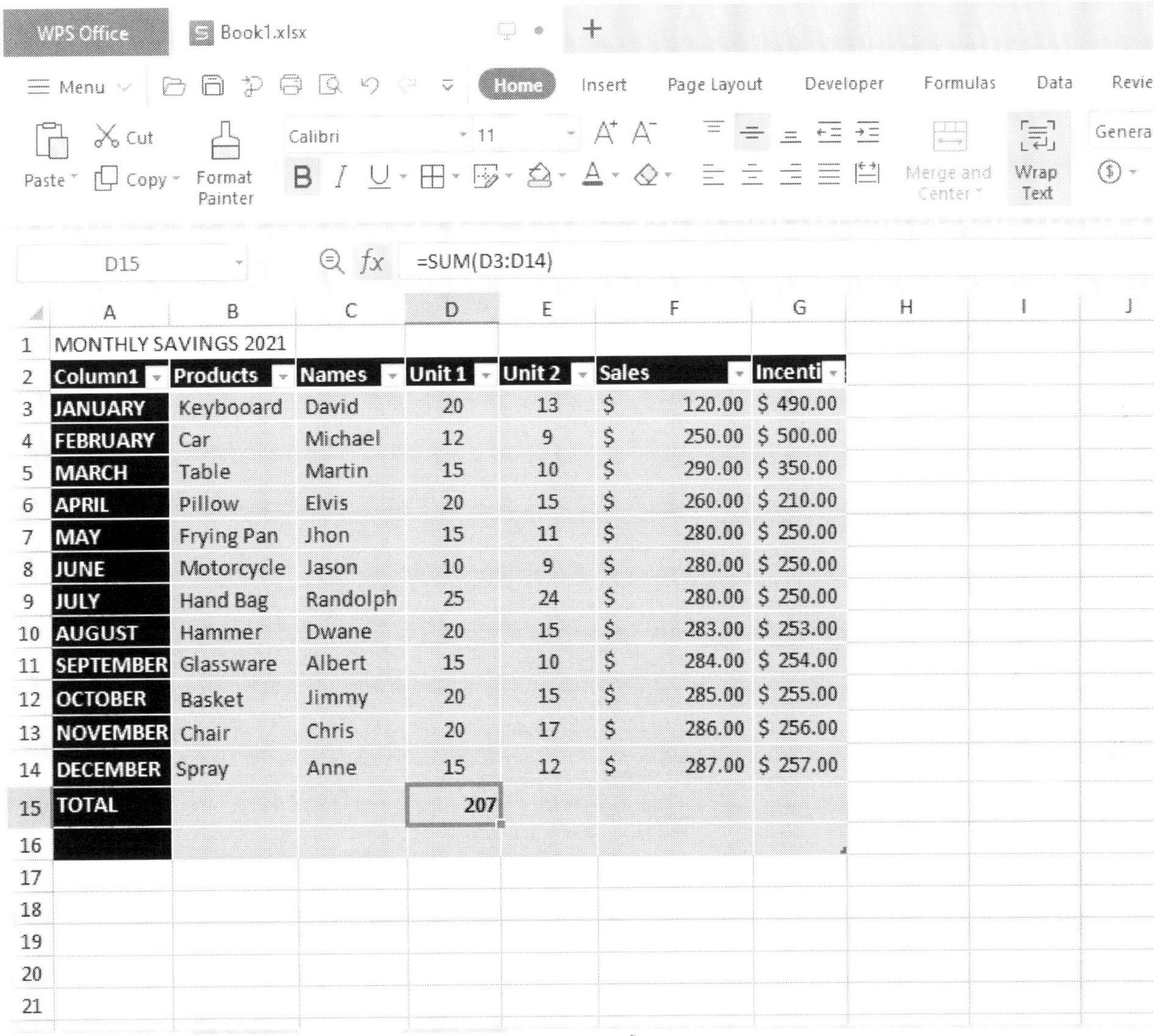

This formula is common to use when summing up a range of cells.

=SUM(D3, E14)

Adds up values in cells D3 and E14

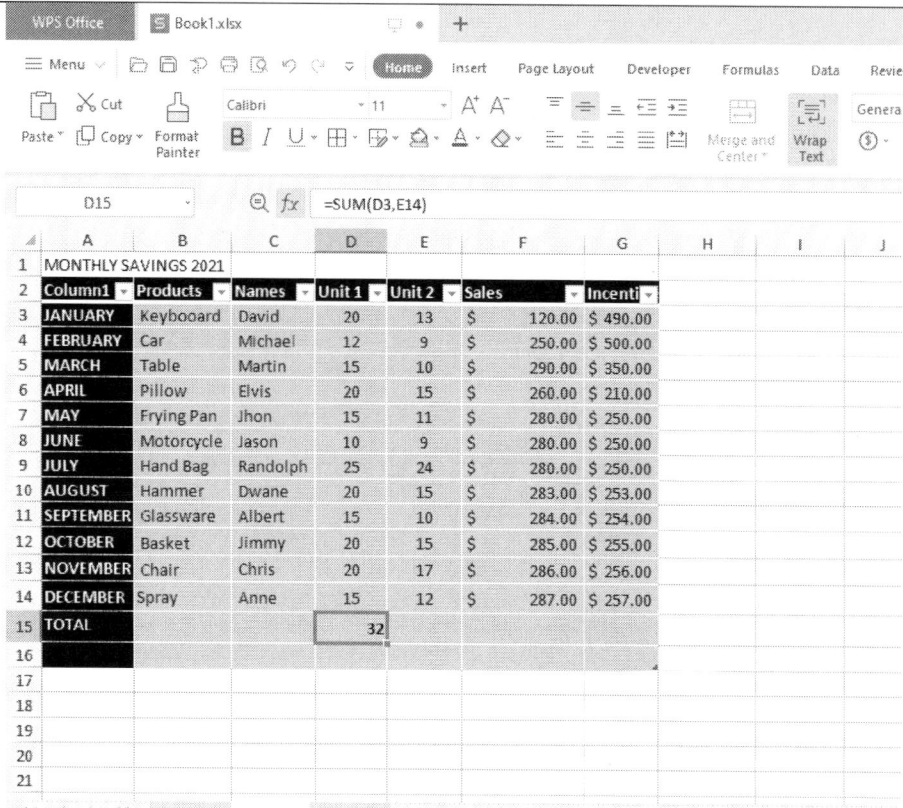

This formula will calculate the total of the values in cells B2 and B6.

AVERAGE

=AVERAGE(B2:B21)

Use this formula to calculate the average.

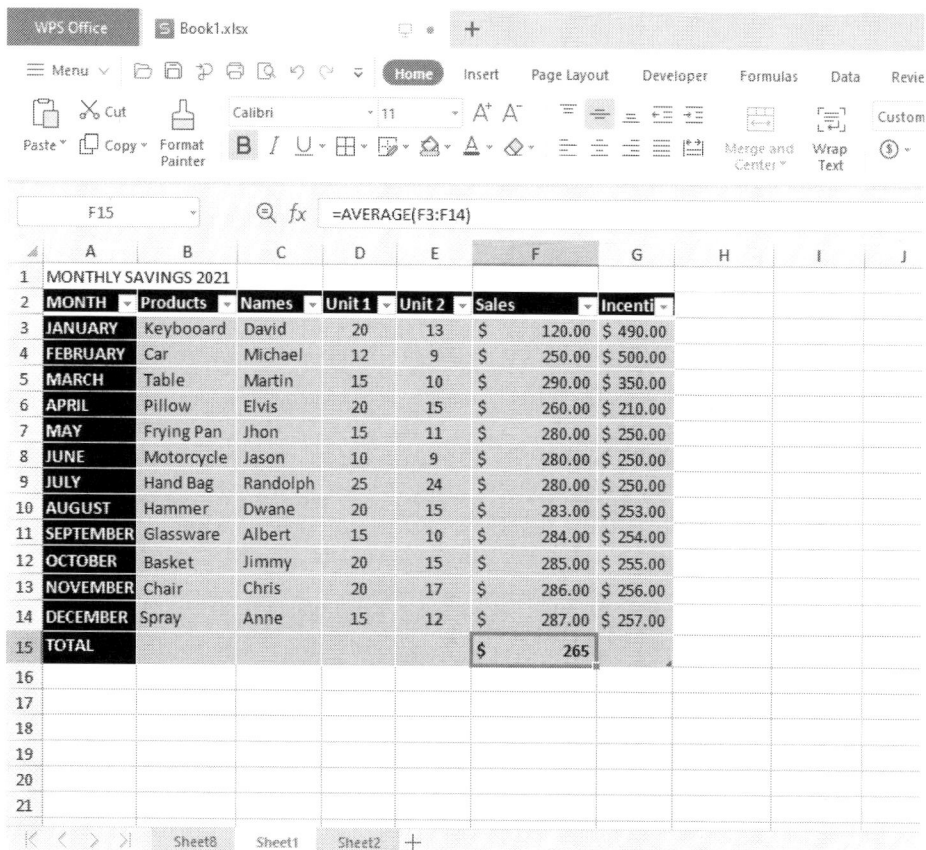

This formula is the most used in Excel.

This sample shows you the total Average of students on their scores using the formula:

=AVERAGE(B2:D2)

MATCH

=MATCH(I5,B3:B7,0)

The Match function will find the position of a certain value in a list and return the relative position number.

This is very useful when you must match information from different locations and you do not know where exactly this information will be.

SUBTOTAL

=SUBTOTAL(1,D3:D14)

The SUBTOTAL() function is one of the most commonly used formulas in Excel. SUBTOTAL() function calculates the total of a range of cells. Depending on what you want, you can select average, count, sum, min, max, min, and others.

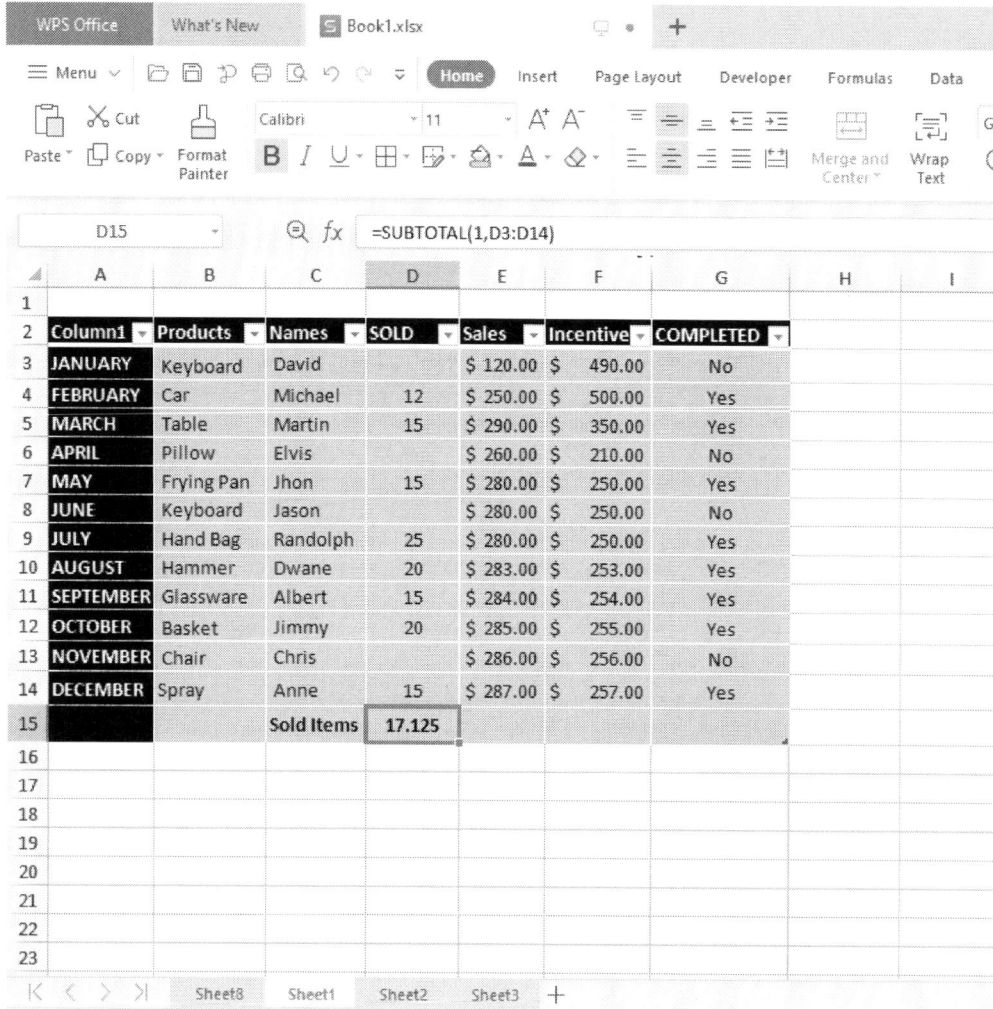

The subtotal calculation on cells ranging from D3 to D14 and in the subtotal list "1" refers to average. This can be exceptionally helpful when creating formulas and performing calculations

IF FUNCTION

The IF function is the most common formula in Excel. You can use it to create a table or chart with changing values.

=COUNTIF(E3:E14,15)

Use this formula to count the number of cells containing the number 15.

This is useful for calculating frequency distributions.

=SUMIF(B3:B14,I3,D3:D14)

This formula will add up all the values in a table where a condition is met.

Counts the number of times "I3" appears in cells D3:D14. The formula outputs the value 30 when "I3" is included in D3 to D14 and 0 otherwise.

=IF(D3<>"","Yes","No")

This formula can be used to calculate the answer of yes or no when a condition is met.

It's very useful when you have several conditions in which you must check whether a certain result has been met or not.

TRIM FUNCTION

Trim Function removes all the characters from a string and places them in front of itself.

=Trim(A2)

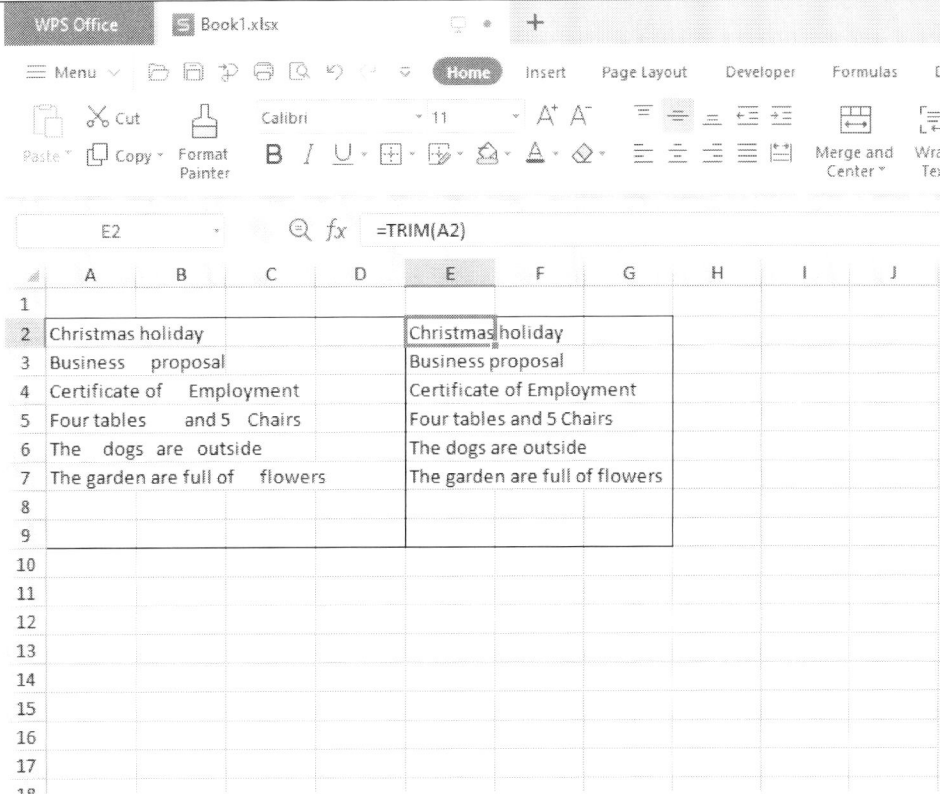

Takes no arguments and will remove all spaces from both ends of a string.

MAX AND MIN

This formula can be used to find the maximum or minimum value of a given range. Let's say you want to find the highest incentives in a list using this formula:

=MAX(F3:F14)

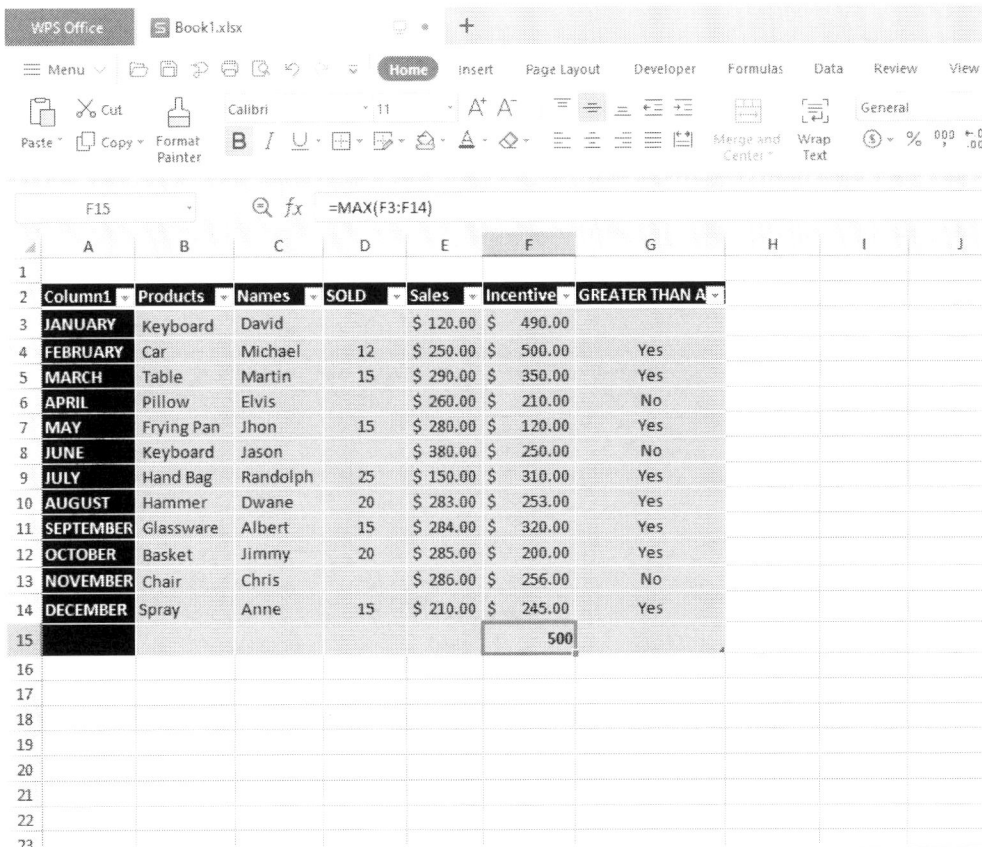

And let's find out the lowest incentives in a list using this formula:

=MIN(F3:F14)

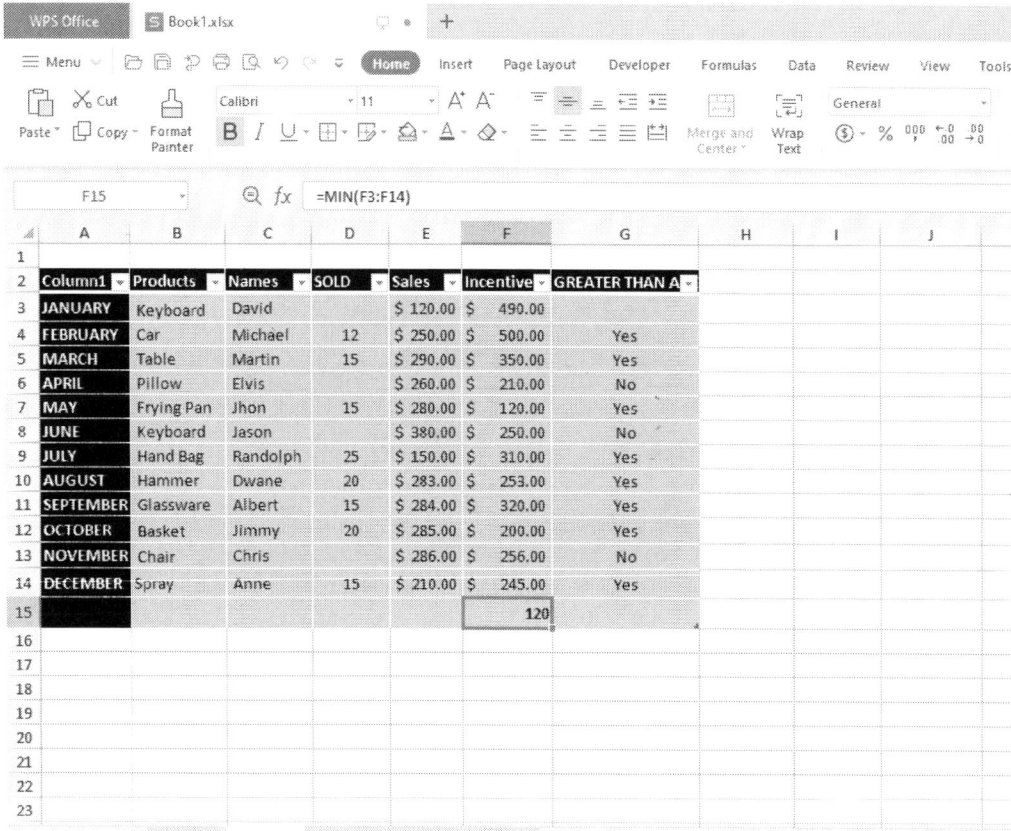

This is very useful to find the highest and lowest value in a list that may exceed the maximum number allowed.

DATE AND TIME FUNCTION

The current date and time can also be determined with two formulas: =NOW() or =TODAY(). Today and now functions can be found in any version of Microsoft Excel. The most common formula is =TODAY(), which displays the date for today.

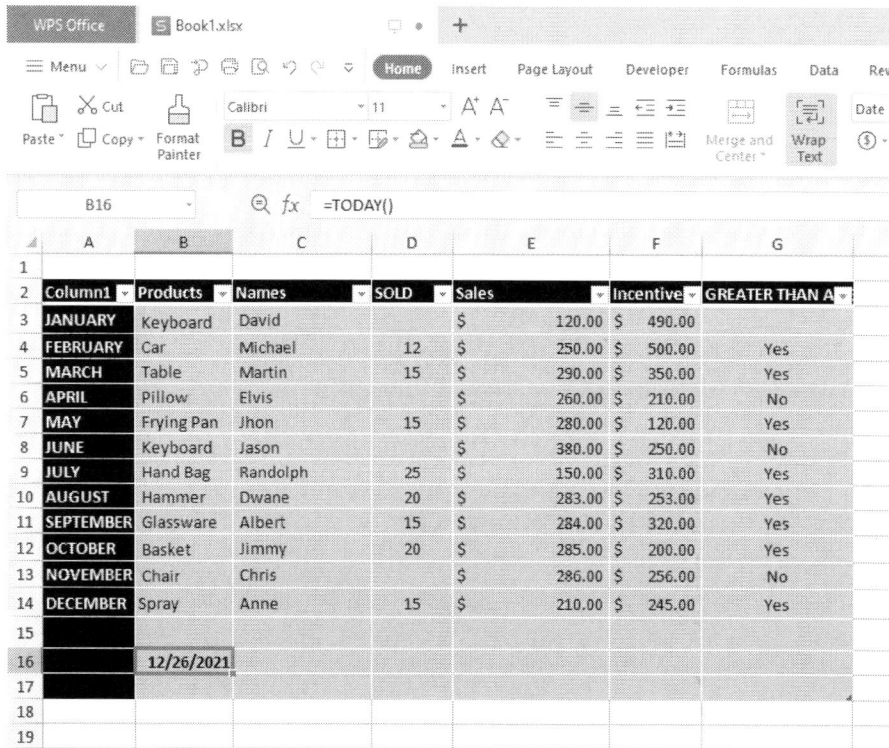

The second most common formula is =NOW(), which displays the date and time for now.

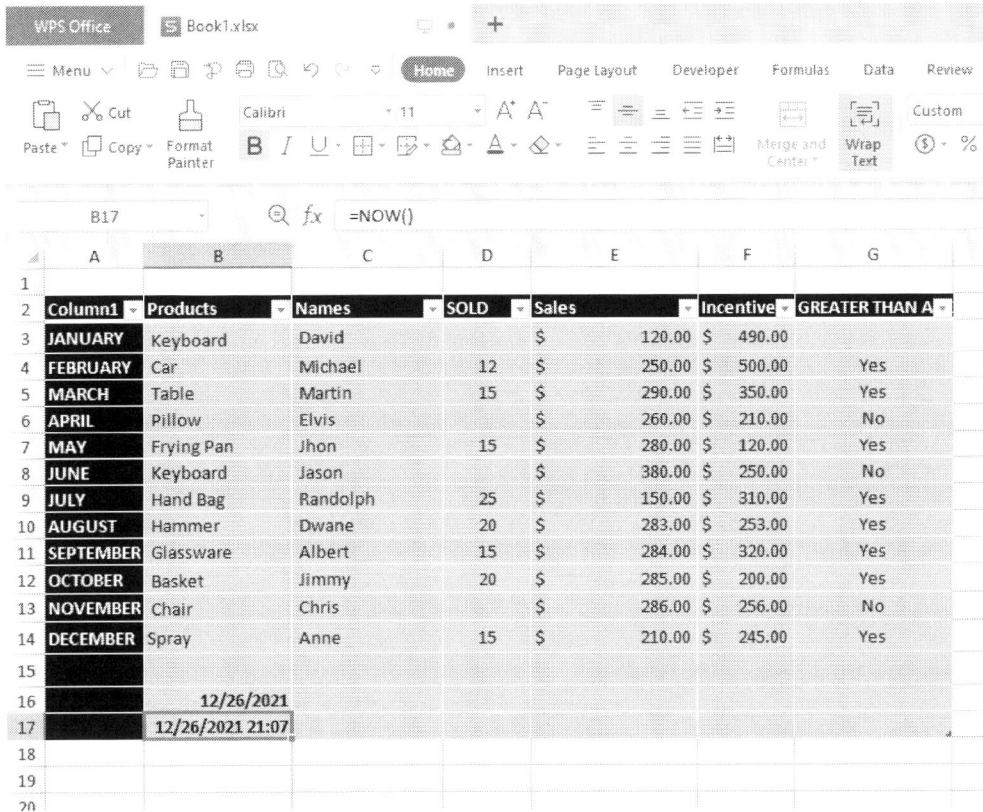

The date and time functions in Excel can be used for a variety of purposes including calculating an employee's work hours, the amount of time until a project is due, or calculating the number of days since your last meeting. Some functions that can be used to calculate the number of days between two dates are DATEDIF, DATEDIF2, DATEVALUE and WORKDAY.

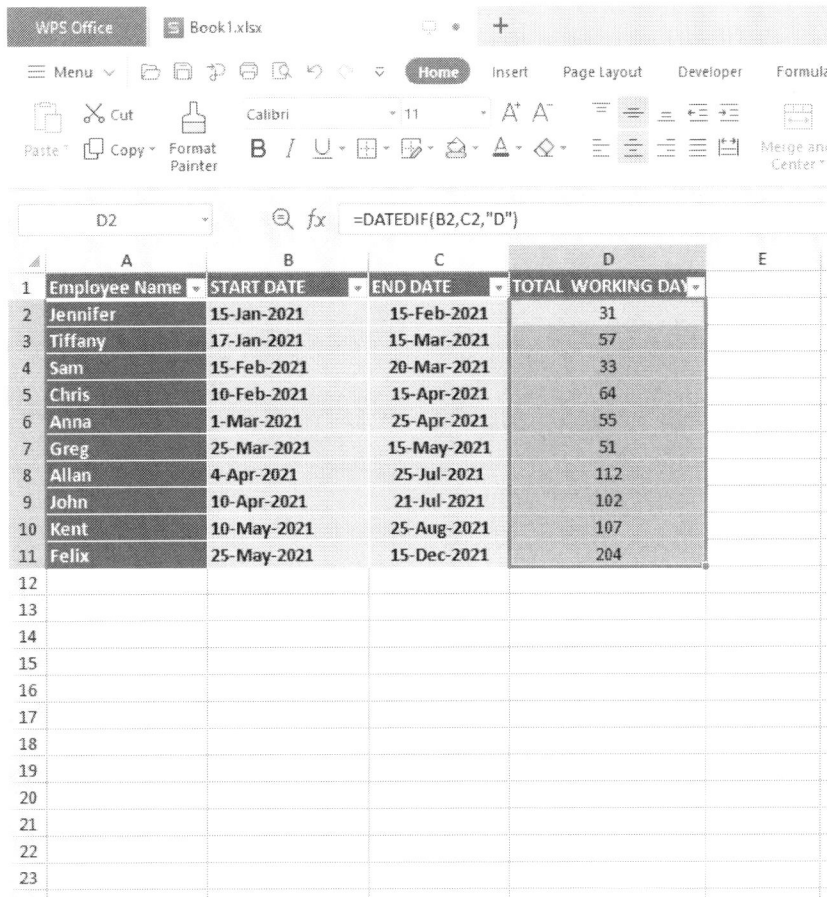

The TIME function can be used to return or calculate any type of time values in Excel, including hours, minutes, seconds and so on. It can also return formatted time values in letters like AM/PM words.

=TIME(B2,C2,D2)

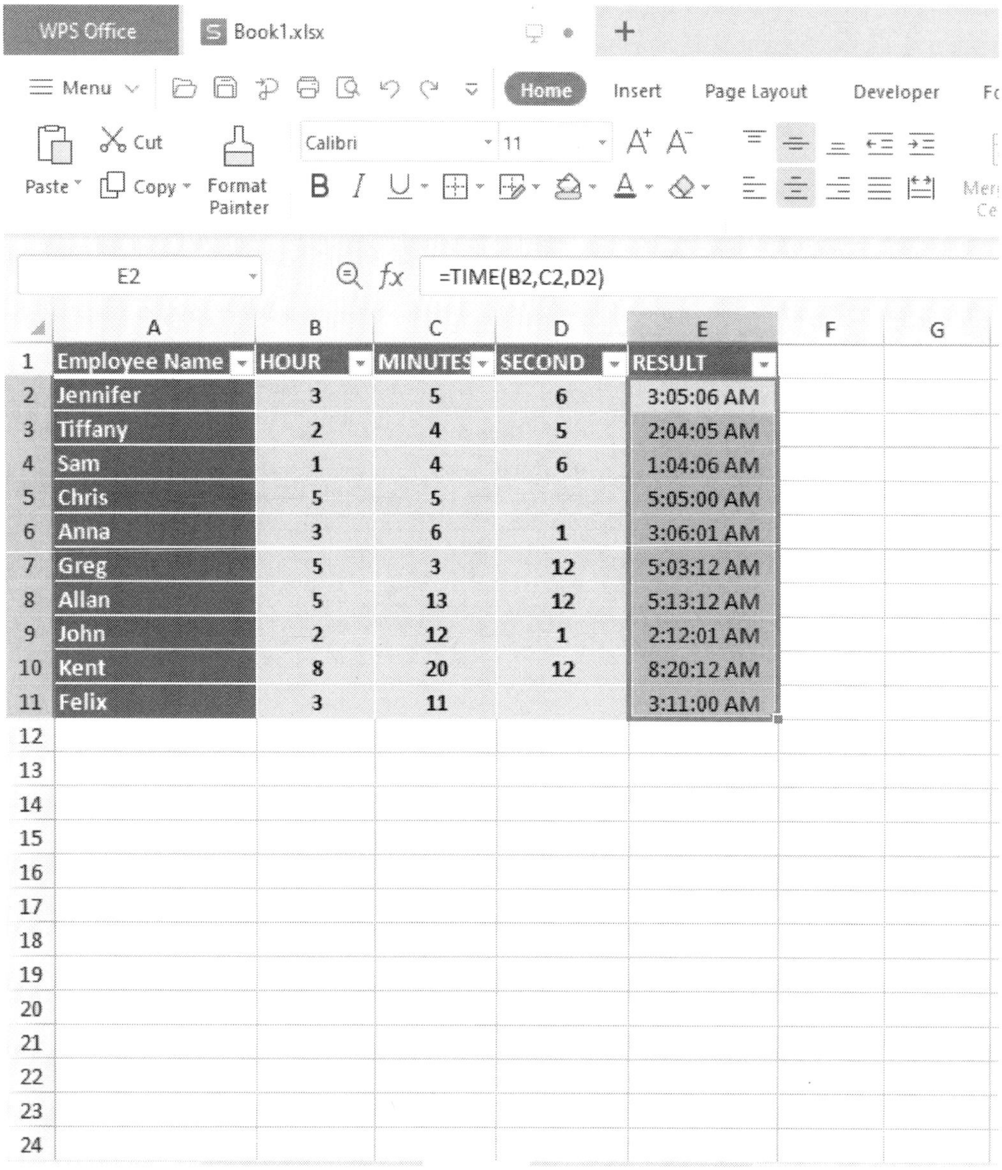

Employee Name	HOUR	MINUTES	SECOND	RESULT
Jennifer	3	5	6	3:05:06 AM
Tiffany	2	4	5	2:04:05 AM
Sam	1	4	6	1:04:06 AM
Chris	5	5		5:05:00 AM
Anna	3	6	1	3:06:01 AM
Greg	5	3	12	5:03:12 AM
Allan	5	13	12	5:13:12 AM
John	2	12	1	2:12:01 AM
Kent	8	20	12	8:20:12 AM
Felix	3	11		3:11:00 AM

Calculating an employees pay for a day, a month or a year is easy by using the TIME function.

Another example to calculate the time that the employee worked an 8 hours shift is one of the very common formulas in excel. The formula in excel for calculating the hours worked is as follows:

=(C2-B2)*24

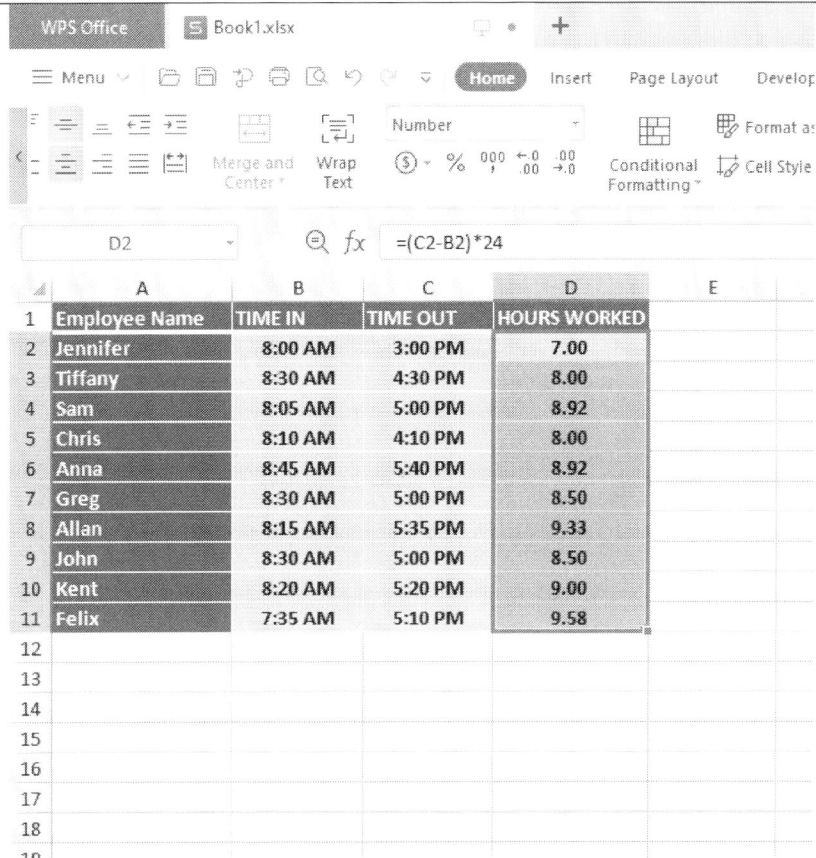

We used the decimal 24 in this formula because the decimal 24 is a factor of 60 minutes and 60 minutes is equal to 1 hour.

Another example is calculating time difference between two date/times from two columns in Excel. This function is very useful to calculate how long it will take to deliver some work at the client site and a lot of other examples where you want to calculate the time.

It is a very common formula in excel,

=TEXT(C2-B2,"HH:MM:SS")

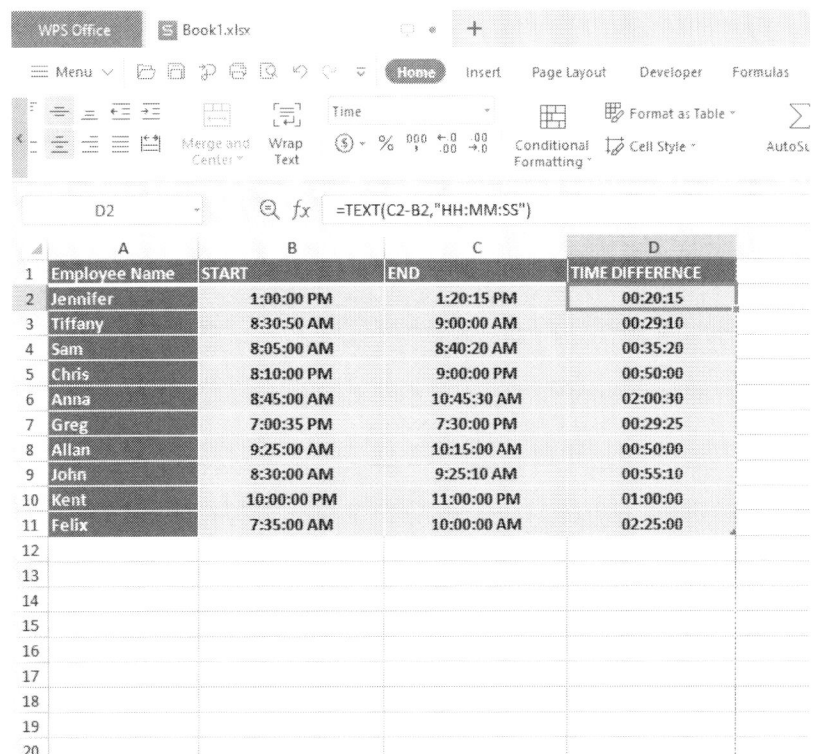

When we give the formula for calculating time difference above, we must write "HH:MM:SS", for hour, minute and second.

Now, we want to know if the employee has delivered the project in 30 minutes or has crossed in 30 minutes.

We will use the IF function, which will return CROSSED or WITHIN to say if the employee has done the job within 30 minutes or not.

=IF(HOUR(D2)>0,"Crossed",IF(MINUTE(D2)>30,"Crossed",IF(AND(MINUTE(D2)=30,SECOND(D2)>0),"Crossed","Within")))

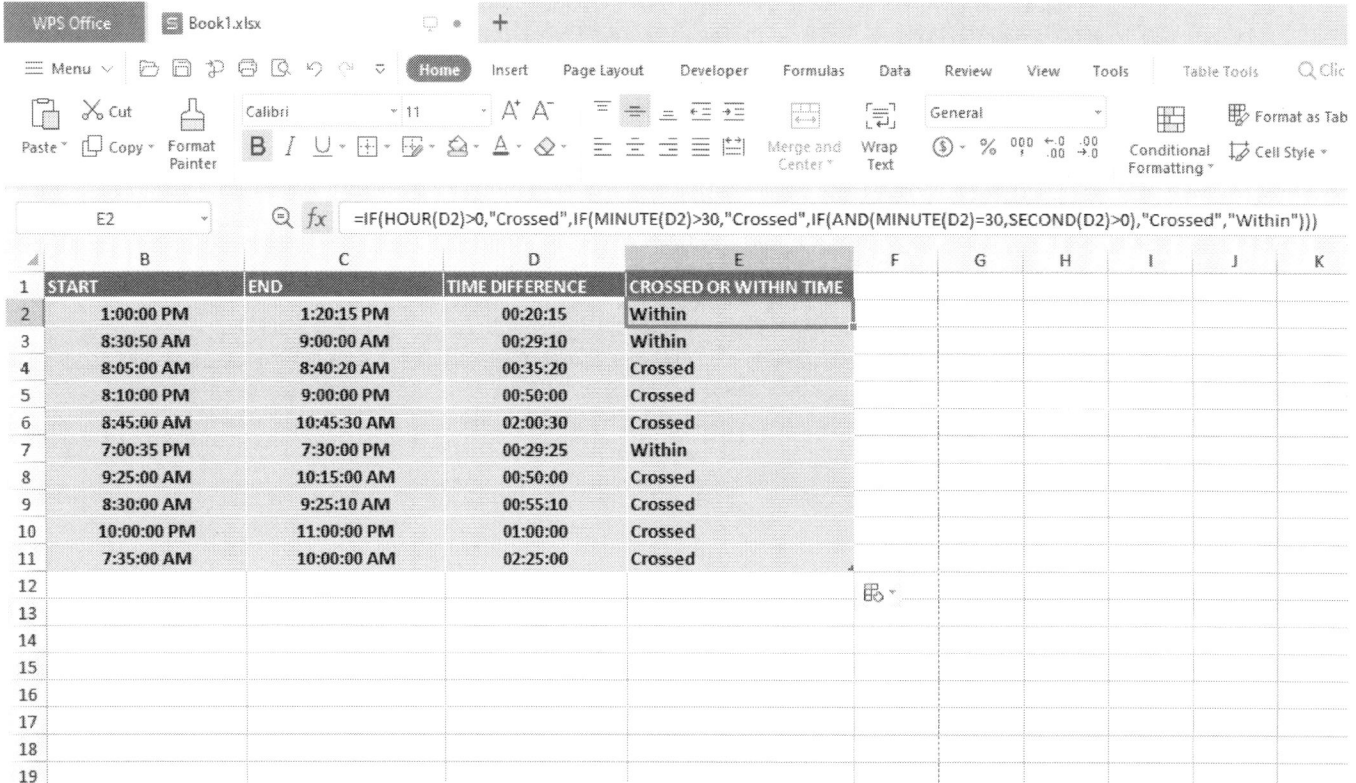

We know that the result in first column is WITHIN, it means that the project has been completed within 30 minutes and for other result is CROSSED, it means the project has taken more than 30 minutes.

VPLOOKUP

You've created the perfect spreadsheet with all sorts of formulas to calculate your net pay. You want to include this formula into your spreadsheet, but you're not sure how.

The VLOOKUP function is a helpful function to use, if you want to search an array of data and return a result that matches your criteria.

The VLOOKUP function serves 2 purposes:

For example, let's say you have a list of information about your employees and their salaries. You can use the VLOOKUP function to retrieve their net pay. The formula is:

=VLOOKUP(G3,A2:D9,4,FALSE)

Using the VLOOKUP function is a very simple formula. It's as follows:
=VLOOKUP(lookup_value,table_array,index_num,match_type)

The formula above gives you the result. Notice that if the lookup value is not found in the table into which you are trying to look up, then Null returns its value.

An alternative to the VLOOKUP is the HLOOKUP function. The HLOOKUP performs a similar function to the VLOOKUP, except that it works horizontally instead of vertically.

Hence, the HLOOKUP function searches from left to right and returns a result based on your specified criteria.

The formula is: =HLOOKUP(lookup_value,table_array,row_num,column_num). The three parameters in this formula are:

1. Lookup value- the value you are searching for in the corresponding cell (C2 or 567).
2. Table Array- where the data is located (A2:D4).
3. Row- number you are searching from (3).
4. False- indicates to an exact match
5. True- indicates an approximate match

For example, if you want to find the total of the column A (for instance, employee code) and the row 3 (for instance, value for employee salary), your formula should look like this: =HLOOKUP(567,A2:D4,3,FALSE)

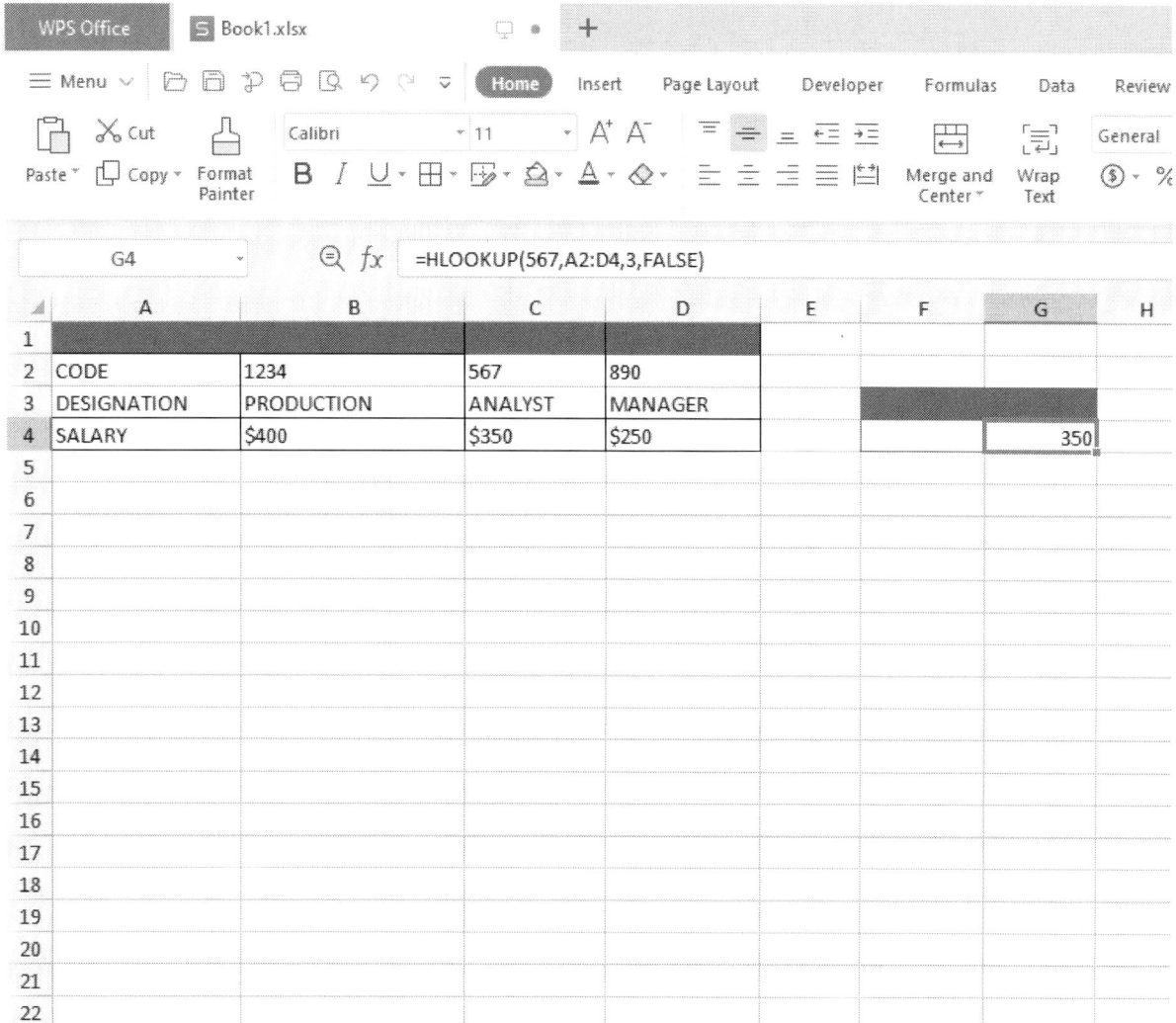

	A	B	C	D	E	F	G	H
1								
2	CODE	1234	567	890				
3	DESIGNATION	PRODUCTION	ANALYST	MANAGER				
4	SALARY	$400	$350	$250			350	

G4 =HLOOKUP(567,A2:D4,3,FALSE)

That's all you must do to create and use a spreadsheet formula.

INDEX

The index formula is an indispensable tool that can be used throughout Excel when working on tables, charts, or graphs. It really becomes invaluable when combined with other formulas such as MATCH, MIN and MAX functions. The index formula is a versatile tool that can be used in many different situations and can be used to solve problems quickly.

The first example is one that can be done with any type of table. The goal of this formula is to identify what month an employee was hired in. By doing this you will be able to restructure the table and have a more refined profile of each employee. In the first column of the table, you can identify the name of each employee. Then in the second column, you can identify which month they were hired and so on.

The formula is as follows:

=INDEX(B2:B17,MATCH(J3,A2:A17,0))

The parameters: =INDEX(array, MATCH(lookup_value,lookup_array,[Match_type])

The formula starts by verifying that you are in the correct column. The next step is to get the correct row for your data point. The formula MATCH(J3,A2:A17,0) does this. It finds index J3 in column A and then locates the corresponding value in column A (the second parameter) at row 2 (the first parameter). The last piece of this INDEX formula is to verify that it returned a blank cell if no match was found. This is indicated with zero (0).

This next example is locating the designation of each employee.

The formula goes with:

=INDEX(C2:C17,MATCH(J3,A2:A17,0))

J5 | fx =INDEX(C2:C17,MATCH(J3,A2:A17,0))

	A	B	C	D	E
1	NAME	HIRED	DESIGNATION	SCHEDULE	SALARY
2	ERICA	JANUARY	PRODUCTION	8AM-5PM	$120
3	ANNA	JANUARY	PRODUCTION	8AM-5PM	$120
4	CHICO	FEBRUARY	PRODUCTION	3PM-11PM	$150
5	GREG	MARCH	ANALYST	3PM-11PM	$150
6	BEN	AUGUST	ANALYST	9AM-6PM	$120
7	CHRIS	MARCH	PURCHASER	9AM-6PM	$120
8	HONEY	JANUARY	PURCHASER	9AM-6PM	$120
9	SAM	SEPTEMBER	ENCODER	6PM-2AM	$150
10	ERIC	SEPTEMBER	ENCODER	6PM-2AM	$150
11	RICHARD	OCTOBER	ENCODER	7PM-3AM	$150
12	JOHN	OCTOBER	TECHNICIAN	7PM-3AM	$200
13	NICKY	JANUARY	TECHNICIAN	7PM-3AM	$200
14	KEN	MAY	CALL REPRESENTATIVE	11PM-7AM	$200
15	BARIE	JUNE	CALL REPRESENTATIVE	11PM-7AM	$180
16	HELEN	NOVEMBER	HUMAN RESOURCEES	11PM-7AM	$180
17	ELLA	JULY	HUMAN RESOURCEES	11PM-7AM	$180

	G	H	I	J
Employee Name:				CHRIS
	HIRED:			MARCH
	DESIGNATION:			PURCHASER

In the images above, we can see how this formula was used to restructure the spreadsheet. We can see that the table is significantly more refined down to two specific employees. An additional benefit of using this formula is that you will be able to identify employees in different tables. This is great for keeping track of all employees and who they are.

XLOOKUP

An Excel function that finds the value of a cell in another row or column. This function will teach you how to use Excel's most popular function, the XLOOKUP . You'll quickly learn that this powerful function can do even more than just scan through a row or column of values-- it can also scan through another sheet of data. Be sure to keep reading to get your first-hand learning experience!

XLOOKUP is used for finding a value in another row or column.

The syntax of XLOOKUP Function is: = XLOOKUP (lookup_value , lookup_array , return_array)

The lookup_value is the value that you are looking for:

- lookup_array: this is the array of values used to search for the lookup_value. This can be a single column or a range of cells.

- return_array: is the result of the function, this is the range or cells that contain the corresponding value from lookup_array

Calculate the maximum bonus each employee can have.

On a separate tab, you can see some informations from the employees such as: ID number, BONUS Percentage and EMPLOYEE name.

The formula returns the highest bonus a particular employee can receive.

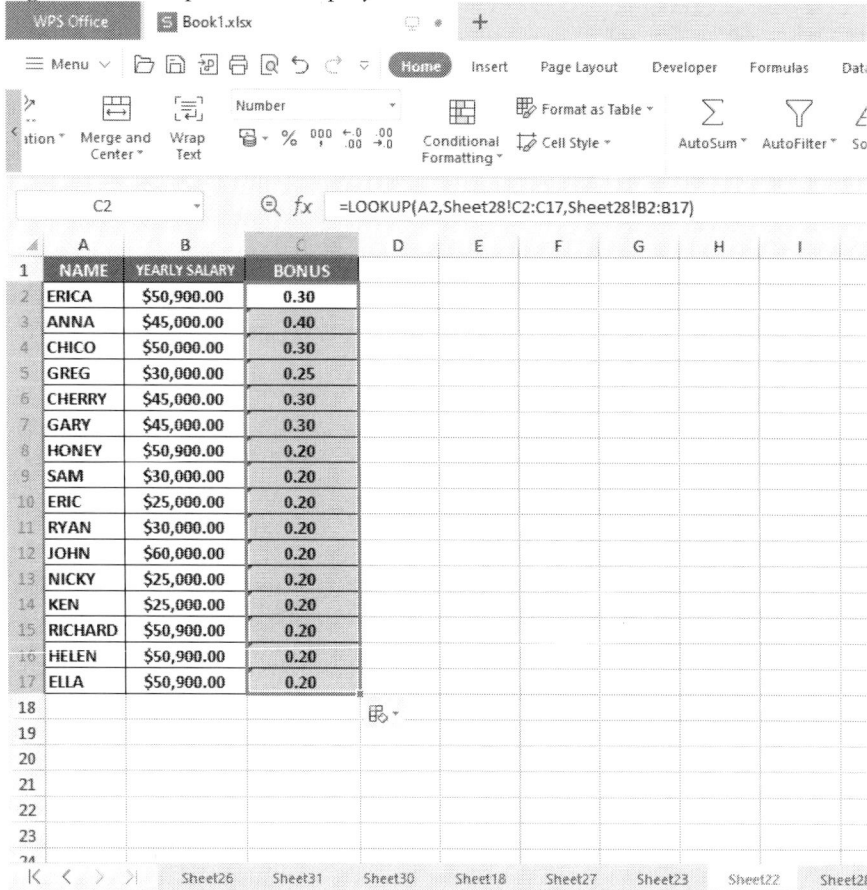

This would be the formula as shown above sample:

=LOOKUP(A2,Sheet28!C2:C17,Sheet28!B2:B17)

This formula looks at all the cells in C2:C17 on Sheet 28 and will find the highest value in B2:B17.

Adding the multiplication in the data will help you get the exact bonus amount on each employee.

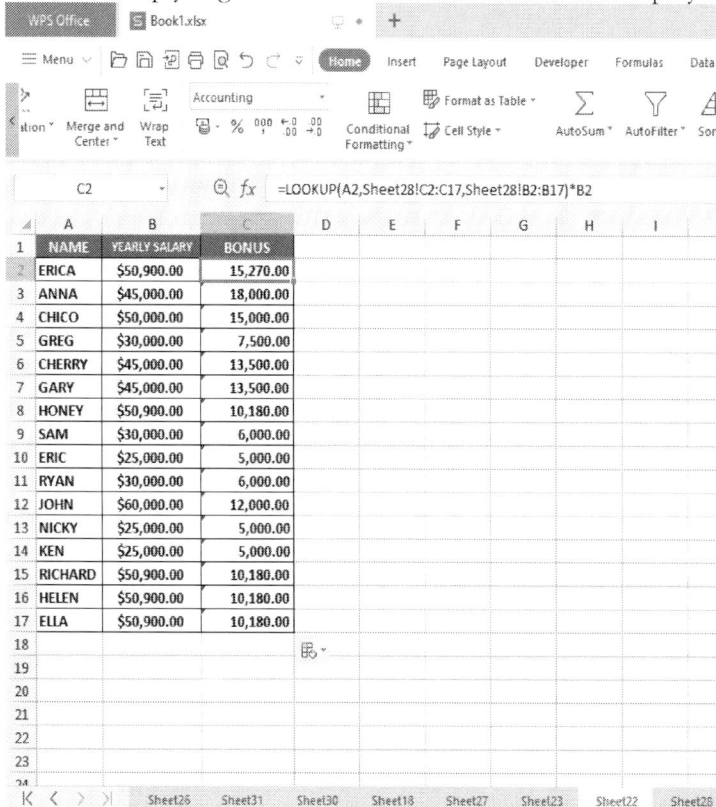

Taking the percentage and multiplying it with yearly salary.

Formula:

=LOOKUP(A2,Sheet28!C2:C17,Sheet28!B2:B17)*B2

This function can be used a number of ways, and it will return different results depending on how you use it. You could use this formula, for example, to look up a product ID number and find out which item it represents.

You can also use this formula when you want to find a value within a column or row. For example, you could use this function to find the number of units sold by each product category.

HLOOKUP

The Hlookup function can help us do some pretty neat things, like use it to lookup up our team's batting average as it changes over time and plot it against their total runs scored. Hlookups are especially useful when you have a data set that changes overtime, such as with some sports teams or music albums. Once you look up your team's batting average, try doing this for a few years and see what you can find.

Another really neat thing you can do is use the Hlookup to look up the date of each workout, based on the date of the workout and time. This would let you create a chart that shows your time vs. pace for each run.

Syntax: Hlookup(lookup_value, table_array, row_num, [range_lookup])

For example, we want to locate a unit price based on a particular Sales Invoice number.

The formula shows:

=HLOOKUP(873,A25:F27,2,FALSE)

Lookup value: This refers to the value we are looking for. (Sales Invoice num 873)

table_array: an array of values you wish to look up. This is what we are referencing in our lookup value. (A25:F27)

row_num: the row number for which you want to return the value from table_array. (row num 2)

range_lookup: A value of FALSE means that HLOOKUP is looking for an exact match. A value of TRUE means that an approximate or close match will be returned. Unless you have a specific reason for looking for an approximate match, you should always use FALSE to return an exact match.

In general, Excel is pretty good at laying things out with the most relevant data at the top. But sometimes you need to get creative with what order you want to see your data in.

Chapter 17.   VARIOUS FORMULAS

This section will demonstrate how to quickly access, view, and utilize Excel formulas. They are applicable for use in simple financial models, calculations for work or school projects, and other accounting tasks. The formulas can also be used to display data generated by a spreadsheet application or another application. It enables users to perform virtually any task, from creating graphs to calculating loan interest to creating business models. The tax calculation formula is one of the most useful Excel formulas if you are planning to take an accounting course but are unsure which calculators you will need. Excel supports two tax types: Pay as you go tax and Pre-tax tax. The first option, pay as you go Tax, is exclusive to businesses with a single employee. However, the Pre-tax tax can be utilized by any type of company or business.

The pre-tax tax uses the formula =B2+D2 to determine the amount of money that must be contributed to taxes each period. With the use of parenthesis "()" or "(", you can group similar calculations into a single cell to simplify the calculations. To determine your total income, any deductions, and your tax liability, each component of the calculation must be added separately.

	NAME	SALARY	TAX RATE	TAXES	TOTAL
1	NAME	SALARY	TAX RATE	TAXES	TOTAL
2	ERICA	$200.00	5.09%	$10	$210.18
3	ANNA	$250.00	5.09%	$13	$262.73
4	CHICO	$280.00	5.09%	$14	$294.25
5	GREG	$300.00	5.09%	$15	$315.27
6	BEN	$350.00	5.09%	$18	$367.82
7	CHRIS	$300.00	5.09%	$15	$315.27
8	HONEY	$330.00	5.09%	$17	$346.80
9	SAM	$320.00	5.09%	$16	$336.29
10	ERIC	$450.00	5.09%	$23	$472.91
11	RICHARD	$430.00	5.09%	$22	$451.89
12	JOHN	$420.00	5.09%	$21	$441.38
13	NICKY	$410.00	5.09%	$21	$430.87
14	KEN	$380.00	5.09%	$19	$399.34
15	BARIE	$350.00	5.09%	$18	$367.82
16	HELEN	$320.00	5.09%	$16	$336.29
17	ELLA	$330.00	5.09%	$17	$346.80
18					

There are two ways to calculate an individual's income: the Gross Income Method and the Net Income Method. The formula for the Gross Income Method is =SUM(B2:D2), where B is your base salary, C is your allowance, and D is your bonus. It is also recommended that your employer permit a certain amount to be deducted from your pay, whether for health insurance or for education. This option is available at the conclusion of the tax calculator and will display as a separate line item below your pay. If you know that your wages have already been taxed by your employer, it is recommended that you select this option.

WPS Office | Book1.xlsx | +

Menu | Home | Insert | Page Layout | Developer | Formulas

Paste | Cut | Copy | Format Painter | Calibri | 11 | A⁺ A⁻ | B I U | Merge and Center

E2 | fx | =SUM(B2:D2)

	A	B	C	D	E	F	G
1	NAME	SALARY	ALLOWANCE	BONUS	TOTAL		
2	ERICA	$200.00	$10.00	$100	$310.00		
3	ANNA	$250.00	$10.00	$100	$360.00		
4	CHICO	$280.00	$10.00	$100	$390.00		
5	GREG	$300.00	$10.00	$100	$410.00		
6	BEN	$350.00	$10.00	$100	$460.00		
7	CHRIS	$300.00	$10.00	$100	$410.00		
8	HONEY	$330.00	$10.00	$100	$440.00		
9	SAM	$320.00	$10.00	$100	$430.00		
10	ERIC	$450.00	$10.00	$100	$560.00		
11	RICHARD	$430.00	$10.00	$100	$540.00		
12	JOHN	$420.00	$10.00	$100	$530.00		
13	NICKY	$410.00	$10.00	$100	$520.00		
14	KEN	$380.00	$10.00	$100	$490.00		
15	BARIE	$350.00	$10.00	$100	$460.00		
16	HELEN	$320.00	$10.00	$100	$430.00		
17	ELLA	$330.00	$10.00	$100	$440.00		
18							
19							
20							
21							
22							
23							

The second method, the Net Income Method, uses the following formula: =E3-F3-G3-H3-I3, where E is Your Total Gross Income Salary, from which taxes, health insurance, car insurance, and savings will be deducted. This formula is slightly more complicated than the previous one, but it is easier to comprehend. This calculation has an advantage over the first because it takes into account potential tax deductions and bonuses, which are not taken into account by other calculation methods..

PRESENT VALUE FUNCTION

PV function returns the present value of an investment based on constant annual payments and an interest rate. The formula has three parameters: the rate, the number of payments (NPER) and the payment made (PMT).

To calculate PV in Excel, enter the following into cell:

=PV(C2,C3,C4,0)

The PMT parameter is useful because it enables you to modify the number of payments made throughout your project, allowing you to observe how your present value calculation varies over time. The NPER parameter represents the number of payments made. The formula will return a value between 0 and 1 that is positive or negative depending on whether there are additional payments to be made. This function's primary purpose is to provide an answer to the question of how much you should invest today in order to save enough money for a future purchase.

FUTURE FUNCTION

The FV Function returns the future value of money in one lump sum with payments and interest received in a series of time periods. This function is valuable for planning purposes and solving business problems. Here is the syntax for the FV Function:

FV(rate, nper, pmt, pv, [fnce])

The FV Function takes six arguments. The Rate argument refers to the percent interest rate per period ([0,1] or 0%). The Nper argument that refers to the number of payment periods (note: periods must be > 0). The Pmt argument that refers to the payment made each period and has a corresponding sign (+ or -). The PV argument refers to present value.

Example, you had loan $1,000 at 10% interest rate. $50 is paid every month for 1 year. How much will you pay for that loan? Let's take an example to understand it:

Let's look at below formula:

=FV(C5/12,C6*12,C4,C3)

In the formula above, the FV Function calculates future value of $1,000 borrowed at 10% interest rate which divide into 12 (months) for 1 year payment multiply into 12 (months) with $50 payment every month. In other words, it calculates amount we need to pay for that loan. The formula returns ($1,732.99).

STANDARD DEVIATION

The standard deviation calculation is another illustration.

The standard deviation measures how far a set of data can vary from its mean. This is crucial information because it indicates how many values in a set are greater or less than a given value. For instance, if you scored 80% on a test, your standard deviation would be 0. (because your score was included twice on the scale). However, if you scored 85% on a test, your standard deviation would be 1 (since only one of those numbers was greater than 85%).

This statistic is used to describe how much a single data point deviates from the mean; it is the squared difference with positive or negative signs.

The standard deviation of a data set is calculated by dividing the data standard deviation by the square root of the total number of data points. Standard deviation is commonly employed in business and finance, particularly in statistical analysis and portfolio management. In computer science, it is also used to calculate numeric properties or compare two things, such as the price-to-value ratio (P/V).

Let's assume you have data from a male and female biceps curl experiment, where you recorded the biceps curl power in pounds on sheet 1 of an Excel file.

FINANCIAL FORMULAS FOR INTEREST AND MORTGAGE CALCULATIONS

The hour is near. The end of the world has arrived. The 2023 version of Excel will no longer be available, and its formulas will be obsolete. But this will not prevent you from calculating your future interest and mortgage payments if you learn how to use these formulas today!

If you have ever attempted to calculate a loan's interest or mortgage payment, you are aware that it is a tedious process. Every time you modify any of the loan's values, it will recalculate everything from scratch.

There is a way to avoid having to re-enter the values for all the loan variables every time you want to make a modification. Excel can accomplish this in a matter of seconds or less by utilizing functions, specifically the PMT function and FV function.

The PMT Function: Loan Interest Calculation Made Easier

The PMT (payment) function is extremely user-friendly. Simply enter the values for the loan amount, interest rate, and number of payments that you wish to calculate. Once you press the Enter key, the monthly payment amount for the loan's duration will be displayed.

syntax: =PMT(rate,nper,pv)

Lets plug in the rate and number of payments that we want to calculate, into our example.

payment=PMT(10%,30,$500)

Let's say that you have a loan amount of $500 and an annual interest rate of 5% on your loan. Your monthly payment will be $50.00 and your total interest for one year will be $350.

PERCENTRANK

This value's percentile rank represents the proportion of values in the dataset that are less than or equal to it. Within a given range, the percentile rank ranges from the lowest percentage value to the highest percentage value. This function returns an error value along with an appropriate message if the dataset contains an uneven number of values.

A common use for the percentile rank is to find if a value is within a given range. For example, if you want to look for sales that are greater than 95% of all sales then you can do: SELECT percentrank(t.sales, 95) FROM sales_date t WHERE t.sales >= 95

or if you want to find the percentage of values that fall between 80% and 90% of all sales you can use:

SELECT percentrank(t.sales, 80, 90) FROM sales_date t WHERE t.sales >= 80 AND t.

The '>9.5' part of the formula tells Excel that we want sales greater than 9.5%.

The syntax is: =Percentrank(array,number, [Num_digits])

The array argument is a range of data, and the number argument is the value to rank.

The third optional [Num_digits] argument specifies how many digits to show after the decimal point. The default value is 0, which means that no decimal places are shown. For example, if the dataset contains 10 numbers and 9 of those numbers fall between 80% and 90%, then:

=percentrank(sales, 80, 90)

	A	B	C		D	E	F	G	H	I
1	SEX	BICEPS (lbs)	STANDARD DEVIATION				SEX	BICEPS (lbs)	STANDARD DEVIATION	
2	F	18.889	=STDEV.S(B:B)				M	29.54545	5.443708828	
3	F	12.1234					M	12		
4	F	11					M	10		
5	F	14.88					M	5.666		
6	F	10.54423					M	13.4563		
7	F	9.23411					M	12		
8	F	11.4377					M	9.342		
9	F	12					M	8.2346		
10	F	7.564					M	15.23331		
11	F	7.3421					M	10.2311		
12	F	11					M	9		
13	F	9					M	13.2458		
14	F	11.9834					M	9.2341		
15	F	10.5632					M	11.3429		
16	F	9.5329					M	9.23134		
17										

This formula uses this piece of data, which was collected from a biceps curl experiment you ran.

If you look at the formula, you'll see that it computes the standard deviation based on the data quantity as well as the number of samples. The formula returns a decimal number so that it can be used in Excel calculations.

Chapter 18.   TRACING FUNCTIONALITY

We will concentrate on tracing Excel functionality. There are several ways to accomplish this, but we will focus on the most common approach. We'll also discuss a few of the benefits that Excel's tracing functionality offers. It is important to note that there are many compelling reasons for doing so, including the ability to track formula changes, discover errors in workbooks, and eliminate manual dependencies. Without further ado, let us begin!

The ability to trace functionality is one of the most important Excel skills to acquire. This skill will provide you with an invaluable resource for troubleshooting and conducting research. The initial step in acquiring this skill is to gain an understanding of what functions are. As you may be aware, there are three types: fundamental, input, and output. To master this skill, it is beneficial to learn as much as possible about each function.

Using functions, you can apply numerical, logical, text, and even cell references from your worksheet to your data set. Frequently, you may use multiple functions simultaneously in the same worksheet. For example, you may wish to add the minimum and maximum values in column B. And you want these two calculations to be performed within a loop so that you can repeatedly traverse the values.

INPUT FUNCTIONS

First, we will discuss input functions. In order to return a result, these functions require an argument. For instance, if you had an unorganized list of homework assignments, you could use the IF function to determine which assignment is due next based on the number of assignments already completed. You may also use a term such as NOW to display the current date and time. Or using TODAY to display only the current date.

OUTPUT FUNCTIONS

In contrast to input functions, output functions do not require input. They instead return a result based on the information provided. For instance, the SUM function takes values and adds them together, but it does not return the final value. You would then use IF, TODAY, or TODAYIF to provide us with that answer.

BASIC FUNCTIONS

Generally, you will utilize fundamental features the most. These are the types of functions that examine the value of a cell or range of cells and return a result. For instance, if you had grades for each student and wanted to determine the average grade for the entire class, you could use AVERAGE. Or if we had a list of numbers that we desired to multiply. We could use the PRODUCT function to multiply them all together and then divide by the number of inputs. The most important functions for our worksheet's objective are the fundamental ones.

INPUT VS. OUTPUT:

This is one of the most important things to remember when using a basic function; its behavior is entirely dependent on the input. For the function to return a result, input must be provided. If no input is provided, the function cannot return a result. However, if you input something, the function will return that value. If your function does not require any input, it is considered an output function. Enjoy!

OUTPUT VS. INPUT:

Importantly, the fact that we are outputting a result does not mean that everything you enter into the formula will be returned as a result. For the function to return a result, you must provide an input. A simple illustration of this is when we perform subtraction on our worksheet. When we must perform a subtraction, we must input a number, which is represented by the number to the left of the equals sign. For instance, if I wanted to subtract 10 from 50, I would enter -10 instead of 10. If you do not enter anything, you will receive an error message.

TRACING FORMULAS

Tracing Functionality in Excel involves identifying the source of a formula. Cell Reference or Named Range would apply if a formula is derived from another cell or cells. Typically, this is performed while locating the source of an error, but it can also be used to determine how something operates.

Each time you copy and paste into Excel, you may find yourself trying to identify the source of a formula. This is straightforward when using formulas, but it frequently causes complications when using sheet functions. When copying a report and attempting to bring the sheets together, or when copying an invoice and attempting to obtain the sum of each charge, this feature is frequently employed. Utilizing the "Trace Precedents" function will assist you in determining what you did and why. To trace the origin of a formula, you must first ensure that Excel contains the formula on your sheet. Next, select the cell(s) or range(s) containing your formula, and then click "Trace Precedents" from the "Formula" menu's drop-down menu.

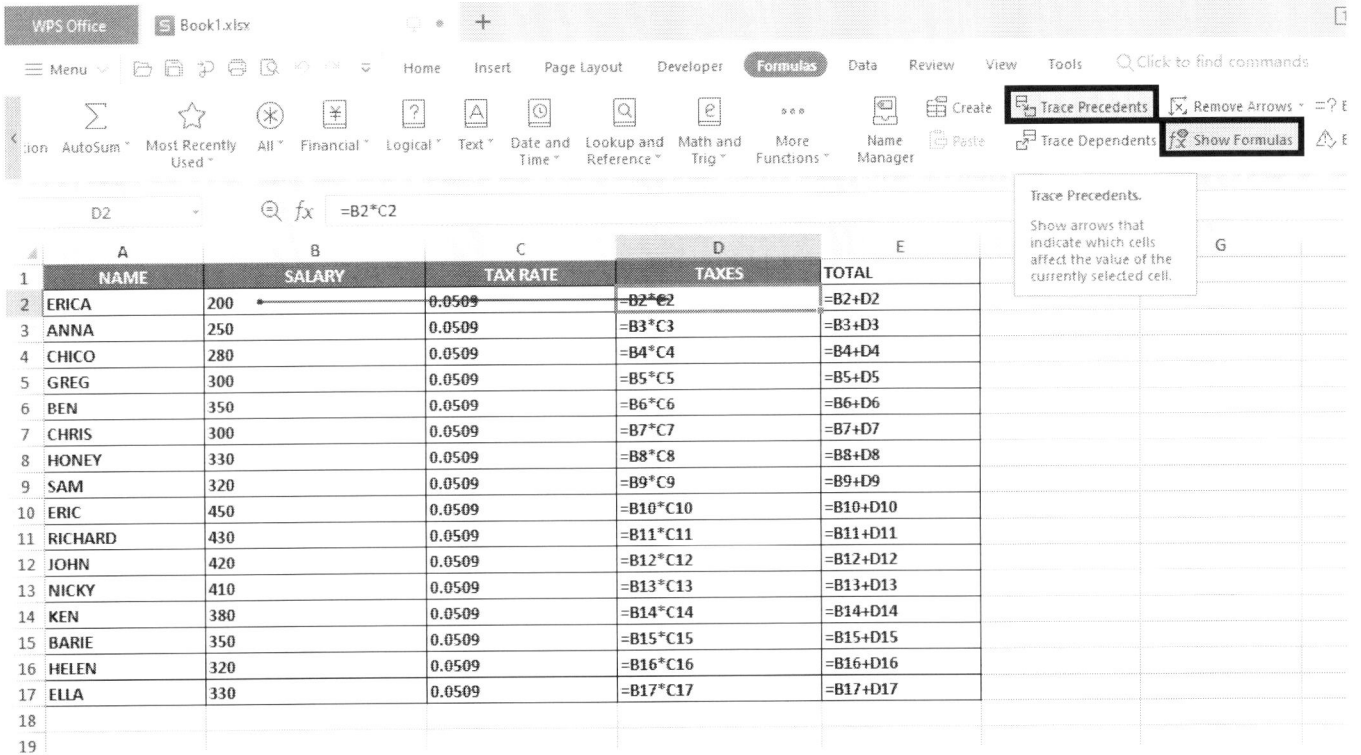

There are several different types of functions one can trace in Excel.

SUMPRODUCT

The most basic function that many people use is SUMPRODUCT(). This simply returns a result based on the values you input into it. For example, we could have a cell that says something like this: 1+2, 3+7 and 9+8. We could take these numbers and put them into SUMPRODUCT and get the result 30.

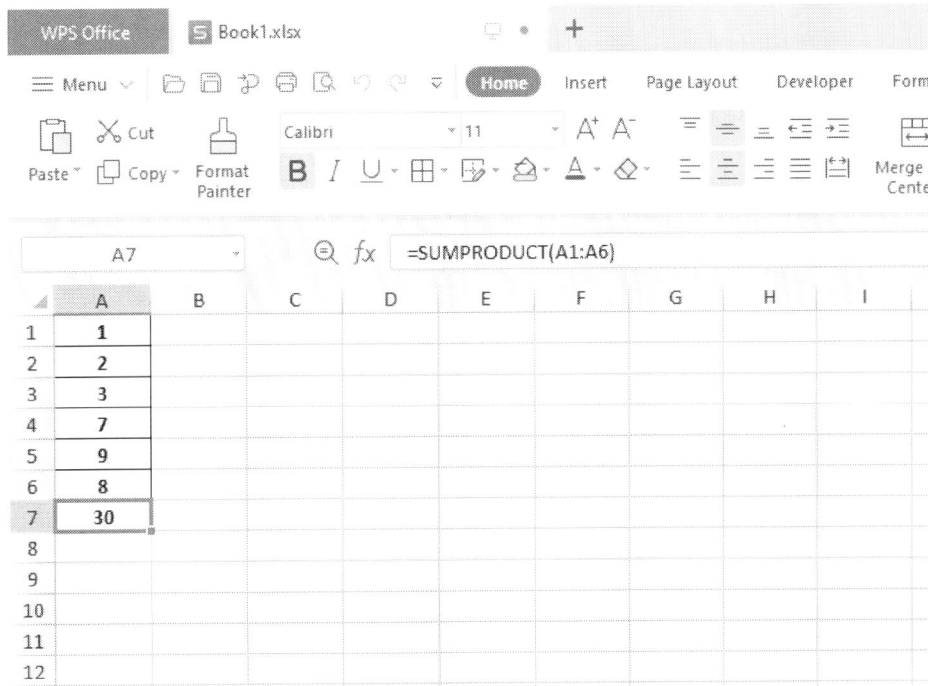

The next type of function we will look at is one that takes information from more than one cell. For example, if I want to take 6 different numbers, multiply them all together and then divide by 4, it will look like this: =SUMPRODUCT(A1*A2*A3*A4*A5*A6/4). This type of formula is most frequently used for an array multiplier for products such as sales figures, inventory, etc.

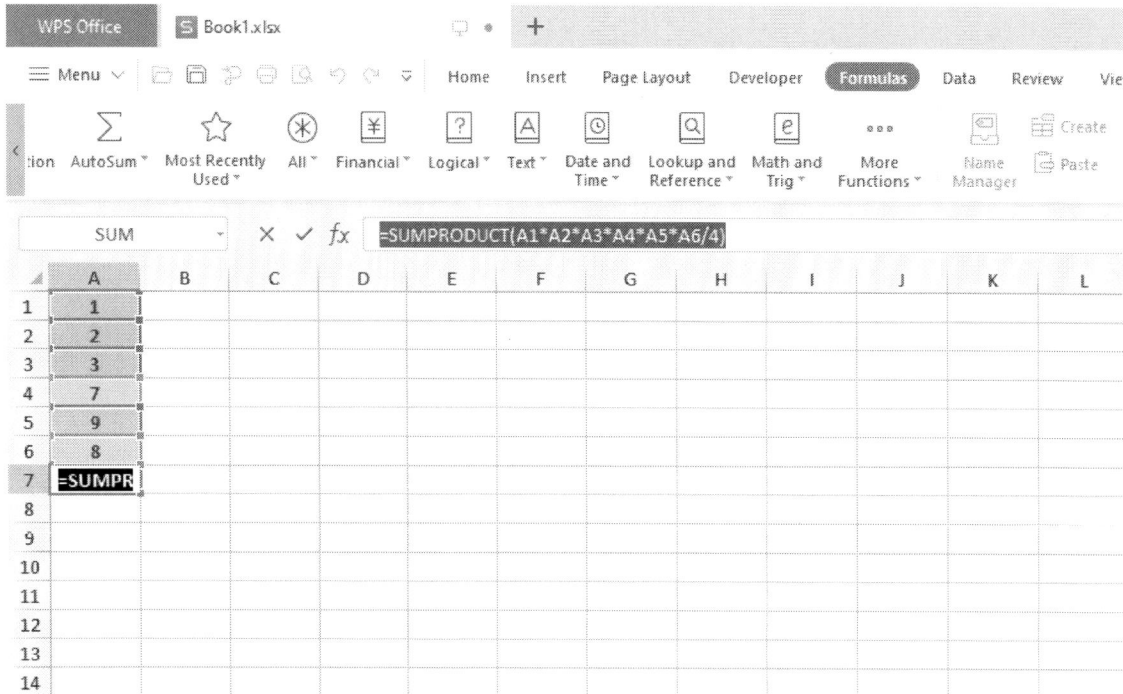

The last type of function that we will look at is a function that takes information from a cell and returns something based on a formula. For example, if we had a value in one cell, and wanted to find its square root, it would look like this: =SQRT(C2).

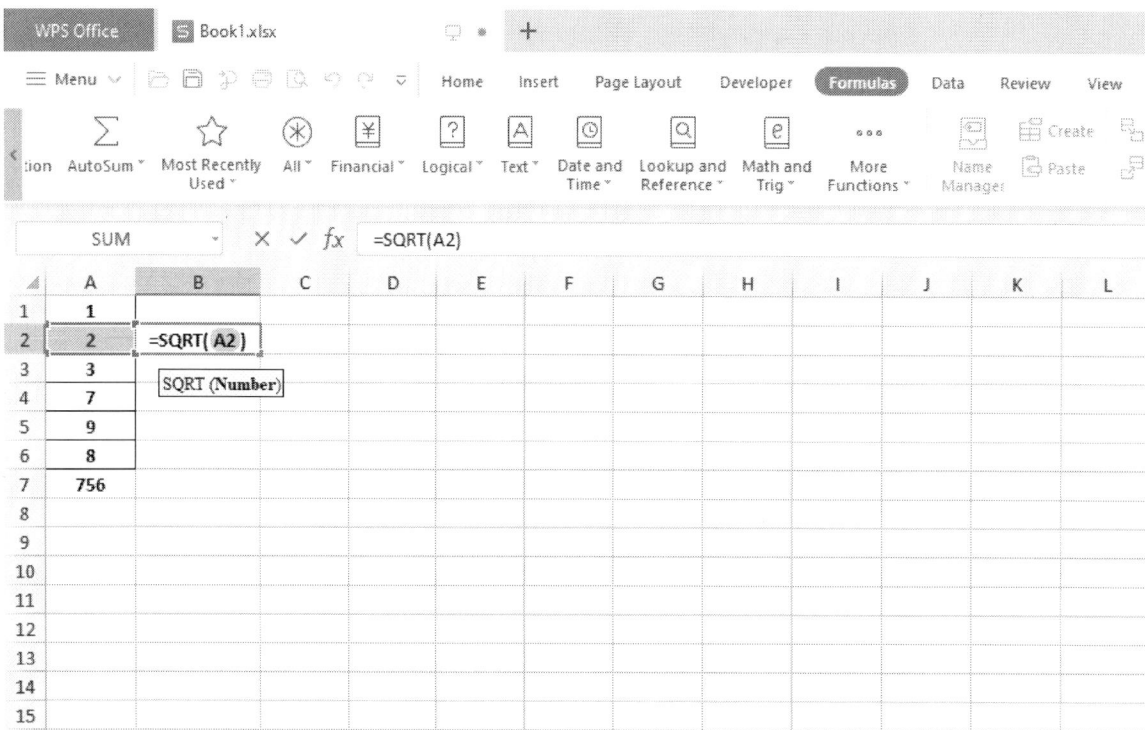

A lot of people like this type of formula because it is easier to write and still just as efficient.

When writing formulas in Excel, there are a lot of functions one can use. The main purpose of this book is to explain many different functions that are available in Excel and how they work.

OTHER LOGICAL FUNCTIONS

A function is an infinite machine that performs a task for us, such as adding 2 and 3 or changing the color of an image. Excel functions typically have names such as "SUM" and "QUOTE". There are two types of Excel functions: logical and numeric, and their names do not always correspond to their underlying mathematical functions.

logical (AND represents AND; OR represents OR; NOT represents NOT) and mathematical (MA means MULTIPLY; DIVIDE BY).

Before delving into the specifics, it is helpful to understand that Excel is similar to a slide rule or a spreadsheet with many advanced features. Excel was designed so that everything works together, but some things work better than others. As we progress, I will attempt to provide precise descriptions of each function.

Examples:

=if(logical_test, [value_if_true], [value_if_false])

the main parts of the logical functions are:

logical_test (that is, the condition)

value_if_true (the value if logical_test = True) value_if_false(the value if logical_test = False)

=and(logical1, [logical2]) =or(logical1, [logical2]) =not(logical)

The "=if" function is a shortcut that allows you to check a logical condition, and if it is true, call another function. If the first part of the "=if" condition is true, all of the following functions in the value_if_true list will run. If the first part of the logical condition is false, none of them will run.

=IFERROR(VALUE, [TEXT])

This is probably not a lot of information to guess that this function might be handy for some error handling. It checks for an error or warning condition and reports it if one exists. If there are no errors, the value is returned. If there is an error, the text of the error is returned.

When you output a formula that contains the word "IFERROR", Excel displays a dialog box with the text of any error that happens.

Note: This function is a built-in function, in which case, it can be used by itself to display an error message. The text inside the brackets will be displayed if there is an error. Otherwise, the value inside the brackets will be used.

=COUNTIF(range, [value_if_true])

This works exactly the same was as =COUNTIF(), except that it counts the number of cells in a range that are not equal to value_if_true.

=disc(transaction date, maturity date, pr, redemption, [basis])

This function calculates the number of days to maturity, based on an interest rate or principal amount and a schedule of principal payments. It also displays the remaining number of days to maturity, compounded daily. To use it, you specify the date to start and when it expires. The first argument is typically the fixed value, but if you want to compute a monthly payment you could use:

=disc(DATE(today), DATE(now), 0.075, 100000, 2 - [basis])

which says to compute a $100,000 payment with an interest rate of 0.075% for 30 years in a 2-periods/month scheme. The result is negative because DATE(today) returns the date today and DATE(now) returns today's date plus one day.

=duration(settlement, maturity, coupon, yld, frequency, [basis])

It computes daily payments for a given coupon and a given maturity. The basis is the annual interest rate.

This function works for fixed rate securities where you want to compute payments at any frequency. It does not work for variable rate securities since it assumes that the annual interest rate is constant.

=sln(cost, salvage, life)

Simplifies the payment of a bond, typically by computing the actual price based on present value factors and then discounting the payments back to present value. The salvage value is the price at which you would sell the bond if you held it until maturity and it paid off by sinking into bankruptcy.

=dollar(decimal_dollar,fraction)

Converts a decimal value to a dollar value and displays the result in standard format.

You may use them to perform calculations or create a financial model around the results which is based on these functions.

Chapter 19. DATA

Excel is an excellent instrument for combining data from multiple sources. To accomplish this, however, you must first import the data from the various sources into Excel. You can do this manually, or you can automate the process using the import function.

IMPORTING DATA TEXT FILE

Excel permits the importation of data from a variety of other file types, including CSV and TXT files. This chapter will guide you step-by-step through the process of importing this type of data into your workbook.

In this example, we are importing data from a text file with a single row and a single column. Select the cell into which you wish to import data.

1.   To get started, click the Data tab on the Excel toolbar.

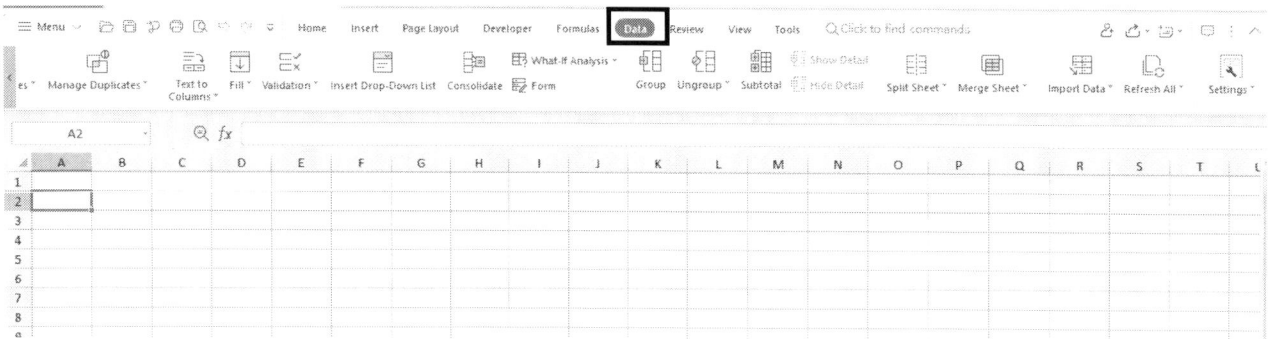

2.   Choose Import Data tools section at the left of your screen. This option allows you to import data from a wide range of sources into Excel.

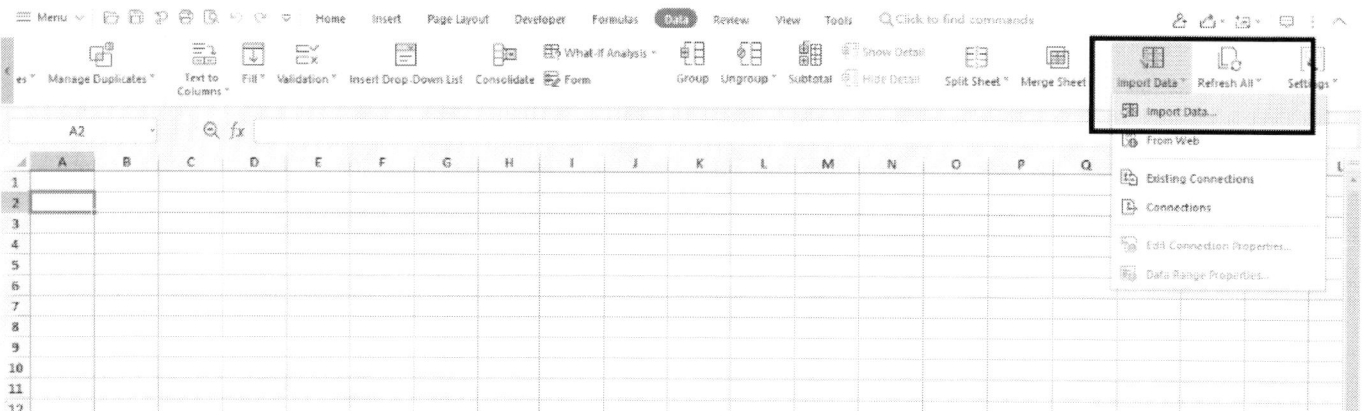

3.   Next, select the text data format.

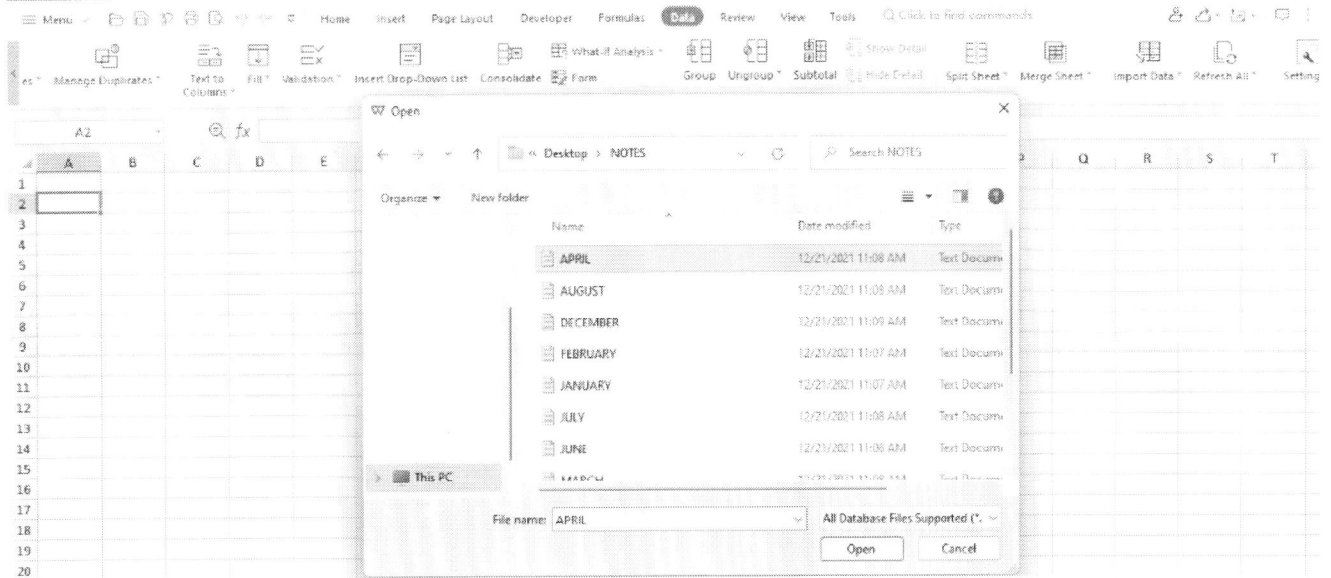

4. Click on the 'Open button to advance to the next page of the wizard and verify that you want to import all data from files, including any charts or graphs they contain, into a new table in your workbook.

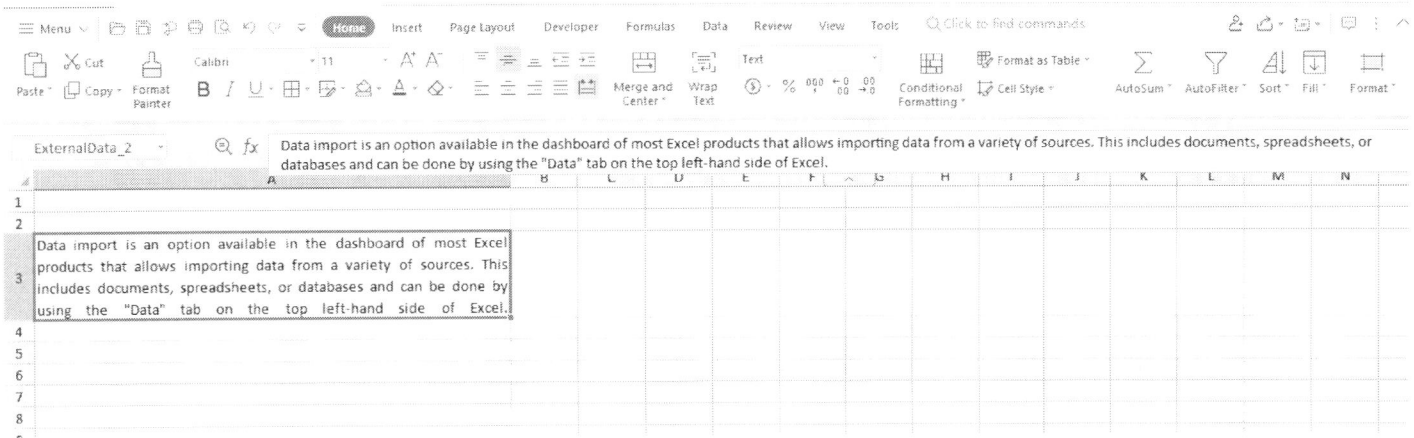

This is extremely simple, yet extremely effective. If you need to import data from a database or website into your spreadsheet, simply copy and paste the information into the first cell of the first sheet.

If your spreadsheet contains many different types of data that don't look quite right next to each other, then there is likely an issue with their formatting. The issue is frequently caused by inconsistent column widths, resulting in misaligned content.

Using the best feature of Numbers, you can fix this in mere seconds. It is called "AutoFormat," and you would use this to fix it. Simply select the cell or cells you wish to format, and then use the drop-down menu that appears to select from the available options. This will almost always result in everything aligning perfectly.

SORTING AND FILTERING

Excel's two most useful features are sorting and filtering. They enable the user to quickly organize data into distinct categories, making it easier to locate the desired information and perform calculations.

Sorting is used to organize data into various categories, with each category sorted in ascending or descending order based on the options selected. The user can also use sorting functions to combine two or more similar data types into a single column and arrange them according to their type. You can sort your data by one of three columns using the sorting function: name, date, or value. This can be accomplished by clicking the button in the upper-right corner of the Excel window. The drop-down menu permits selection of the column to sort by. If you wish to sort your data by the column "name," for instance, simply select "Name" from the drop-down menu. If you want to sort your data by a date column, simply select "Date" from the drop-down menu, and so on.

When there are too many records for a spreadsheet and you do not want them all displayed in one table, you use filtering. You can exclude rows that contain specific values in their column headers without having to manually modify them. For instance, if you were an event planner, you could filter out all non-category-specific records, which would save you a great deal of time when planning the event. Filtering is also useful for removing unnecessary data from a spreadsheet, allowing it to operate more quickly and efficiently.

Excel offers two filtering options:

AUTO FILTER

AutoFilter is the default and most user-friendly filtering option, but it has limited filtering options. The advantage of AutoFilter is that you can select items from the filtered list using drop-down menus. AutoFilter is useful when you need to filter out rows or combine multiple columns into one category.

ADVANCED FILTER

Advance Filter is the option that enables deeper row and column filtering. Users must first determine how they wish to filter the data and which columns will be used for this purpose. Advanced filters are useful in a variety of circumstances, such as when you want to exclude rows based on multiple criteria or perform calculations on the filtered data.

DATA VALIDATION

This is when you want Excel to check whether the data in your cells are in a certain range.

Validation criteria are composed with Whole number, Decimal, List, Date, Time and Text length.

Whole Number Criteria

For instance, if you want to ensure that your product's price does not exceed $400, you can add validation criteria by selecting cells and clicking Data Validation on the Data Tab. Set the Minimum amount and maximum value for the Whole Number option.

Input message

This is an optional message that can be displayed in a pop-up box when you click on the cell.

Error Alert

This is another optional feature that will shows if the data you entered does not match the validation criteria. You can set the style, Title and the error message.

This is an example of how it looks like when the data in your cells are not in a certain range.

Decimal Criteria

If you have a product that has a decimal point, let's say your product is priced at $12.50. You can add validation criteria based on this condition by selecting cells and clicking Data Validation on the Data Tab. Select the Decimal option and set the Data to "Less Than" and set the Precision and set Minimum amount.

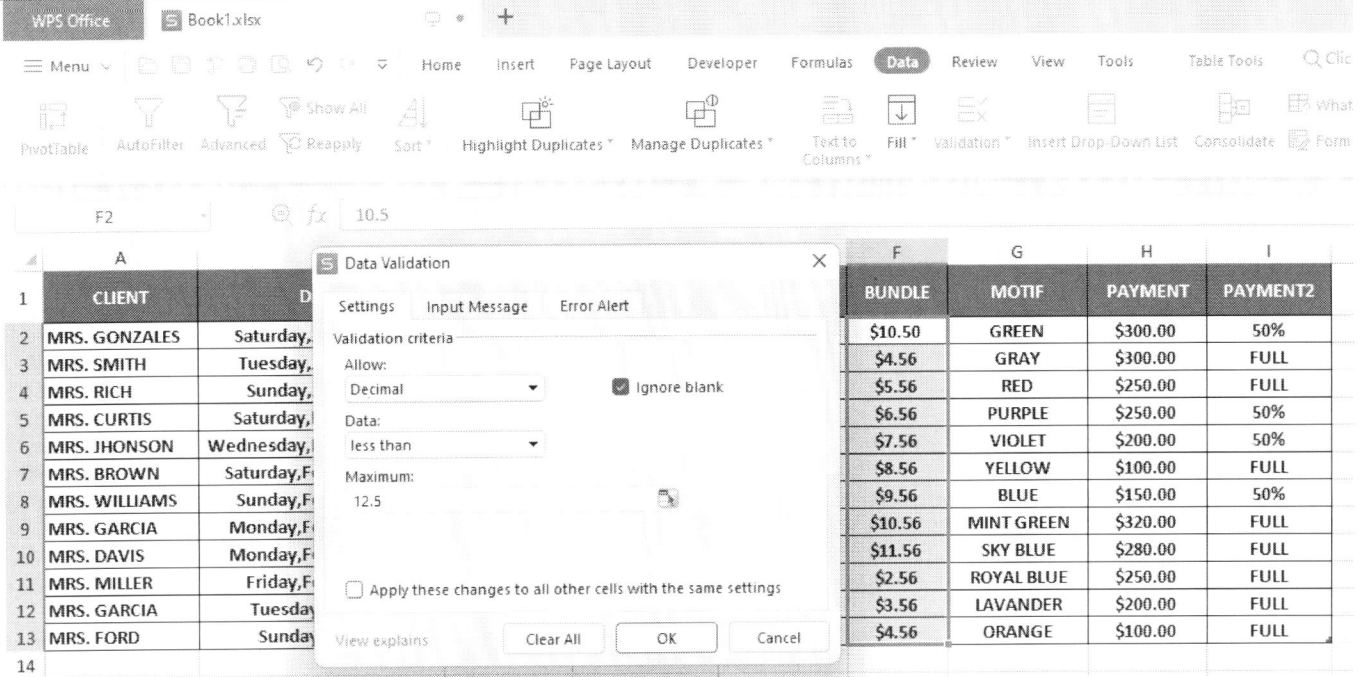

List Criteria

If you want to make sure that the data in your cells are from a certain drop down list, List criteria is the best option for you if you want to add validation on your cell based on a specific range of data.

Step 1: Create a new list for your source list.

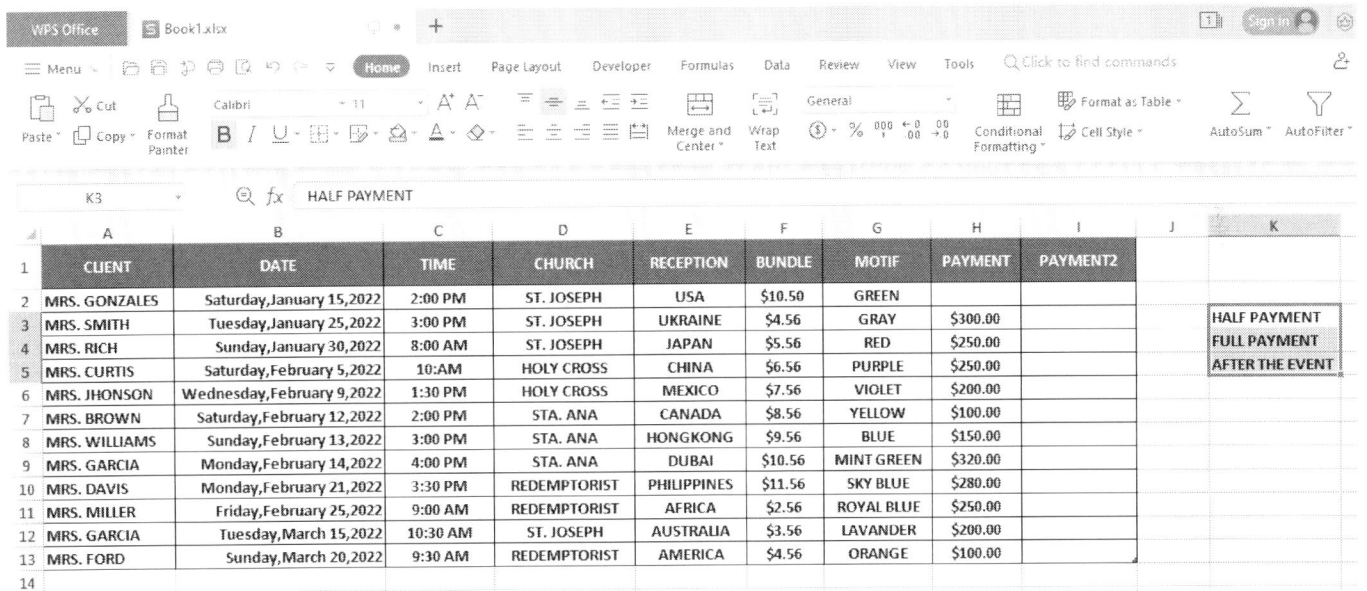

Step 2: Select cells that you want to add validation and go on a Data Tab and select List under Data Validation.

Step 3: Click the small square on the right side of the tab to get the list of your source.

Step 4: Select the list of your source.

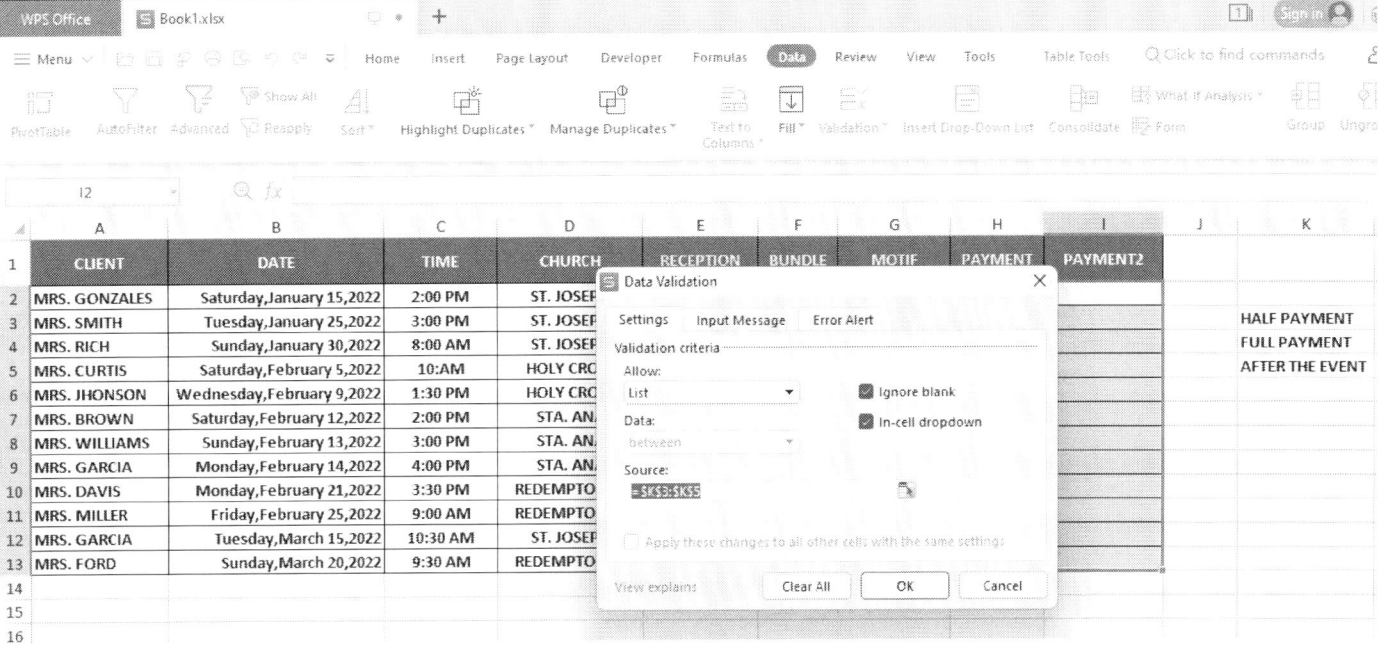

Step 5: Now, click OK to see the result. (Do not forget to delete your source list after setting up the validation)

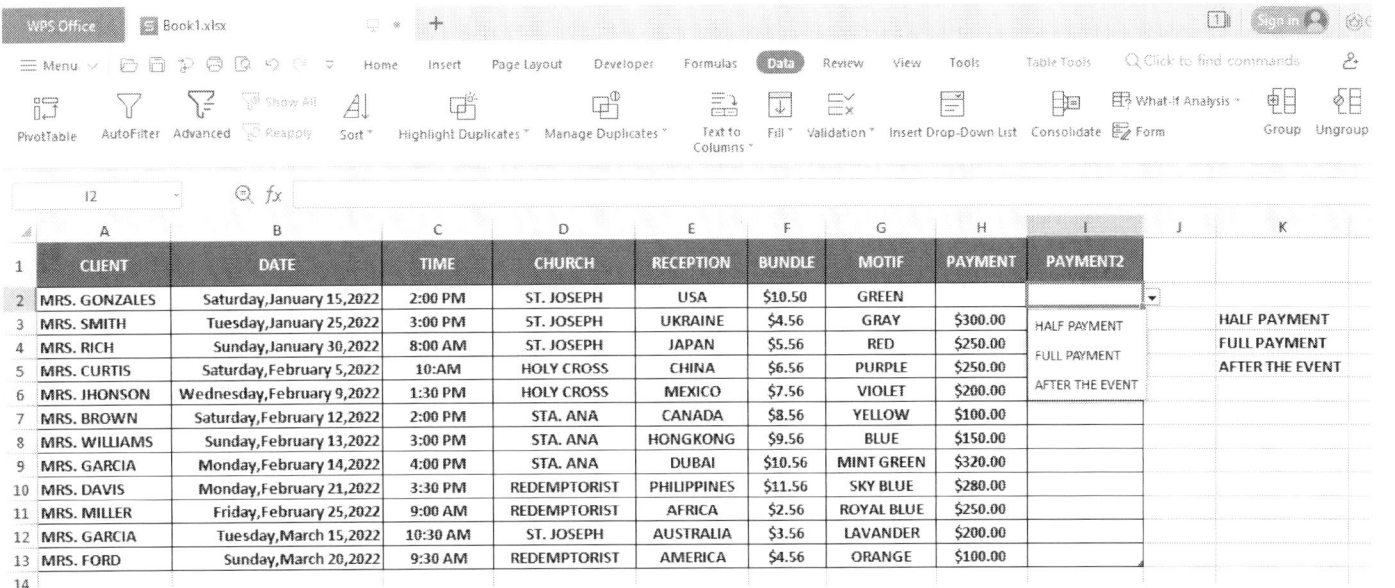

Date Criteria

If you have a schedule that requires a certain date, let's say the event will get expired after it reaches its target date. This is the perfect time to add validation on your cell based on the date by selecting cells and clicking Data Validation on the Data Tab. Select the Date option and input your date in a drop down box.

Let's assume the target date will be on March 14, 2022. Set the end date on March 15, 2022.

Notice the date on cell B13 (March 20, 2022), and when you click "Ok" you will then notice the red color on the cell.

	CLIENT	DATE	TIME	CHURCH	RECEPTION	BUNDLE	MOTIF	PAYMENT	PAYMENT2
1									
2	MRS. GONZALES	Saturday,January 15,2022	2:00 PM	ST. JOSEPH	USA	$10.50	GREEN		HALF PAYMEN
3	MRS. SMITH	Tuesday,January 25,2022	3:00 PM	ST. JOSEPH	UKRAINE	$4.56	GRAY	$300.00	
4	MRS. RICH	Sunday,January 30,2022	8:00 AM	ST. JOSEPH	JAPAN	$5.56	RED	$250.00	
5	MRS. CURTIS	Saturday,February 5,2022	10:AM	HOLY CROSS	CHINA	$6.56	PURPLE	$250.00	
6	MRS. JHONSON	Wednesday,February 9,2022	1:30 PM	HOLY CROSS	MEXICO	$7.56	VIOLET	$200.00	
7	MRS. BROWN	Saturday,February 12,2022	2:00 PM	STA. ANA	CANADA	$8.56	YELLOW	$100.00	
8	MRS. WILLIAMS	Sunday,February 13,2022	3:00 PM	STA. ANA	HONGKONG	$9.56	BLUE	$150.00	
9	MRS. GARCIA	Monday,February 14,2022	4:00 PM	STA. ANA	DUBAI	$10.56	MINT GREEN	$320.00	
10	MRS. DAVIS	Monday,February 21,2022	3:30 PM	REDEMPTORIST	PHILIPPINES	$11.56	SKY BLUE	$280.00	
11	MRS. MILLER	Friday,February 25,2022	9:00 AM	REDEMPTORIST	AFRICA	$2.56	ROYAL BLUE	$250.00	
12	MRS. GARCIA	Tuesday,March 15,2022	10:30 AM	ST. JOSEPH	AUSTRALIA	$3.56	LAVANDER	$200.00	
13	MRS. FORD	Sunday,March 20,2022	9:30 AM	REDEMPTORIST	AMERICA	$4.56	ORANGE	$100.00	
14									

This means that the cell is not valid for any date that is after the inputted date.

To check this error, simply click the drop down tab and select edit formula the press OK.

| | B13 | | × ✓ fx | 3/20/2022 | | | | | |

	A	B	C	D	E	F	G	H	I
1	CLIENT	DATE	TIME	CHURCH	RECEPTION	BUNDLE	MOTIF	PAYMENT	PAYMENT2
2	MRS. GONZALES	Saturday,January 15,2022	2:00 PM	ST. JOSEPH	USA	$10.50	GREEN		HALF PAYMENT
3	MRS. SMITH	Tuesday,January 25,2022	3:00 PM	ST. JOSEPH	UKRAINE	$4.56	GRAY	$300.00	
4	MRS. RICH	Sunday,January 30,2022	8:00 AM	ST. JOSEPH	JAPAN	$5.56	RED	$250.00	
5	MRS. CURTIS	Saturday,February 5,2022	10:AM	HOLY CROSS	CHINA	$6.56	PURPLE	$250.00	
6	MRS. JHONSON	Wednesday,February 9,2022	1:30 PM	HOLY CROSS	MEXICO	$7.56	VIOLET	$200.00	
7	MRS. BROWN	Saturday,February 12,2022	2:00 PM	STA. ANA	CANADA	$8.56	YELLOW	$100.00	
8	MRS. WILLIAMS	Sunday,February 13,2022	3:00 PM	STA. ANA	HONGKONG	$9.56	BLUE	$150.00	
9	MRS. GARCIA	Monday,February 14,2022	4:00 PM	STA. ANA	DUBAI	$10.56	MINT GREEN	$320.00	
10	MRS. DAVIS	Monday,February 21,2022	3:30 PM	REDEMPTORIST	PHILIPPINES	$11.56	SKY BLUE	$280.00	
11	MRS. MILLER	Friday,February 25,2022	9:00 AM	REDEMPTORIST	AFRICA	$2.56	ROYAL BLUE	$250.00	
12	MRS. GARCIA	Tuesday,March 15,2022	10:30 AM	ST. JOSEPH	AUSTRALIA	$3.56	LAVANDER	$200.00	
13	MRS. FORD	3/20/2022	9:30 AM	REDEMPTORIST	AMERICA	$4.56	ORANGE	$100.00	
14									
15		⚠ **EXPIRED!!!**							
16		TARGET DATE: March 14, 2022							
17		Press [Enter] again to confirm							

This means that the cell is not valid for any date that is after the inputted date.

Time Criteria

An hour's difference can cause a lot of confusion. To prevent that, you can use a Time Criteria which will give you specific times. To set up this kind of validation, select cells and click Data Validation from the Data Tab. Select the Time option and input the time in the pop up box.

| Menu ∨ | | | Home | Insert | Page Layout | Developer | Formulas | **Data** | Review | View | Tools | Table Tools | Q Clic |

PivotTable AutoFilter Advanced Reapply Sort Highlight Duplicates Manage Duplicates Text to Columns Fill Validation Insert Drop-Down List Consolidate Form

| | C2 | | fx | 2:00:00 PM | |

	A	B	C					PAYMENT	PAYMENT2
1	CLIENT	DATE	TIME						
2	MRS. GONZALES	Saturday,January 15,2022	2:00 PM					$300.00	HALF PAYMENT
3	MRS. SMITH	Tuesday,January 25,2022	3:00 PM					$300.00	
4	MRS. RICH	Sunday,January 30,2022	8:00 AM					$250.00	
5	MRS. CURTIS	Saturday,February 5,2022	10:00 AM					$250.00	
6	MRS. JHONSON	Wednesday,February 9,2022	1:30 PM					$200.00	
7	MRS. BROWN	Saturday,February 12,2022	2:00 PM					$100.00	
8	MRS. WILLIAMS	Sunday,February 13,2022	3:00 PM					$150.00	
9	MRS. GARCIA	Monday,February 14,2022	4:00 PM					$320.00	
10	MRS. DAVIS	Monday,February 21,2022	3:30 PM					$280.00	
11	MRS. MILLER	Friday,February 25,2022	9:00 AM					$250.00	
12	MRS. GARCIA	Tuesday,March 15,2022	10:30 AM					$200.00	
13	MRS. FORD	Friday,March 11,2022	9:30 AM					$100.00	

Data Validation ×

Settings | Input Message | Error Alert

Validation criteria

Allow:
Time ▼   ☑ Ignore blank

Data:
between ▼

Start time:
5:00:00 AM

End time:
5:00:00 PM

☐ Apply these changes to all other cells with the same settings

View explains   Clear All   OK   Cancel

Text Length

If you have a product that has several words in its name, this will be a great way to ensure it can only contain specific characters. Find the cell where you want to use the validation. Select Data Validation on the Data Tab and click Text Length.

Now you can see that it is only allowed to have less than 10 characters in a cell.

If you enter more than 10 characters, you will get an error message.

To enter a word in cell B14, double-click on the red colored cell and type in your word and click Enter. You will then notice that the red color changes back to black. This means that your entry is valid now.

Data validation is essential for your spreadsheets in order to prevent errors in your workbook. When entering data into a worksheet, you should verify the accuracy of the data to prevent errors. This is how Data Validation in Excel operates.

REMOVE DUPLICATES

If you want to be absolutely certain that what you have entered is a unique record, you should eliminate duplicates before using the value in Excel. Creating a list of duplicate entries on the screen for data entry has no effect. It is a complete waste of time.

Copy and paste your list in order to preserve the original set. Now, select "REMOVE DUPLICATE" by clicking the HIGHLIGHT DUPLICATE icon in the toolbar.

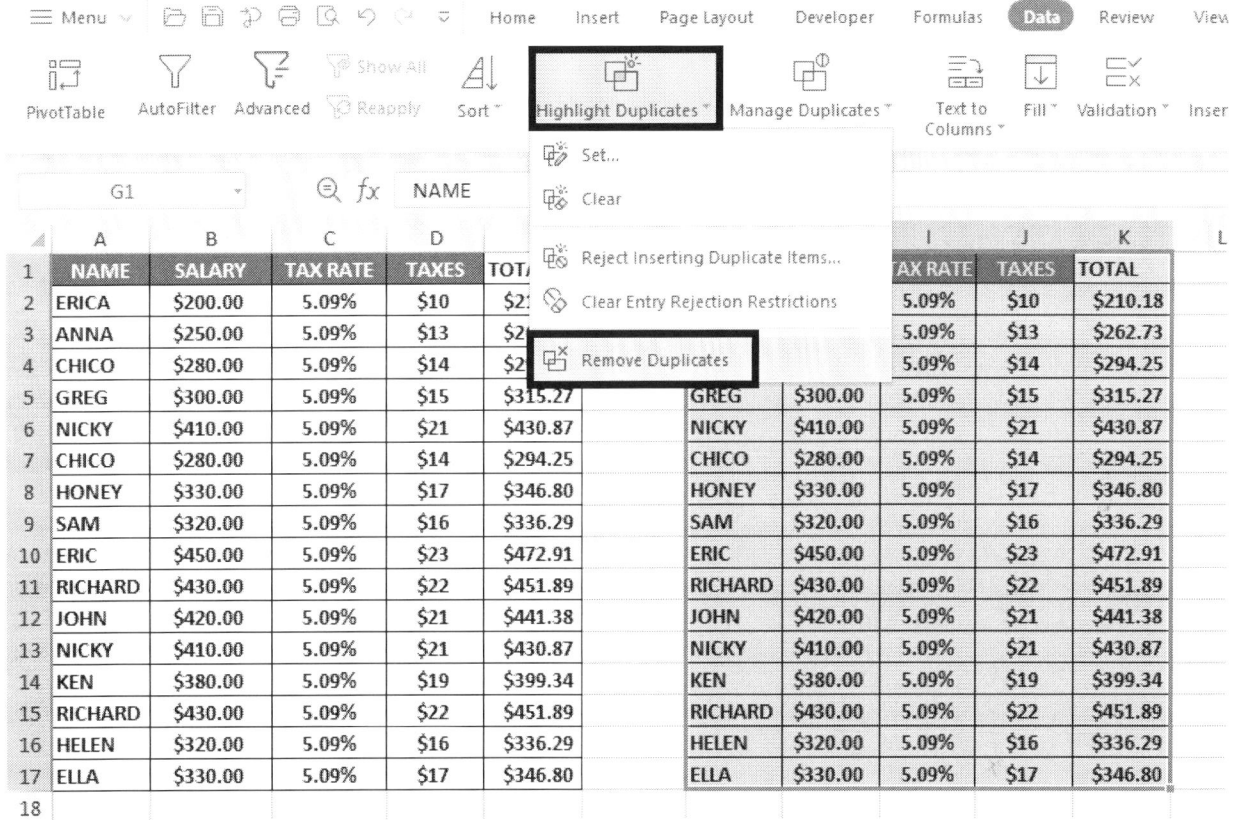

	A	B	C	D					TAX RATE	TAXES	TOTAL	L
1	NAME	SALARY	TAX RATE	TAXES	TOT							
2	ERICA	$200.00	5.09%	$10	$2				5.09%	$10	$210.18	
3	ANNA	$250.00	5.09%	$13	$2				5.09%	$13	$262.73	
4	CHICO	$280.00	5.09%	$14	$2				5.09%	$14	$294.25	
5	GREG	$300.00	5.09%	$15	$315.27		GREG	$300.00	5.09%	$15	$315.27	
6	NICKY	$410.00	5.09%	$21	$430.87		NICKY	$410.00	5.09%	$21	$430.87	
7	CHICO	$280.00	5.09%	$14	$294.25		CHICO	$280.00	5.09%	$14	$294.25	
8	HONEY	$330.00	5.09%	$17	$346.80		HONEY	$330.00	5.09%	$17	$346.80	
9	SAM	$320.00	5.09%	$16	$336.29		SAM	$320.00	5.09%	$16	$336.29	
10	ERIC	$450.00	5.09%	$23	$472.91		ERIC	$450.00	5.09%	$23	$472.91	
11	RICHARD	$430.00	5.09%	$22	$451.89		RICHARD	$430.00	5.09%	$22	$451.89	
12	JOHN	$420.00	5.09%	$21	$441.38		JOHN	$420.00	5.09%	$21	$441.38	
13	NICKY	$410.00	5.09%	$21	$430.87		NICKY	$410.00	5.09%	$21	$430.87	
14	KEN	$380.00	5.09%	$19	$399.34		KEN	$380.00	5.09%	$19	$399.34	
15	RICHARD	$430.00	5.09%	$22	$451.89		RICHARD	$430.00	5.09%	$22	$451.89	
16	HELEN	$320.00	5.09%	$16	$336.29		HELEN	$320.00	5.09%	$16	$336.29	
17	ELLA	$330.00	5.09%	$17	$346.80		ELLA	$330.00	5.09%	$17	$346.80	
18												

Now, click the HIGHLIGHT DUPLICATE in toolbar and select "REMOVE DUPLICATE".

| | Menu ˅ | | | | | | Home | Insert | Page Layout | Developer | Formulas | **Data** | Review | View | Tools | Click t |

| PivotTable | AutoFilter | Advanced | Show All / Reapply | Sort ˅ | Highlight Duplicates ˅ | Manage Duplicates ˅ | Text to Columns ˅ | Fill ˅ | Validation ˅ | Insert Drop-Down List | Conso |

G2 | fx | ERICA

	A	B	C	D	E	F
1	**NAME**	**SALARY**	**TAX RATE**	**TAXES**	**TOTAL**	
2	ERICA	$200.00	5.09%	$10	$210.18	
3	ANNA	$250.00	5.09%	$13	$262.73	
4	CHICO	$280.00	5.09%	$14	$294.25	
5	GREG	$300.00	5.09%	$15	$315.27	
6	NICKY	$410.00	5.09%	$21	$430.87	
7	CHICO	$280.00	5.09%	$14	$294.25	
8	HONEY	$330.00	5.09%	$17	$346.80	
9	SAM	$320.00	5.09%	$16	$336.29	
10	ERIC	$450.00	5.09%	$23	$472.91	
11	RICHARD	$430.00	5.09%	$22	$451.89	
12	JOHN	$420.00	5.09%	$21	$441.38	
13	NICKY	$410.00	5.09%	$21	$430.87	
14	KEN	$380.00	5.09%	$19	$399.34	
15	RICHARD	$430.00	5.09%	$22	$451.89	
16	HELEN	$320.00	5.09%	$16	$336.29	
17	ELLA	$330.00	5.09%	$17	$346.80	
18						
19						

Remove Duplicates ✕

Please select one or more columns that contain duplicates.

☑ My data has headers

ⓘ Spreadsheets ✕

3 duplicates are found and have been deleted. 13 unique values are remained.

OK

3 duplicates are found;
13 unique values will be left after delete.

[Remove Duplicates] [Cancel]

Now, check for duplicates in the list to find which one is the same as what you are looking for.

And that is how the list of duplicate records is removed.

Chapter 20.   CODING

VB macros are helpful in Excel. The VB Editor has an abundance of built-in and add-in commands that can be utilized for a variety of purposes. Macros can be used to generate customized reports, automate repetitive tasks, and even create new functions. It has been part of the system for a long time, and it is such an effective programming tool that the majority of users are unaware of its existence. This chapter will provide information on what VBA can do and how to use it. Once you have mastered the fundamentals, you can determine whether this tool meets your needs or if there are superior alternatives available. In either case, it will provide you with a fresh perspective on spreadsheet creation.

Microsoft Office includes three versions of Visual Basic for Applications, which can be accessed via their respective menus. These menus should say "Developer's Tools" or something similar when accessed. Visual Basic, Visual Basic for Applications (VBA), and VBScript are the three options. Each individual is unique and interprets specific commands differently. In Visual Basic, the MsgBox function can be used without quotation marks, but in VBA, it must be enclosed in quotation marks. VBScript will complain if they are omitted. If you do not know which language to use and remain consistent with it throughout your macro, it will not function properly. The first option after accessing the menu is to create a new project. This option is available for all VB languages. For the sake of usability, we will concentrate on VBA. By selecting this option, Microsoft's Visual Basic Editor will launch and a new project with a default module will be created. The module is the container for the code, which may consist of a single function or thousands of lines of code. To activate code written in VBA, it must be entered into the module. This is accomplished by selecting NEW from the FILE menu and entering the module's name (no spaces). After entering the code, all other commands will become accessible. To execute a macro or function, you must click VIEW and select either EDIT or TOOLS from the drop-down menu. When you select the TOOLS option, a window containing all available tools will open. The VBE is the easiest to use because it contains all the Visual Basic Editor's commands. It will operate in the background.

The remaining options are for code analysis and debugging. There are multiple methods for debugging VBA code. Clicking DEBUG and SELECT TRACE TOOLS will bring up a window from which you can choose specific commands for your debugging needs. You can also use the SCREEN command to validate your code's output. To view the actual VBA code, navigate to FILE > Open and select the module containing your code. It will open in the Visual Basic Editor, allowing you to view the code, and it will function without the DEBUG command.

Most people struggle with VBA because they do not understand what it does to their spreadsheets. It will be difficult to distinguish between VBA and the free version of Excel. Numerous spreadsheets contain code, but it is impossible to determine what it does or how it is structured. Even if you understand the language, modifying something that has already been created can be intimidating. Occasionally, it will be necessary to take notes as you learn potentially useful new commands. You will find that some commands closely resemble their equivalents in standard English, but with minor variations.

Chapter 21.   MACROS IN MICROSOFT EXCEL AND REMINDERS

A macro is a recording of how you need to act, such as performing some calculations. Using macros in Microsoft Excel will expedite the opening and closing of your workbook. You can also use them to remind yourself of important tasks, such as creating a "to-do" list or scheduling a meeting. You can also automate repetitive tasks with macros. Since your action steps are now recorded in a macro, you no longer need to write them down by hand.

A macro can be used to:

1.   Calculate or modify a series of numbers, values, or text automatically.
2.   Display specific information in a cell automatically.
3.   Repeat a set of instructions or actions periodically.
4.   Edit the contents of an entire workbook at one time by running a single command.

The created macros can also remind you of tasks due at the beginning of the week or month. For instance, you will create a macro that sends you an email every time you open a particular workbook, so that when it is complete, you will know the exact time it was created. Thus, if something goes wrong or something else occurs in the future, there will be no confusion regarding what action was taken and when it was taken. You can also use macros to facilitate the completion of daily repetitive tasks. This can be accomplished by selecting and recording specific tasks as macros. For instance, if you like to print a headings page whenever you begin a new project, you can record the necessary steps using the macro recorder. Then, instead of having to re-record the steps each time you need it, you will only need to remember to click "Apply" on your keyboard.

To record and playback macros in Microsoft Excel, click the Developer tab after enabling the "Developer" option in Excel's menu. You will see the Macro dialog box there.

When you do so, you will be prompted to record your actions or simply open the Visual Basic Editor. Excel will begin recording everything that occurs on your screen if you choose to record your steps. When you are finished recording, you must click the Stop Recording button on the Developer tab to stop the recording. If you choose to open the Visual Basic Editor instead, you can view and modify your macro code. Then, once your macro is complete, click "Record" in the Macro dialog box to create it. This option enables you to store multiple macros in a single location and run them sequentially by selecting a specific sequence from a drop-down menu.

Excel macros are effective tools for automating repetitive tasks, but they can also be confusing. You may wonder what will occur in the event of an error or system failure. Therefore, you should only consider using macros if you are familiar with their proper application. For instance, it would be a great idea to create macros that print documents or workbooks in a random order, so that even if something goes wrong the next time they are opened, you will still have a valid copy.

Additionally, it is crucial to remember that macros are easily corrupted because they typically do not retain information about their previous executions. Therefore, only the most frequently utilized macros should be recorded and kept in one location.

If you need to edit the macro, you can open the Microsoft Visual Basic for Applications window by pressing Alt + F11 on your keyboard. Then, to access your macro, navigate to Tools > Macro > Macros. There will be a sheet with a recorded list of macros once it is opened. The main code window will then appear, where you can edit your macro code. After that, the Visual Basic Code Editor will display a line of code. When you right-click a line, a menu of Excel and other program commands that can be used on that line will appear. To insert one of them, simply double-click the command or drag and drop it into your code window.

Click "Save" before closing the macro to save it. The macro recorder in Microsoft Excel is a useful function that can greatly accelerate your work. Nonetheless, if you do not know how to use them properly, recording macros can be dangerous. If you wish to begin recording your actions, you must be aware of all the risks and determine which types of actions will have a significant impact on your workbook if something goes wrong.

You can also use Macros to remind yourself of the upcoming meeting with your boss, work-related tasks, or anything else you must not forget in the future. You can record a macro that will send yourself an email every time you open a particular workbook, so that when it is complete, you will know exactly when it was created.

It is essential to realize that macros are not designed to enter data; per company policy, this must be done manually. The macro should be used to save time and effort by performing tasks that ordinarily require the use of keyboard shortcuts, rather than tracking the location of the mouse and repeatedly clicking keys.

ADVANTAGES OF MACRO IN EXCEL

Macros have many benefits, including:

1. They can facilitate your work.
2. They can assist you in not forgetting any important tasks or deadlines. You can remind yourself of tasks or deadlines by playing the macro at a specific time or date, when your workbook is opened, or when "something" occurs on your screen, such as opening a file or clicking a button.
3. With the help of macros, you can complete daily tasks that are repetitive.
4. When a project is assigned to you, you can use them to ensure that you have the necessary information on hand. This can save you a great deal of trouble when the time comes to submit the report or answer questions in group meetings.

DISADVANTAGES OF MACRO IN EXCEL

While macros are handy, there are also some disadvantages:

1. They may not always function depending on the version of Microsoft Excel you are using or if your macros have become corrupted.
2. They can be confusing to use for the first time. It is crucial to remember that macros are not intended to directly create and edit your workbook.
3. It can be difficult to train new employees because they may not know how to use macros correctly; therefore, they should be familiar with macros before being given the responsibility of creating and editing macros.
4. 4. Your organization's security settings may prohibit them. Additionally, they can be disabled by the organization's antivirus software.
5. To effectively utilize macros, you must learn the correct keystrokes.

In Microsoft Excel, macros can be a valuable and time-saving tool, but you must ensure that you use them correctly. It may be tempting to simply record your actions and create a macro, but if you don't know what you're doing, this can be dangerous. Instead, choose an important daily task, record the process of completing it with all the required steps, and then use the macro each day when the task needs to be completed.

If you want to explain something in a meeting before the actual meeting, you should also avoid sending the same email to all of your colleagues and clients. Instead, create a macro that will send a unique email to each recipient based on who you select. Thus, it will be simple to make adjustments if something does not go as planned.

Chapter 22.   EXCEL SHORTCUTS AND TIPS

Are you a novice Excel user? Complicated menus and formatting suggestions can make a spreadsheet appear more difficult than it actually is. Fortunately, there are numerous shortcuts that you should be familiar with before beginning your spreadsheet. These tips are designed to save you time and boost your productivity while enhancing your appearance. Whatever the case, beginners will appreciate having these helpful shortcuts at their disposal!

KEYBOARD SHORTCUTS

The following are some of the most used shortcuts to save time and increase productivity:

CTRL + C: Copy the item immediately to the right

CTRL + V: Paste the item that was copied to the right

CTRL + Z: Undo last action

ALT + SHIFT + . : Strikethrough (This will delete the cell contents of the cells selected.)

Can be used with a letter to highlight all cells beginning with that letter.

CTRL + I: Change the font formatting of the entire row or column.

ALT + SHIFT + O: Creates a chart from data in a selected range.

ALT+F11: Shows the Microsoft Visual Basic Editor window, where you can access all VBA code for your workbook.

That's a lot of shortcuts, but it's worth remembering them-- especially when you're working with spreadsheets. Once you start applying these shortcuts, you'll wonder how you ever got by without them!

FORMATTING TIPS

In addition to the above-listed keyboard shortcuts, there are also dozens of formatting shortcuts that can be used to enhance your documents. These tips will not only help you produce legible worksheets and documents, but they will also save you time.

1. The small curved arrow on the Home key can be used to quickly navigate between cells.
2. When entering a value, you should typically enter it in one cell and then press SHIFT to copy it to all adjacent cells. This will result in an exact value as opposed to a fraction of each adjacent cell.
3. In Excel's formula bar, there are numerous shortcuts that can be used to create formulas more quickly. There are shortcut key combinations that can be used to generate formulas that automatically appear on the right side of the formula bar.
4. Excel's "AutoComplete" feature will save you time if you frequently type words that are similar to one another. This feature detects the most frequently used words in your document and automatically fills them in. It does not work with all problematic words, such as "and," but it does work well with the majority of words, such as "city."
5. Change your view if you are working with a large spreadsheet with numerous columns, but you only want to see the column in which you are currently typing. You can accomplish this by pressing "Ctrl" and selecting "View." There will be a box containing three view options beneath this tab: View as single column, View as double columns, and View as gridlines on. Select "View as single column," and only that column will appear on the screen.
6. You can use the "Go To Second Column" feature in Excel if you are dealing with a large number of columns, which means you have a lot of information to review. This function allows you to quickly navigate to the second column of the worksheet. To accomplish this, press SHIFT+F9, which jumps to the second column and remains there until the keys are released.
7. It is advisable to leave ample white space in your spreadsheet. This makes the information you've included easier to read and gives the impression that there is more content than there actually is. It also makes it easier to quickly locate pertinent information.
8. Use a different ink pen to write in your spreadsheet. You can create your own color-coding system by using different-colored ink. This is extremely helpful if you are working with a very large document or if you are using multiple fonts and want to visually distinguish between them.
9. When working with graphics, don't forget to use the "Alignment" option under the "Format" menu. You can also utilize "Line Spacing." This can significantly enhance the appearance of your spreadsheet's graphics.
10. When using columns, you will find that they are simple to modify and manipulate. You can accomplish this by pressing "Home" followed by the arrow to the right of it. This will allow you to change the orientation of an entire column without much effort.

11. Excel allows you to change the font quite easily. Simply press "F11" to access the "Font" menu, then select a different font. This is extremely useful if your document contains only one font type.

12. If you're having trouble with very long names, it's a good idea to use the label feature to complete your spreadsheet. This feature can separate names into individual labels and make your document easier to read once it has been completed.

13. When working with very large documents, you may notice that the sorting process takes longer than usual. This could be due to the quantity of information being entered. Try using the Excel "Sort" function.

14. When sorting "Columns" (or "Rows"), selecting a column or row and pressing "Tab" sorts that area first. If the desired column or row does not appear in the drop-down menu, it is likely because the entire column or row has not yet been selected.

15. Using the arrow keys to navigate a worksheet is significantly faster than using the mouse.

16. Don't overlook color-coding your spreadsheets! You can accomplish this in a number of ways, including: using a different font color, using a unique background color, or using both!

17. If you wish to combine cells, you can use the "Home" button. By pressing "Ctrl" and the left button, you can merge cells by rows, and by pressing "Shift" and the right button, you can merge cells by columns.

18. When working with a spreadsheet containing a large amount of data, use the feature that allows you to filter data out of your document based on various criteria. This is easily accomplished by clicking "Data" at the top of your spreadsheet. Thereafter, you can select the criteria you wish to filter out by clicking "Filter"

19. You can easily hide columns or rows in a spreadsheet by clicking the "View" tab at the top of the document and selecting "Hide Columns" or "Hide Rows."

20. Right-clicking on any of your cells will reveal a long list of options that make it easier to format your document. Just be careful in your selections!

21. If you are typing in a very large area, it is advisable to reduce the font size of your text significantly. Thus, more information can be displayed on a single page without requiring as much scrolling.

TOOLS SHORTCUTS

If you have time, the best course of action is to manually enter each key combination on your keyboard. The shortcuts allow you to access Excel more quickly than if you followed each step in this guide individually.

1. To launch Excel from Word, select "Home," "Start," and then "Excel." This will open a new Excel workbook-formatted document.

2. If you don't have time to use all the shortcuts in this guide, at least try to use the ones in the "File" menu. This can be accessed by pressing "Ctrl" followed by "F11." Save as, Save, Save As Another File, New Workbook/File, Open Workbook/File, Close Workbook/File, Print Preview, and Exit are essential file commands.

3. To create a new workbook, select "New" and then click on "Workbook."

4. Select "File" from your toolbar, and then click "Open" to access your workbook. This will display a dialog box where you can select the Excel file to open.

5. Select "File" from the toolbar and then "Open" to access a second Excel file saved in the same folder as the original.

6. You can also access this dialog box's options by pressing "Ctrl" and "O."

7. If you want to save your file as a different file type, click "Save As" and then choose the desired format.

8. If you're using a more recent version of Excel, click "Options" in the upper-right corner of the screen, then click "Save." When you do this, a dialog box will appear that allows you to control where and how your documents are saved.

9. If you want to access your file directly from the open program's menu, press "Alt" and select "File" along the top of the screen.

10. Simply press "Ctrl" and "F4" to close an Excel file without first saving it. This will prompt you to save any unsaved changes before closing the file.

11. To exit Excel without being prompted to save documents, press "F12" followed by "Yes."

12. Check out the Print Shortcuts section of this manual if you wish to print your document on a different printer than your default one.

13. To add a file extension to an existing Excel document, select "File" and then "Info." Then, select the "Save" tab and check the box beside "Add To File Name."

14. When viewing a file, you can rename it by pressing "F2" and entering the new name.

15. If you would like to print your spreadsheet, select "File" and then "Print." Then, click the printer from which you wish to print and choose the desired print options.

16. To determine which version of Excel you are using, press "Ctrl" and "Q" followed by "About." This will display a dialog box displaying the exact version number.

17. To determine how much space your spreadsheet occupies on your computer, press "Ctrl" and "Q." Then, click the "Size" tab near the top of the screen to find out how many megabytes the file is consuming.

18. To zoom in or out of a spreadsheet, hold down the "Ctrl" key and click the "+" or "-" signs on the toolbar's top.
19. To access the files you've used most recently, click "File" and then "Open Recent." This will display a dialog box containing the most recently accessed files.
20. To copy the entire row in which the cursor is currently located, press "Alt" followed by "down arrow." Press "Alt" followed by "up arrow" to copy all cells directly above your cursor.
21. To cut the entire row in which the cursor is located, press "Ctrl" and then click the "X" button. Hold "Ctrl" and click on the box at the top of your screen to delete the cells directly above your cursor.
22. To move the entire row in which the cursor is located, click on the empty space on the left side of the screen and drag it to the desired location. Click on the empty space at the top of the screen and drag it to the desired location if you want to move the cells directly above your cursor.

These are only a few of the things that can be accomplished with Excel. You can use an abundance of shortcuts and functions to make your work simpler, quicker, and more efficient. Remember to take things slowly when learning Excel for the first time. You can always return and learn the shortcuts in the future.

Chapter 23. NEWEST FEATURES 2023

Amazingly, Microsoft Excel has grown to be a potent and valuable tool for many people worldwide, especially businesses. There are many new features in the next release of Microsoft Excel that will help people even more. The lists of new features useful for business users, especially in the finance industry, are given below.

New chart types

In the next version of Microsoft Excel, there will be six new chart types: waterfall, box, whisker, Pareto, histogram, and funnel. These new chart types will make it easier to understand data and data patterns by providing visualization methods like those used in Excel but with additional features that help users to communicate the impact of data better.

Import pictures and convert the table

In the next version of Microsoft Excel, you can import images or other file formats and convert them into a table format. Microsoft has created new functions and a macro that people can use.

Image function

This new picture function in Excel 2023 will let you insert images into a cell. The new "Image" format will let you insert images like a picture file and attach them to text or import images from a web page.

New filter function

The filter function of Microsoft Excel has been updated, and it now supports more than 600 new filters, which will make working with large data sets easier for business users and help them find relevant information faster.

Big data analysis improvements

There are several improvements for analyzing big data. One of them is that when combining multiple tables in a single query, Microsoft Excel will be able to use this feature for tables and any other kind of data. There are also several improvements regarding performance that will allow users to run queries much faster, especially when there are large data sets.

More advanced formulas

In the next version of Microsoft Excel, other valuable functions for advanced formulas will be available. The best feature of these new formulas is that they are not limited to a single cell. The user can edit a formula in one cell and then attach it to any other cells in the workbook at any time.

Hyperlink in comments

When working on a formula, the new version of Microsoft Excel will allow you to add hyperlinks in the comment. This will be very helpful for people sharing their workbooks with others, as comments often contain links to cell references and other information that others need to know.

Leading Zeros

People who use Microsoft Excel will know that there are times when you have to look backward and forward in rows or columns because there are a lot of zeros or decimal places in data. In the next version of Microsoft Excel, it will be possible to delete all decimals from the right, left, top, or bottom of a column. You will also be able to keep values intact, which is especially good for financial data.

VBA improvements

Microsoft has made significant updates to the VBA language in the next version. One of them is that it will be effortless for users to create new functions and procedures. There will also be a new option to make all procedures in a workbook run automatically, which is especially good for macros.

Linked drawings in charts

The next version of Microsoft Excel has made it possible to link charts with drawings that users can use instead of using embedded charts. This will let users change the size or format of the drawing and see the changes reflected in the chart almost immediately. You will also find new drawing tools in Microsoft Excel to help you create and modify graphics.

Screen Sketch mode

Many people working with Microsoft Excel might not know that the next version of this application has a new screen sketch feature that lets the user draw an image on the screen and then send it to other users or copy it to a word processing program. This feature is handy for people who work on different computers simultaneously and want to share information or ideas with others.

Keyboard shortcut customization

In the next version of Microsoft Excel, users can customize keyboard shortcuts for all commands, including predefined ones. This will allow users to use keyboard shortcuts that best fit their personal preferences, knowledge, and practices.

Improved query Support

The next version of Microsoft Excel supports more data source types from external databases and data warehouses. With the new version, you can save external queries in a single file and then use these queries in other spreadsheets. You can also share these queries with others by using links.

Data Modelling

Data modeling has always been a challenge for business users, and Microsoft Excel 2023 is designed to help users solve their problems with relational databases. The new version will allow you to define relationships between tables, which means that you can label and sort data in one table from the other. From the next version, you will be able to use multi-valued fields as primary keys, and Microsoft Excel will also be able to validate and generate keys automatically in many cases.

New pivot table modes and features

There are two new pivot table modes. One of them is called 'slice and dice', which lets users define multiple fields as slicers and then define the layout of a report in a series of 'dice'. The other option is an interactive grid where you can drag the data to reorder it. This way, you can construct a grid that displays data in a different order. The new version of Microsoft Excel will improve the experience of Pivot Table by making these tables more interactive. You can now apply pivot table formatting simultaneously, and you do not have to use design to do it one by one. The changes will also make it easier to edit formulas within Pivot Table fields. You will now be able to apply formatting to all fields or each field separately, and at the same time, you can also produce a custom-calculated field.

Search fields in PivotTable

This feature lets users create a field that lets them search for data in multiple fields simultaneously and will also provide support for the 'boundary search' functionality. This way, you can search for information within specific ranges.

Protect sheets and Manage Protection

The new version of Microsoft Excel will allow users to protect sheets so that other users cannot accidentally delete data from them. The latest version will also allow you to set different levels of sheet protection. This will be a significant change both for individuals and businesses.

Microsoft Excel will have new options for how you work with your data which is an excellent reason to upgrade. With the latest version, Microsoft Excel will provide you with more efficient tools and make the entire work process much more manageable. All these new features are designed to help you to spend less time working as well as helping you save time for data sharing and analysis.

Also, the new version of Microsoft Excel will allow you to improve your efficiency by using data from external databases and data warehouses. With this, your workload will be considerably reduced, and it is through this feature that Microsoft Excel will allow you to maximize the value of apps.

Chapter 24.   BONUSES – VIDEO LECTURES AND TEMPLATES

Even if this book is very detailed and contains a lot of pictures and examples, we know that to have other sources of information can help to improve faster your skills and bring you to the next level.

For this reason, there are two bonuses that we want to share with you:

1)   a thirty videos' lectures playlist that you can find at this link:

Video Lectures

2)   Over 100 templates that you can use at your convenience at this link:

Free Excel Templates Ready to Use

Chapter 25. BONUS - ACCOUNTING SPREADSHEET IN LESS THAN 15 MINUTES!

Most of the people think that it is very difficult to create a spreadsheet in Excel. Some of us don't even know how to create one.

In accounting spreadsheets, the main job of the user is to collect all the data into a single place and then perform operations on that data. As a matter of fact, you can have your own spreadsheet in 10 minutes only if you are following these steps.

For creating accountancy spreadsheets, you need:

Step 1: Open MS Office Excel program.

Step 2: Create a new spreadsheet and save it as "accounting spreadsheet".

Step 3: Write the important information in your accounting spreadsheet.

The sample below shows the Company Sales for 2021.

Step 4: In the other sheet, we will create various formulas to perform various operations on your data.

Step 5: Write down the information in the other sheet.

Step 6: Drag the columns and now go to the "Insert" row and click on "Formula" option.

Step 7: Insert formula "SuppliesTypes" for your data with no space and click "OK".

Step 8: Go back to your first data sheet and set the formulas in the Debt Balance cells you have defined and type "PaymentStatusTypes".

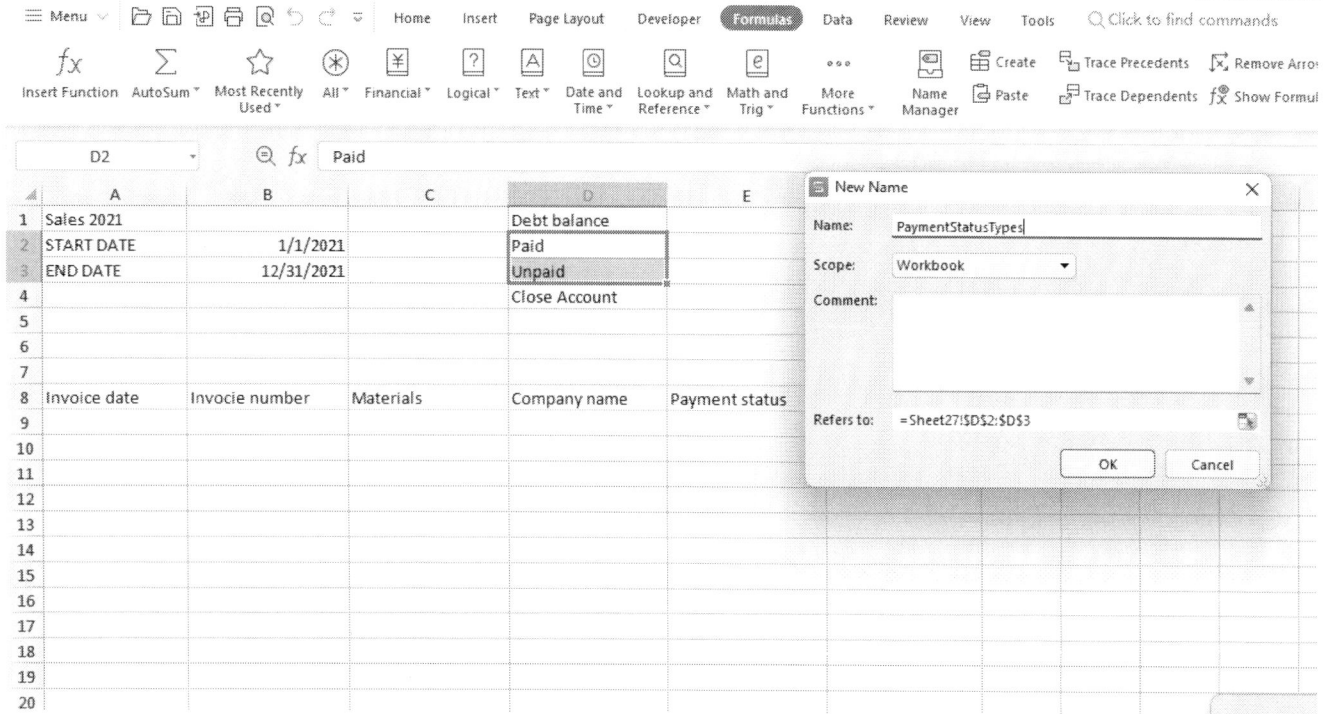

Now we need to insert various formulas in "Payment Status" column. This is to make the spreadsheet to sort the details for you.

Step 9: Navigate the Payment Status column and select "Data" and allow "List" in the settings.

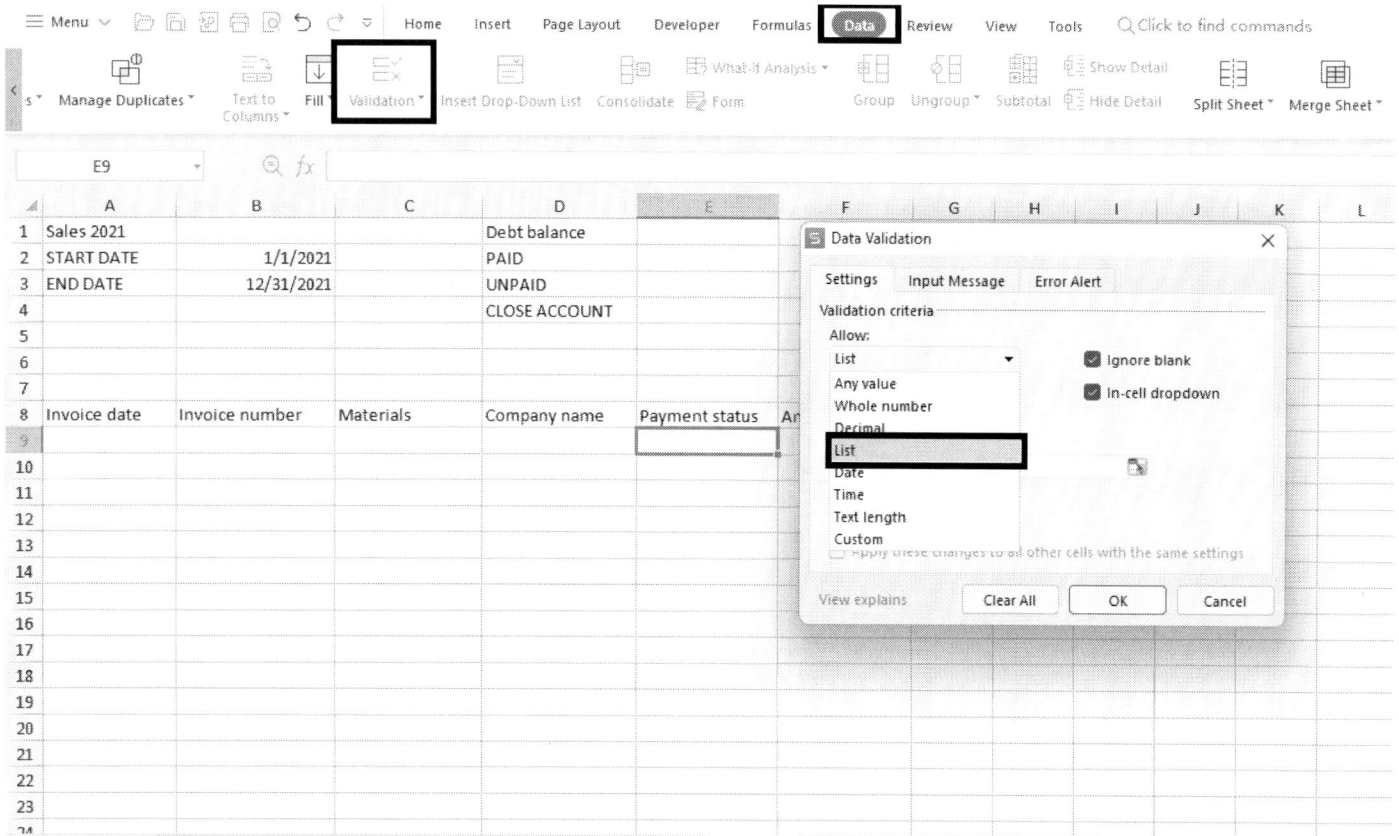

Step 10: Insert "=PaymentStatusTypes in the source area and click "OK."

This is to allow us to select the payment status instead of typing in a single number.

Now, repeat the process in "Materials" column to easily have access in your data. Remember on the second sheet you've created. Insert the source "=SuppliesTypes" and click "OK".

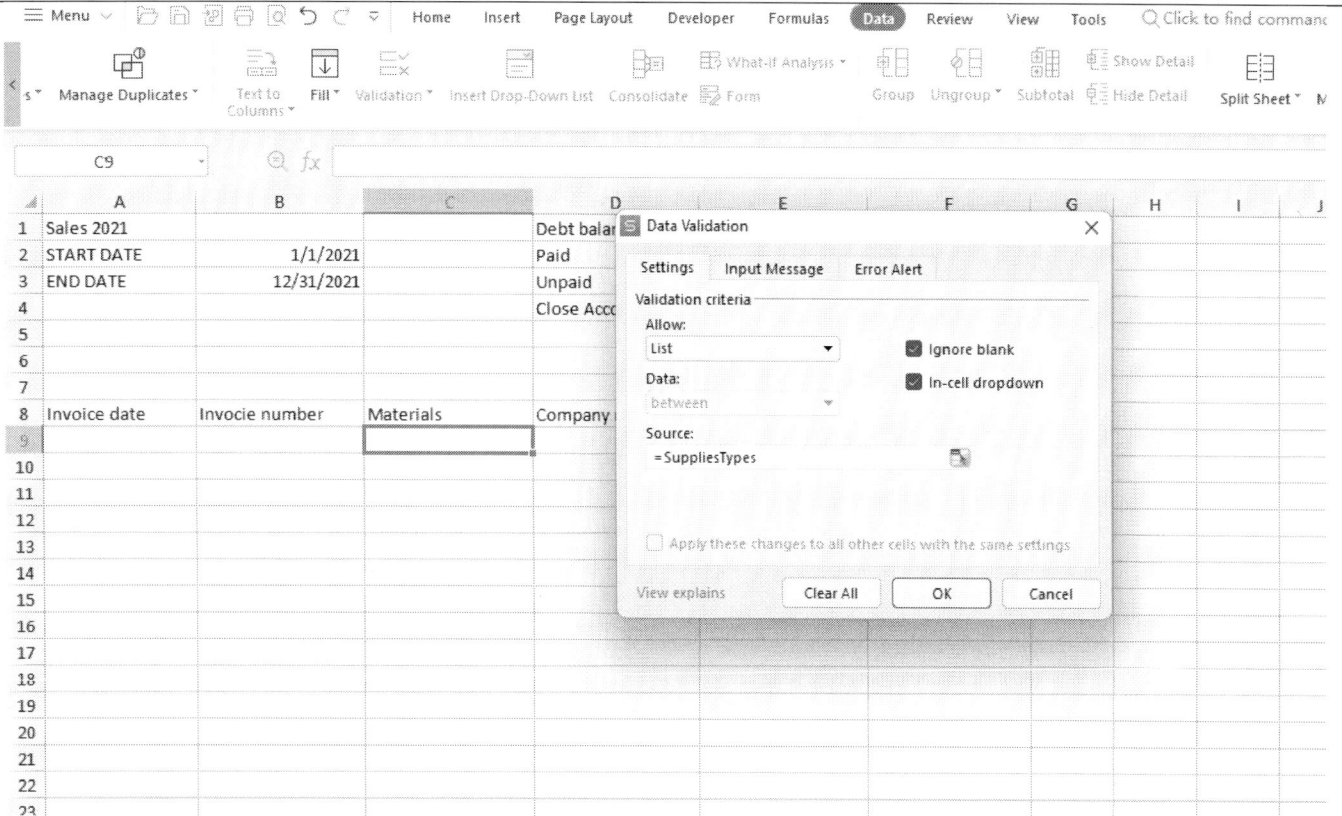

This is to allow the program to easily sort out the data you have inserted by creating formulas that can be copied and pasted automatically, making it easier for other people to use. So, whenever you enter a new row of data in your spreadsheet, it will update all the existing rows automatically.

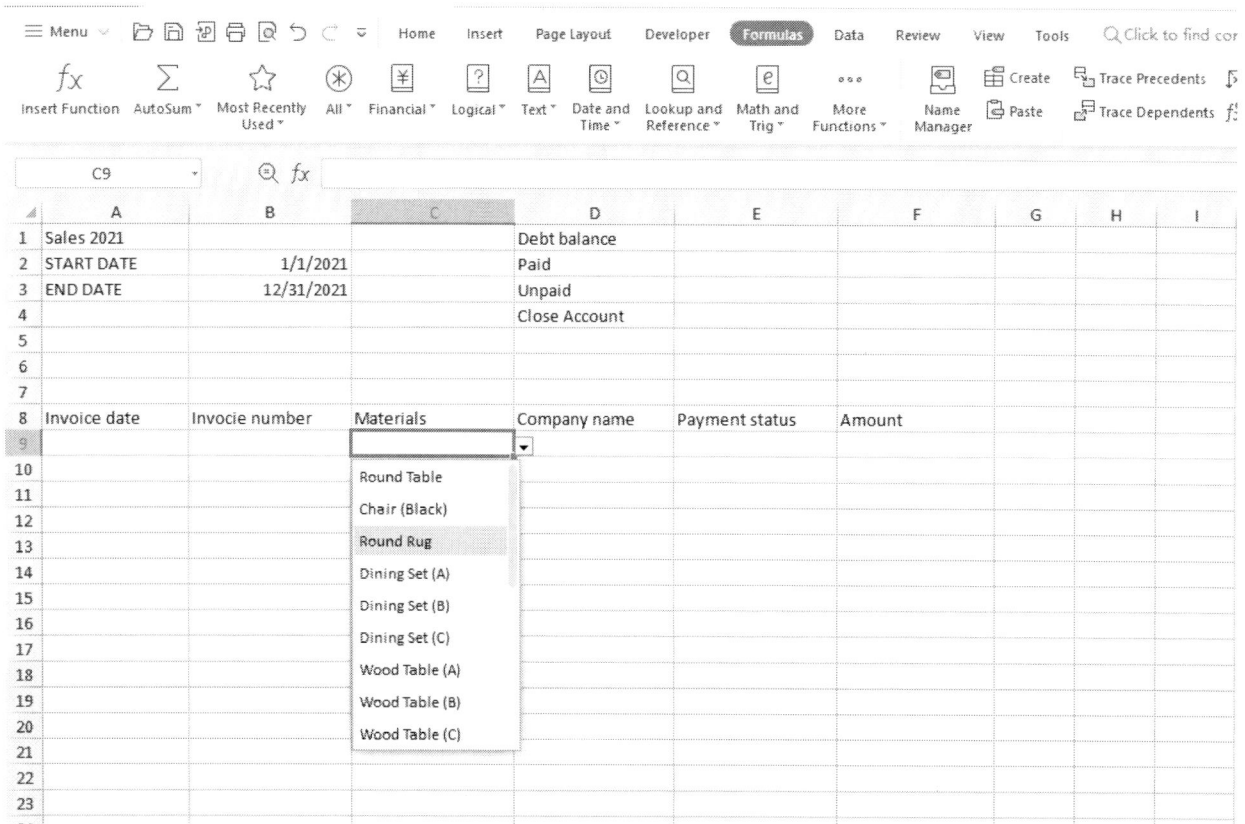

Now, enter the other information in your data and apply some formatting and a template look a little more professional.

Excel 2023

	A	B	C	D	E	F	G
1	**Sales 2021**			Debt balance			
2	START DATE	1/1/2021		Paid			
3	END DATE	12/31/2021		Unpaid			
4				Close Account			
5							
6							
7							
8	Invoice date	Invocie number	Materials	Company name	Payment status	Amount	
9	1/15/2021	872	Round Table	ABC Company	Unpaid	$150.00	
10	1/16/2021	873	Dining Set (A)	DEF Company	Paid	$200.00	
11	1/17/2021	874	Wood Table (A)	GHI Company	Unpaid	$130.00	
12	1/18/2021	875	Chair (Black)	JKL Company	Paid	$100.00	
13	1/19/2021	876	Round Carpet	MNO Company	Unpaid	$140.00	
14	1/20/2021	877	Dining Set (A)	PQR CompanY	Paid	$120.00	
15	1/21/2021	878	Wood Table (B)	STU Company	Paid	$150.00	
16	1/22/2021	879	Round Rug	VWX Company	Unpaid	$270.00	
17	1/23/2021	880	Dining Set (B)	YZA Company	Paid	$250.00	
18	1/24/2021	881	Big Square Carpet	BCD Company	Unpaid	$110.00	
19	1/25/2021	882	Spoon Holder	EFG Company	Unpaid	$200.00	
20	1/26/2021	883	Spoon Holder	HIJ Company	Unpaid	$320.00	
21	1/27/2021	884	Knife Organiser	KLM Company	Paid	$330.00	
22	1/28/2021	885	Wood Table (B)	NOP Company	Paid	$230.00	
23	1/29/2021	886	Dining Set (B)	QRS Company	Unpaid	$200.00	
24							

Account of 2021

	Supplies Type	TOTAL
1	Round Table	
2	Chair (Black)	
3	Round Rug	
4	Dining Set (A)	
5	Dining Set (B)	
6	Dining Set (C)	
7	Wood Table (A)	
8	Wood Table (B)	
9	Wood Table (C)	
10	Round Carpet	
11	Big Square Carpet	
12	Knife Organiser	
13	Spoon Holder	
14	Fork Holder	
15	Grocery Racks (3 ply)	
16	Grocery Racks (4 ply)	
17	Grocery Racks (5 ply)	
18	Furit Organiser	
19	Shoe Organiser	
20	Fry Pan (Small)	

We will now create formulas to calculate the total amount on each data using the sumif command.

Step 11: Select the range of "Payment Status" and click the "Formula" in the home tab and define new name and set this "PaymentStatusRange" and click "OK".

Do the same process in the range "Amount" and set it "AmountRange" with no spaces.

Now, return to the second sheet where "Supplies Type" located and enter our sumif commands to calculate the amount of all Materials Types sold in 2021.

Step 12: Select cell D4 and enter the following command

=SUMIF(MaterialsRange,C4,AmountRange)

Once we have entered the formula successfully the total amount will appear in the data.

Step 13: Return to the first sheet calculate all the paid and unpaid in our data sheet. Select cell E2 and enter the following command:

=SUMIF(PaymentStatusRange,D2,AmountRange)

☰ Menu ∨		Home	Insert	Page Layout	Developer	Formulas	Data	Review	View	Tools

fx Insert Function | Σ AutoSum ⁻ | ☆ Most Recently Used ⁻ | ⊛ All ⁻ | ¥ Financial ⁻ | ? Logical ⁻ | A Text ⁻ | ⊙ Date and Time ⁻ | Lookup and Reference ⁻ | Math and Trig ⁻ | More Functions ⁻ | Name Manager | Create / Paste

| SUMIF | ⁻ | × ✓ *fx* | =sumif(PaymentStatusRange,D2,AmountRange) |

	A	B	C	D	E	F	G
1	**Sales 2021**			Debt balance			
2	START DATE	1/1/2021		Paid	=sumif(PaymentStatusRange, D2 ,AmountRange)		
3	END DATE	12/31/2021		Unpaid	SUMIF (Range, Criteria, [Sum_range])		
4				Close Account			
5							
6							
7							
8	Invoice date	Invocie number	Materials	Company name	Payment status	Amount	
9	1/15/2021	872	Chair (Black)	ABC Company	Paid	$150.00	
10	1/16/2021	873	Dining Set (A)	DEF Company	Paid	$200.00	
11	1/17/2021	874	Wood Table (A)	GHI Company	Unpaid	$130.00	
12	1/18/2021	875	Round Carpet	JKL Company	Paid	$100.00	
13	1/19/2021	876	Round Carpet	MNO Company	Unpaid	$140.00	
14	1/20/2021	877	Dining Set (A)	PQR CompanY	Paid	$120.00	
15	1/21/2021	878	Wood Table (B)	STU Company	Paid	$150.00	
16	1/22/2021	879	Round Rug	VWX Company	Unpaid	$270.00	
17	1/23/2021	880	Dining Set (B)	YZA Company	Paid	$250.00	
18	1/24/2021	881	Big Square Carpet	BCD Company	Unpaid	$110.00	
19	1/25/2021	882	Spoon Holder	EFG Company	Unpaid	$200.00	
20	1/26/2021	883	Spoon Holder	HIJ Company	Unpaid	$320.00	
21	1/27/2021	884	Knife Organiser	KLM Company	Paid	$330.00	
22	1/28/2021	885	Wood Table (B)	NOP Company	Paid	$230.00	
23	1/29/2021	886	Dining Set (B)	QRS Company	Unpaid	$200.00	

This formula says calculate the total of all instances where the value of D2 appears in Payment Status Range and from the Amount Range add these totals up.

≡ Menu ∨ 🗀 🗎 🗐 🖶 🔍 ↺ ↻ ▽   Home   Insert   Page Layout   Developer   **Formulas**   Data   Review   View   T

fx	Σ	☆	✳	¥	?	A	🕐	🔍	🔍	*e*	∘∘∘	🗔	⊞ Creat
Insert Function	AutoSum ˅	Most Recently Used ˅	All ˅	Financial ˅	Logical ˅	Text ˅	Date and Time ˅	Lookup and Reference ˅	Math and Trig ˅	More Functions ˅		Name Manager	🗎 Paste

E2 ▾   🔍 *fx*   =SUMIF(PaymentStatusRange,D2,AmountRange)

◢	A	B	C	D	E	F	G
1	**Sales 2021**			Debt balance			
2	START DATE	1/1/2021		Paid	1530		
3	END DATE	12/31/2021		Unpaid			
4				Close Account			
5							
6							
7							
8	Invoice date	Invocie number	Materials	Company name	Payment status	Amount	
9	1/15/2021	872	Chair (Black)	ABC Company	Paid	$150.00	
10	1/16/2021	873	Dining Set (A)	DEF Company	Paid	$200.00	
11	1/17/2021	874	Wood Table (A)	GHI Company	Unpaid	$130.00	
12	1/18/2021	875	Round Carpet	JKL Company	Paid	$100.00	
13	1/19/2021	876	Round Carpet	MNO Company	Unpaid	$140.00	
14	1/20/2021	877	Dining Set (A)	PQR CompanY	Paid	$120.00	
15	1/21/2021	878	Wood Table (B)	STU Company	Paid	$150.00	
16	1/22/2021	879	Round Rug	VWX Company	Unpaid	$270.00	
17	1/23/2021	880	Dining Set (B)	YZA Company	Paid	$250.00	
18	1/24/2021	881	Big Square Carpet	BCD Company	Unpaid	$110.00	
19	1/25/2021	882	Spoon Holder	EFG Company	Unpaid	$200.00	
20	1/26/2021	883	Spoon Holder	HIJ Company	Unpaid	$320.00	
21	1/27/2021	884	Knife Organiser	KLM Company	Paid	$330.00	
22	1/28/2021	885	Wood Table (B)	NOP Company	Paid	$230.00	
23	1/29/2021	886	Dining Set (B)	QRS Company	Unpaid	$200.00	

Step 14: Simply drag down one line so the formula is also applied to the unpaid line and enter any amount on Debt Balance in E1.

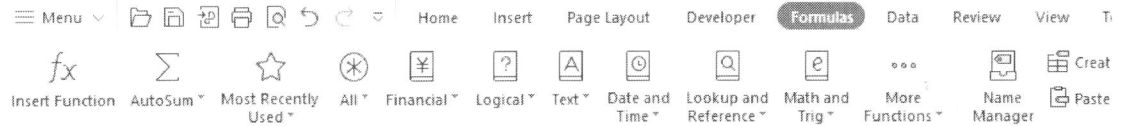

≡ Menu ∨ 🗀 🗎 🗐 🖶 🔍 ↺ ↻ ▽   Home   Insert   Page Layout   Developer   **Formulas**   Data   Review   View   T

fx	Σ	☆	✳	¥	?	A	🕐	🔍	🔍	*e*	∘∘∘	🗔	⊞ Creat
Insert Function	AutoSum ˅	Most Recently Used ˅	All ˅	Financial ˅	Logical ˅	Text ˅	Date and Time ˅	Lookup and Reference ˅	Math and Trig ˅	More Functions ˅		Name Manager	🗎 Paste

E2 ▾   🔍 *fx*   =SUMIF(PaymentStatusRange,D2,AmountRange)

◢	A	B	C	D	E	F	G
1	**Sales 2021**			Debt balance	500		
2	START DATE	1/1/2021		Paid	1530		
3	END DATE	12/31/2021		Unpaid	1370		
4				Close Account		🖺 ▾	
5							
6							
7							
8	Invoice date	Invocie number	Materials	Company name	Payment status	Amount	
9	1/15/2021	872	Chair (Black)	ABC Company	Paid	$150.00	
10	1/16/2021	873	Dining Set (A)	DEF Company	Paid	$200.00	
11	1/17/2021	874	Wood Table (A)	GHI Company	Unpaid	$130.00	
12	1/18/2021	875	Round Carpet	JKL Company	Paid	$100.00	
13	1/19/2021	876	Round Carpet	MNO Company	Unpaid	$140.00	
14	1/20/2021	877	Dining Set (A)	PQR CompanY	Paid	$120.00	
15	1/21/2021	878	Wood Table (B)	STU Company	Paid	$150.00	
16	1/22/2021	879	Round Rug	VWX Company	Unpaid	$270.00	
17	1/23/2021	880	Dining Set (B)	YZA Company	Paid	$250.00	
18	1/24/2021	881	Big Square Carpet	BCD Company	Unpaid	$110.00	
19	1/25/2021	882	Spoon Holder	EFG Company	Unpaid	$200.00	
20	1/26/2021	883	Spoon Holder	HIJ Company	Unpaid	$320.00	
21	1/27/2021	884	Knife Organiser	KLM Company	Paid	$330.00	
22	1/28/2021	885	Wood Table (B)	NOP Company	Paid	$230.00	
23	1/29/2021	886	Dining Set (B)	QRS Company	Unpaid	$200.00	

Step 15: Complete this section by using the simple formula.

=+E2+E1-E3

	A	B	C	D	E	F
1	Sales 2021			Debt balance	500	
2	START DATE	1/1/2021		Paid	1530	
3	END DATE	12/31/2021		Unpaid	1370	
4				Close Account	=+ E2 + E1 - E3	
5						
6						
7						
8	Invoice date	Invocie number	Materials	Company name	Payment status	Amount
9	1/15/2021	872	Chair (Black)	ABC Company	Paid	$150.00
10	1/16/2021	873	Dining Set (A)	DEF Company	Paid	$200.00
11	1/17/2021	874	Wood Table (A)	GHI Company	Unpaid	$130.00
12	1/18/2021	875	Round Carpet	JKL Company	Paid	$100.00
13	1/19/2021	876	Round Carpet	MNO Company	Unpaid	$140.00
14	1/20/2021	877	Dining Set (A)	PQR CompanY	Paid	$120.00
15	1/21/2021	878	Wood Table (B)	STU Company	Paid	$150.00
16	1/22/2021	879	Round Rug	VWX Company	Unpaid	$270.00
17	1/23/2021	880	Dining Set (B)	YZA Company	Paid	$250.00
18	1/24/2021	881	Big Square Carpet	BCD Company	Unpaid	$110.00
19	1/25/2021	882	Spoon Holder	EFG Company	Unpaid	$200.00
20	1/26/2021	883	Spoon Holder	HIJ Company	Unpaid	$320.00
21	1/27/2021	884	Knife Organiser	KLM Company	Paid	$330.00
22	1/28/2021	885	Wood Table (B)	NOP Company	Paid	$230.00
23	1/29/2021	886	Dining Set (B)	QRS Company	Unpaid	$200.00

Step: 16: Apply some formatting and a template look a little more professional.

	A	B	C	D	E	F
1	Sales 2021			Debt balance	500.00	
2	START DATE	1/1/2021		Paid	1,530.00	
3	END DATE	12/31/2021		Unpaid	1,370.00	
4				Close Account	660.00	
5						
6						
7						
8	Invoice date	Invocie number	Materials	Company name	Payment status	Amount
9	1/15/2021	872	Chair (Black)	ABC Company	Paid	$150.00
10	1/16/2021	873	Dining Set (A)	DEF Company	Paid	$200.00
11	1/17/2021	874	Wood Table (A)	GHI Company	Unpaid	$130.00
12	1/18/2021	875	Round Carpet	JKL Company	Paid	$100.00
13	1/19/2021	876	Round Carpet	MNO Company	Unpaid	$140.00
14	1/20/2021	877	Dining Set (A)	PQR CompanY	Paid	$120.00
15	1/21/2021	878	Wood Table (B)	STU Company	Paid	$150.00
16	1/22/2021	879	Round Rug	VWX Company	Unpaid	$270.00
17	1/23/2021	880	Dining Set (B)	YZA Company	Paid	$250.00
18	1/24/2021	881	Big Square Carpet	BCD Company	Unpaid	$110.00
19	1/25/2021	882	Spoon Holder	EFG Company	Unpaid	$200.00
20	1/26/2021	883	Spoon Holder	HIJ Company	Unpaid	$320.00
21	1/27/2021	884	Knife Organiser	KLM Company	Paid	$330.00
22	1/28/2021	885	Wood Table (B)	NOP Company	Paid	$230.00
23	1/29/2021	886	Dining Set (B)	QRS Company	Unpaid	$200.00

This process will help you to save many times and money in the future because you can create your own spreadsheets with eases and do calculations without having to go to a finance professional.

If you are ready with above steps then you are creating your own accountancy spreadsheets with ease. You can repeat this process if need to create more accountancy spreadsheets.

Chapter 26.   FAQS

The Microsoft excel FAQs are a helpful guide that addresses some of the most common questions and frequently asked problems about this application. It is an easy-to-read document that you can always keep on hand when you have questions about what excel does or how to do specific tasks.

Gain insight into how Microsoft excel works, determine which formulas are used most often, and learn what the various apps do in this article. This document will provide an excellent resource for users looking for information on how to use or make calculations with Excel. It is also a valuable way for beginners to learn what excel does and how you can start using the app.

Operate this guide as a source of information that will help you to understand how to use the various features of Microsoft excel.

Frequently Asked Questions about Microsoft Excel

Q. How does Microsoft excel work?

A. Microsoft excel is a spreadsheet application that can be used for all tasks. It offers a user-friendly way to create spreadsheets that contain data and information. You can organize the data into rows and columns and save the file as an Excel spreadsheet.

Q. How do I open the program?

A. Launch the Microsoft excel program by double-clicking on its icon on your desktop or in your programs list.

Q. What types of tasks can I perform with Microsoft excel?

A. The Microsoft excel program can be used for an assortment of tasks. These include setting up a household budget, creating a recipe book, managing finances, and organizing your life in general. In addition to these practical uses, you can use it to create spreadsheets for things like analysis or college budgets and schedules.

Q. Can I create financial spreadsheets with Microsoft excel?

A. Yes, you can also use the Microsoft Excel program to create financial spreadsheets. These spreadsheets can include loan payments, savings plans, and budgets.

Q. What does Excel do?

A. Microsoft excel is a spreadsheet application that allows you to organize and display data in rows and columns. Using this program, many tasks can be completed, including setting up a household budget or recipe book, managing finances, creating personal documents, and editing photos. The program can be used for just about any type of task that you need to be done.

Q. How do I create a spreadsheet?

A. To create a spreadsheet, begin with the menu options, which can be accessed by clicking on the top menu bar and selecting "File" at the top of the menu. The "File" option is located on the left side of this bar. From this location, click on "New" then select "Spreadsheet." This will launch the blank spreadsheet and allow you to start adding data and information.

Q. How do I format cells?

A. Formatting cell is one way to make your spreadsheets more eye-catching and easier to understand. There are several ways to format cells, including changing the color, font style, or alignment of the text. To apply this, choose the cell or range of cells that you would like to change, then click on "Home" from the menu bar at the top of your screen. From here, select the options that you would like to apply.

Q. How do I create a chart in Excel?

A. To create a chart, you must first open the spreadsheet that contains your data and information. From here, select the "Insert" option from the menu bar at the top of your screen, then click on "Chart." This will show a new pop-up window where you can select different types of graphs to use. Once you have chosen a chart type, click on "OK," and you will be prompted to enter additional details such as labels and titles.

Q. How do I save my worksheet?

A. Saving your work is an essential part of using the Microsoft Excel program. You can either choose to save your work as you are creating it or save it later. Keeping it as you create it will allow you to resume your work if you need to leave or close the program. You can also set multiple versions of the same file, which is useful should you need to go back and set changes or corrections to your original work.

Q. How do I use the autosum feature?

A. To use the autosum feature of Microsoft Excel, select the cells you would like to sum and then click on "Data" from the menu bar. From here, select "AutoSum," which is located at the bottom of the drop-down menu. This will instinctively add all your selected cells and automatically fill in any blank spaces with zeroes.

Q. What does autofill do?

A. Autofill is a handy tool that can help to save time when using Microsoft excel. Using autofill is one way to organize and track multiple tasks that you need to complete, such as paying bills and planning out your finances.

Q. How do I remove rows, columns, or text?

A. There are a range of ways to remove rows, columns, or text within a spreadsheet. To delete a row, click on the "Home" button on your menu and select "Delete." This will take you back to the previous screen, where you can choose which cells you would like to delete. To delete text, select the cell containing the text you would like to remove and click on "Home" again, then choose "Delete." To delete a column, select the column and click on "Home," then select "Delete."

Q. How do I calculate percentages in Excel?

A. Calculating percentages in Microsoft excel is a great way to display information visually and save time when calculating totals. There are range ways that you can complete this task, including using the percentage key on your keyboard or using formulas and functions.

Q. How do I find an average in Excel?

A. Finding averages in Microsoft excel is a great way to compare different numbers and find out how they stack up against your data. There are several ways to complete this task, including using the "Sum" formula, using the "Average" function, or using autofill.

Q. What do Paste Values do?

A. Paste values are a function that automatically updates the rest of the spreadsheet based on the information that you pasted. This is helpful if you use an Excel database or Google doc to update several different spreadsheets at once.

Q. How do I create a row number?

A. Creating row numbers in Microsoft excel is easy because it can be done simply by clicking on a cell and selecting "Row and Column" from the drop-down menu. From here, choose "Insert Row Number." This will automatically add a number based on the total number of rows in your spreadsheet.

Q. How do I create a column number?

A. Creating column numbers in Microsoft excel is easy because it can be done simply by clicking on a cell and selecting "Columns" from the drop-down menu. From here, choose "Insert Column." This will automatically add numbers based on the total number of columns in your spreadsheet.

Q. How do I use conditional formatting?

A. Using conditional formatting to color-code data is a great way to track and organize information. This is especially valuable when working on multiple spreadsheets at once, such as managing your finances, tracking your latest purchases, or creating a pie chart for each month.

Q. How do I insert a hyperlink?

A. Inserting hyperlinks in Microsoft excel is quick and easy when using the "Hyperlink" function located on the "Insert" option at the upper of your screen. Simply enter the link that you would like to use and then click on "Hyperlink."

Q. How do I sort a column?

A. Sorting in Microsoft excel is a great way to organize and track information. When sorting a column, simply click on the "Home" button on your menu bar and click on "Sort." From here, select what type of sorting you would like to complete, such as alphabetically or numerically.

Q. How do I insert pictures to my spreadsheets?

A. Adding pictures to Microsoft excel spreadsheets is quick and easy. Just click on "Insert" in the menu bar at the top of your screen, then select "Picture." This will launch a new window that you can use to upload your picture from your favorite images hosting sites, such as Picasa or Flickr.

Q. How do I change font colors in Excel?

A. Changing colors in Microsoft excel is a great way to emphasize different parts of your spreadsheet because of its versatility. You can choose a different font, outline text using bold, or set the background color. To change the font color, simply click on "Home" on your menu bar, select "Font," and select an option. If you want to create the text bolder, simply right-click on the cell and select "Bold." If you're going to set the background color, click on the "Page Layout" option on your menu bar, then choose "Background."

Q. Why do I make a graph?

A. Graphs in Microsoft excel are a great way to compare different numbers or categories. You can use graphs to compare sales over time, create pie charts or line charts and create scatterplots that show trends over time.

Q. What is an XML file, and how do I open one?

A. An XML file is a text file that includes data in a structured format. This is helpful for compatibility between different computer applications. To open an XML file, click on "Open" in the menu bar and select "Choose Windows." Then simply browse your computer until you find the XML file you would like to open.

Q. How do I send an Excel email?

A. Sending emails with Microsoft excel is a great way to stay organized and share your information with others easily. All you need are your contacts and the link to download your spreadsheet. They can then download any information they need, such as recent purchases or employee paychecks.

Q. What is a pivot table?

A. Pivot tables are great for displaying data on two different sheets of a spreadsheet at once, so making one will help you keep track of how much money you spend each month and how much interest you paid on your bills.

Q. How do I create a chart with multiple series?

A. Creating multi-series graphs in Microsoft Excel is very easy and can be done by clicking on "Insert" on the option bar and then selecting "Chart." From here, you will want to use the drop-down menu and select "Pie Series." This will create a new series that you can use to create your graph.

Q. What does the error saying "You cannot delegate access to worksheet 'insert sheet name' because it is not a trusted source"?

A. This error shows up when someone tries to access a spreadsheet you have shared with them through an app such as Google docs. To fix this error, simply click on "File" then "Info." Under the Protection tab, select "Trusted Sources" and choose anyone you want to be able to access your spreadsheets.

Q. What is the great way to collaborate with other people on a spreadsheet?

A. When trying to collaborate on a spreadsheet, it is helpful to use Microsoft excel's "Shared with me" option. This will let you or your coworkers to open the same spreadsheet and add information. This is an excellent way for people to track their expenses.

Q. What does the error saying "This workbook contains links to other files that are stored on your computer so you can use them in this workbook. The files are automatically updated when you open this file, but if the file has been moved or renamed on your computer, clicking one of these links won't update the link correctly"?

A. This error shows up when an invalid link is used in the spreadsheet, like when someone goes to a different location on their computer and opens an older version of the same workbook. To fix this error, simply right-click on the cell that contains the link and select "Delete Link."

Q. Can I send a spreadsheet as an attachment?

A. Sending a spreadsheet as an attachment is very useful if you are collaborating with coworkers or partners that you do not work with all the time. You can quickly send them the information they need to see, such as your weekly or monthly expenses.

Q. What does the error saying "This workbook is locked. If you need to update it, unlock it and then save it again"?

A. This error shows up when someone tries to open an excel file that is locked by someone else using the same computer. Simply unlock the spreadsheet by clicking on "File" and "Info," then select the Protection tab to fix this error.

Q. How do I change my background color?

A. The background color is a great way to customize and brand your spreadsheet or document, so it stands out from others. Click on " Home " to change the background color, click on "Home" then select "Background." Select a new color in the drop-down menu.

Q. How do I get rid of a comment?

A. Click on the "Comments" tab toward the top of your screen. Then select "Delete Comment" and click on the cell that contains the comment you want to get rid of.

Q. How do I make my spreadsheet printable?

A. This is a great way to keep track of important documents and stay organized. To make your spreadsheet printable, click on "Page Layout" in the menu bar, then select "Page Setup." Then under margins, select "None" on both sides.

Q. What does the error saying "Cannot open file c:\list1.xls from the location C:\Users\Teddi Klein\Documents\Excel\My Workbooks" mean?

A. This error shows up when Excel cannot open a file that has the same name as another file inside of your "Documents" folder. Simply delete the old excel file and rename it to fix this error.

Q. What are Microsoft Excel's features?

A. Microsoft Excel does not have a set feature list. It is designed to help users create different worksheets, lists, and graphs in a spreadsheet format that can easily be shared with other people or saved for future use. Users can have multiple views of their workbook from the main menu and can also save their workbooks so that they can be shared securely with others who may or may not have Excel installed on their devices

Q. What is compatibility?

A. Compatibility is an application's ability to run on different devices, operating systems, and software versions. Microsoft Excel is compatible with Windows 2002 and above, including Windows 10. Microsoft Excel also has a version for Mac OS X. Microsoft Excel can be used to create spreadsheets from any data source that's compatible with Excel's file format.

Q. What is a workbook?

A. A workbook is a file that's created by an Excel program. Each workbook contains one or more worksheets, which are sheets. The worksheet name shows up at the top of each sheet and can have lists, charts, and columns of data.

Q. What is a sheet?

A. A sheet is a single area within a workbook. It has cells, each with its cell address, but no other functionality beyond displaying data and running formulas (see below).

Q. What are timesheet templates?

A. Timesheets are templates used to track time spent on specific tasks and help you bill your clients correctly. Excel has different built-in timesheet templates, or you can create one (here is an excellent guide on creating your own).

Q. What is an Excel template?

A. Templates are files that provide a basic structure for your workbooks. Using a template as a beginning point for a new workbook can help you quickly create organized and professional-looking worksheets.

With the help of this FAQS, your queries about Microsoft excel are solved.

We hope this will be helpful for you and guide you to understand your software and master your skills to create promising projects.

Conclusion

Microsoft Excel is one of the most commonly-used applications in the world. You'll need to know your way around functions and formulas to use them efficiently and productively. It's used to present data in charts and tables, calculate automatically, and manage large volumes of data. Excel has countless features that you need to be familiar with. But it's also easy to use, and there is no need to have any prior experience. This means that anyone who knows how to work with a spreadsheet can learn how to use Microsoft Excel proficiently. The basics are handled in the first steps. You need to understand the standard and advanced functions to stay on task. The navigation and formatting options will help you create a data table that is appropriately formatted. You'll be able to make an effective chart with relative ease after flipping through the pages in this guide. When you have the basic knowledge of how Microsoft excel works, you can build on those skills and add creativity. These points will help you build skills for a lifetime. Not many people will regret the time spent learning how to master Microsoft excel. You can share your charts with the entire world. The possibilities of what you can do are numerous. Even if you don't plan to use excel every day, it's still worth your time to learn how it works beforehand. This will provide you with a good head start on creating your first spreadsheet or chart. Each new skill you learn will be easier to master Microsoft excel. You can develop your skills faster if you search for answers to specific problems. Keeping your skills sharp is easy once you know how to use Microsoft excel. You can find a solution to your questions with a few search terms and the web. This book is created to help you master Microsoft Excel and get answers to your questions. Reducing your learning curve increases the amount of work you can accomplish each day. Be sure that you're on the right track by reading those tips before pressing on with this guide. You'll acquire the skills you need more easily after studying this guide. If you improve your skills as outlined in this guide, it will benefit your life in many ways. If you're seeking for a great way to master the MS excel functions, look no further!

THE END

Manufactured by Amazon.ca
Bolton, ON